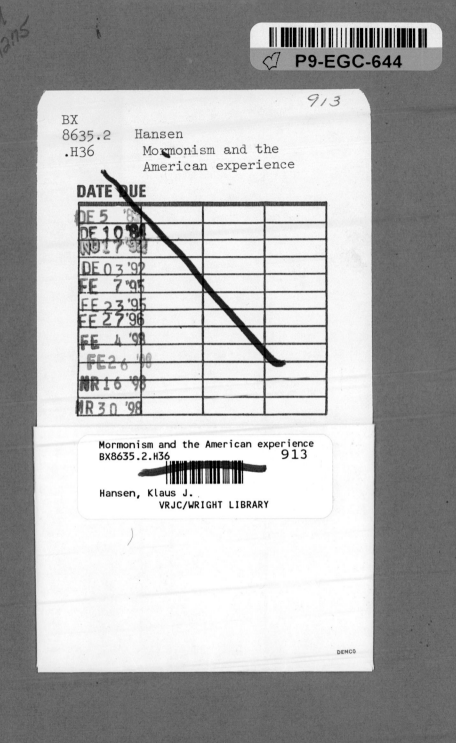

Chicago History of American Religion
Edited by Martin E. Marty

William A. Clebsch, *American Religious Thought: A History* (1973)
Edwin Scott Gaustad, *Dissent in American Religion* (1973)
Joseph L. Blau, *Judaism in America: From Curiosity to Third Faith* (1976)
Donald G. Mathews, *Religion in the Old South* (1977)
William G. McLoughlin, *Revivals, Awakenings, and Reform: An Essay on Religion and Social Change in America, 1607–1977* (1978)
Robert S. Ellwood, Jr., *Alternative Altars: Unconventional and Eastern Spirituality in America* (1979)

Mormonism and
the American Experie

Mormonism and the American Experience

Klaus J. Hansen

The University of Chicago Press   Chicago and London

The University of Chicago Press, Chicago 60637
The University of Chicago Press, Ltd., London

Library of Congress Cataloging in Publication Data

Hansen, Klaus J
  Mormonism and the American experience.

  (Chicago history of American religion)
  Bibliography: p.
  Includes index.
  1. Mormons and Mormonism.   2. Mormons and Mormonism
in the United States.   I. Title.
BX8635.2.H36   289.3'73   80-19312
ISBN 0–226–31552–5

For my father and my mother

Contents

Foreword

In the year in which this book first appeared, the *Yearbook of American and Canadian Churches* listed 222 formally organized churches in North America. Two years earlier there appeared *The Encyclopedia of American Religions* with its accounting of nearly 1,200 churches, sects, and cults. The Church of Jesus Christ of Latter-day Saints is only one of these. It is also the only denomination whose career is to be observed at book length in this series. The reasons for the editorial choice demand explanation.

The suspicious reader some years ago might have mused that the Mormons, the more popular name for the Church, are simply so exotic and esoteric that the public cannot resist hearing about them. True, there is something tantalizing about the story of Mormon origins and development, but, as Klaus Hansen clearly shows, by 1980 the Mormons had grown to be so much like everyone else in America or, perhaps, had so successfully gotten other Americans to be like them, that they no longer inspired curiosity for wayward ways. Had the editor wanted to appeal to readers' curiosities about the exotic, he would have done better to choose the People's Temple Christian Church of the Reverend James Jones, who did not make it into the *Yearbook* but who was in the Encyclopedia.

Exoticism? The public would be better advised to pursue it in Feraferia, Abilitism, Scientology, the Prosperos, the Aetherius Society, or the Giant Rock Space Convention, spiritual groups that turn up in discussions of the religion at the American margins. Or, for something more domestic-sounding, straight out of the *Encyclopedia*'s second volume, "Kennedy Worshippers." This group with 2,000 members and a Memorial Temple in Los Angeles, claims contact with the late president's spirit and reports on healings that occurred when they prayed to his spirit. Compared with such groups, the Mormons are just folks down the block.

Nor can the case of their inclusion be based on size. The same *Yearbook* records 2,486,261 members, which leaves it behind a dozen other groups. While internationally it climbed from one million to four million members after mid-century, the Church of Jesus Christ of Latter-day Saints had plenty of company in the growth ranks. During the same period, African Christianity grew from 25 million to 75 million, and other world religions experienced selective growth on at least as rapid a scale. The Church of God of Cleveland, Tennessee, grew more rapidly than the Mormons, but merits no volume in this series. Location? If anything, location would handicap the Mormons. As Professor Hansen shows, they are swarming in the Third World; as anyone who has driven around the nation's capital must know, they have a giant temple there; as millions of Americans know, missionaries knock on doors everywhere. But their base remains Utah and its surrounding area, which is not a crossroads for most citizens.

The wealth and public posture of the Church do commend it for inquiry. Since all faithful members tithe their wealth and time and since the leadership includes astute investors, the riches of the Church are enormous. But even being comparable to the *"Fortune's* 500" firms is not enough to awaken scholarly interest on the scale the Mormon enterprise does. The rejection of black males from the priesthood kept the Church in the news until recently, and its fierce opposition to the Equal Rights Amendment—even to the point of excommunicating a supporter of the ERA who offended leadership—makes Mormonism a page one item. But Roman Catholicism and other religious groups dominate the news of church and state without awakening curiosity on the Mormon scale. We chose the Mormons for inclusion in this series for a reason that Klaus Hansen places at the center of his work. This series is called the "Chicago History of American Religion," and few case studies of a particular group could offer more promise in its context.

Religion, first: in what I think is a stunning chapter on death, Hansen shows how this faith helped and helps its members cope with the unwelcome reality, indeed the terror, of dying. Its theology and practice were designed to make the transition from earthly life easier, and Mormon doctrine and rites reinforce the members who, in common, find meaning through it. Classically, religions have to come to terms with death, and the Church of Jesus Christ of Latter-day Saints qualifies as a religion and not a mere communitarian or business venture on these terms.

Second, history. Today the narrative historian—and Hansen spins a good narrative, as the long first chapter demonstrates—must call upon all the social sciences and humanities to illuminate the story being told. Mormonism, because of the puzzles surrounding its origin and the paradoxes of its development, necessitates a full-range approach, as Hansen shows. Because of his own curiosities and skills, the author comes up with what strikes me as a tour de force use of other disciplinary methods, as if he were writing a textbook but not letting the textbooky character show.

What did occur to inspire Mormon founder Joseph Smith's claim that he had seen visions and been given a set of golden plates and the instruments for translating them into the decisive *Book of Mormon*? The library is full of two kinds of books. One is by and for believing Mormons, but despised by everyone else. It simply assumes the divine and supernatural intrusion into American history on a hill in New York, and all the rest follows. The other is by

"Gentiles" and against believing Mormons. It treats the
revelation and its consequences as mere charlatanry.
Readers of the two types have nothing in common.

Such approaches are out of date, and they never did do
justice to the character of religious claims. Hansen writes
in such a way that the Saints can revisit their history,
perhaps being bruised here and there by the contexts in
which the story appears or the questions are raised, but
still with a sense that the story is respected, that the events
have their own integrity. Gentiles, which means everyone
else, can visit someone else's history, perhaps being asked
to suspend elements of disbelief here and there, but they
never lose their footing in the way evidence has to be
appraised in the modern academy. Between sheer super-
naturalism and pure naturalism, whatever both of them
are, are countless options, and Hansen lifts some of them
up for view.

If at times he verges on speculative or marginally scientific theories—as when he deals with Julian Jaynes's
highly controversial bicameral view of the mind as it experiences the divine—Hansen quickly wins the skeptical
reader back by showing how the Jaynesian approach can be
a "metaphor" for inquiry. He draws on other controversial
and sometimes speculative psychological theories that derive from Freud, Jung, Adler, and others, without getting
drawn into sectarian debate between their schools—
schools which are often as distanced from each other as are
religious sects from their rivals.

As with psychology, so with anthropology, when he dis-
cusses Mormon ritual and myth; or sociology, in Max
Weberian elaborations on the role of the leader or the
factor of economic doctrine. And Hansen has to draw on
the humanities, as well. The *Book of Mormon* exacts literary
and hermeneutical finesse from those who have to con-
front the canonical claims its believers make. There is
plenty of philosophy of history in the Hansenian accounting of processive revelation. And it goes without saying

that the author has to make use of sophisticated historiographical techniques.

The danger in all this is that one could come up with little cameo performances by the Jungs and the Webers and lose the plot. But Hansen integrates them naturally into his own plot. And that plot has to do with the third legitimating word in our series: American.

The Mormons' book of revelation includes the American landscape, as few other religions in America do. While African, Asian, and European religions were imported during the past five centuries, and while the Saints certainly drew on the European heritage as this heritage passed through New England, in other respects it was homegrown. The Mormon trek meant an encounter with the landscape in New York, Ohio, frontier Missouri and Illinois, and undeveloped Utah. The founding documents of the United States received honor in Mormon expounding.

Yet for all the apparent Americanism, Mormonism was consistently seen as un- and anti-American. Its founder wanted to run for president of the United States, wanted to set up a counterkingdom. The practice of polygamy offended all non-Mormons. Warfare between the United States and partisans of the Mormon kingdom was a virtually unique expression of holy war on North American soil. To critics reposed in the Protestant empire, Mormonism was worse than Roman Catholicism, infidelity, and barbarism.

Today, as Hansen shows, Mormons are very American, sometimes super-American. They confirm the hunch many of us have that the American environment is itself seen as revelatory and redemptive by many religious groups, and the Mormons are a prime case study. How the environment worked on them and how they brought Americans to adapt to their ways, or to see some wisdom in those ways, makes up much of the plot of this book. When Hansen toys with words like "bourgeoisification" and em-

bourgeoisement," terms he imports gingerly from other
social sciences into his narrative, he comes close to a secret
that helps religions adapt to the American majority way
and helps the American way to be ever changed as a result
of such encounters.

To detail how Hansen thinks the Mormons have acted
and reacted, and how larger America reacted and acted,
would be to deprive his plot of suspense. It is time for him
to make his case.

MARTIN E. MARTY
The University of Chicago

Preface

The Mormons are on the march. In 1980, the year of their sesquicentennial, more than 28,000 missionaries were spreading the message of their founder Joseph Smith from Iceland to Chile, from Berlin to Hong Kong, from New York to Honolulu. Such efforts are paying dividends. In 1947 there were scarcely more than a million Latter-day Saints in the world, most of them in the United States, and the overwhelming majority of these in Utah. In 1980, of nearly 4.5 million believers in the divine mission of Joseph Smith, about a million were located outside of the United States. According to current projections, within fifteen years foreign Mormons may well outnumber their American coreligionists.

While these statistics may be of interest and even importance, especially to contemporary Mormons, they have little to do with my reasons for writing this book. In fact, I believe that the importance of Mormonism for American history may well be inversely related to the size of its membership. Between 1830 and 1890—the years that circumscribe the major portion of my study—the Saints grew from a handful of members to a community of about 200,000. Yet it was during those first sixty years that Mormonism was at its most active—even militant—in insisting on having its say in that agonizing debate over the meaning of America.

By the turn of the century it had become clear that there
was no place for a traditional, antipluralist Mormon kingdom in the pluralistic society of twentieth-century
America. To the degree that Mormons have made their
peace with modern America—and vice versa—they have
become just one more tolerated and finally highly respectable minority. That they have become active and approv-
ing participants in a modern America whose boundaries
are defined by a liberal consensus may not be a bad thing.
But it does mean that Mormonism in its modern version
does not tell us very much about contemporary American
society and culture that we don't know already. It is of
interest to the historian, however, how this transformation
has come about.

Surprisingly few historians have addressed themselves
to this question, in spite of the fact that the outpouring of
works on Mormonism, according to one observer, "has no
parallel in the history of any other religious group in
America—with the single exception of the Puritans of
Massachusetts Bay, the grandfathers of us all."[1] Much of
this literature is polemical. For more than a century Gentiles and Saints attacked and counterattacked with the
printed word. As passions cooled, more objective accounts
appeared. In recent years, professional historians have
produced an impressive list of scholarly monographs. The
time may well have come to stand back and ask: what does
it all mean? This book is one of several recent attempts to
arrive at an answer to that overwhelming question.

In a work of this kind an author incurs many debts. I am
especially grateful to the Historical Department of the
Church of Jesus Christ of Latter-day Saints and the director of its history division, Leonard J. Arrington, as well as
the director of the archives and library division, Donald T.
Schmidt, under whose auspices I pursued research as a
summer fellow in 1974, as well as on several other occa-
sions. At Yale University I enjoyed the hospitality of the
Graduate School and the Department of History as a fellow, with access to the magnificent Mormon collection in

the Beinecke Library. At Princeton University Alfred L.
Bush—who has assembled one of the finest Mormon collections outside Utah—was a generous host. I am also
grateful to the staffs of the following institutions: the
Huntington Library; the Western History Center of the
University of Utah; the Utah State University Library; the
Utah State Historical Society; the archives and the special
collections at Brigham Young University Library; and the
Douglas Library at Queen's University.

I wish to thank Queen's University for a sabbatical leave
as well as research awards for travel, typing, and xeroxing.
The Canada Council provided a generous leave fellowship.

Martin Marty suggested that I write this book. His infectious enthusiasm and patience were instrumental in
helping me complete the work. I have also received invaluable criticism, conversation, and encouragement from
several other scholars who have read portions of the
manuscript—Leonard Arrington; David Brion Davis,
Howard Lamar, and David Musto of Yale University;
Lawrence Foster of the Georgia Institute of Technology;
Joy Parr of Queen's University; Robert Schwarz of St.
Lawrence University; and Ronald Walters of the Johns
Hopkins University.

Six scholars read the entire manuscript. Jan Shipps of
Indiana University/Indianapolis provided the insights and
caveats of one of the outstanding "Gentile" scholars of
Mormonism. Davis Bitton, of the University of Utah and
the Historical Department of the Church of Jesus Christ of
Latter-day Saints, made some factual corrections, checked
some glib excesses, and provided the critical perspective of
one of the most knowledgeable and objective of Mormon
historians (though I did not always follow his advice). My
colleagues Robert Malcolmson and James Stayer were
especially helpful in saving me from infelicities and lapses
of logic. They, as well as George Rawlyk, aided immensely in my effort to communicate a somewhat esoteric topic to a larger audience. Many of the ideas in
this book were subjected to the sometimes irreverent

scrutiny of my graduate seminar in American thought and culture, where Gordon Pollock made me rethink the idea of the Kingdom of God and Mario Creet, who also read the entire manuscript, teased the idea of the corporate nature of the Kingdom of God out of my reluctant subconscious. Shirley Fraser proved to be an unusually efficient typist, and without the expert aid of Kevin Quinn it would have been impossible to produce the index on time.

As for Joan Hansen, she did read a portion of the manuscript and made her usual, perceptive comments on form and content. Her main contribution to this book, however, has been in merely being. Like Eric, Chris, Evan, and Britt, she has also been a reminder of Emerson's dictum that "books are for the scholars' idle times."

"What matters in a myth, a belief, is ... Does it enable us to live, to keep going? ... The crucial question isn't Can you prove it? but Does it give us a handle on the reality that otherwise would overwhelm us?"

John Updike, *The Coup*

The Birth of
Mormonism

An angel from on high
The long, long silence broke.
Mormon hymn by
Parley P. Pratt

I

When on April 6, 1830, Joseph Smith, Jr., assembled
some thirty of his followers in the log house of Peter
Whitmer in the village of Fayette in western New York to
organize officially "The Church of Christ" (commonly
known today as the Mormon church), the new religion had
already accumulated a colorful prehistory that had its beginnings when the results of a stupendous natural catastrophe and the private misfortunes of the Joseph Smith,
Sr., family intersected at a decisive moment to trigger a
necessary cause for the birth of Mormonism.

The natural catastrophe was the volcanic eruption, in
1815, of Mount Tambora in the Dutch East Indies (today
known as Indonesia), one of the most violent eruptions in
modern times, far surpassing in destructive force the more
famous eruption in Krakatoa in 1883. The explosion
shortened the top of the mountain by some 4,500 feet and
ejected about 25 cubic miles of debris into the strato-
sphere, reflecting sunlight back into space and thus reduc-
ing the amount of radiation to the earth. Reaching the
northern latitudes in the summer of 1816, this dust cloud
had particularly adverse effects on the weather in New
England, Eastern Canada, and Western Europe, leading to
widespread crop failures. It was as a result of the catas-
trophic summer of "eighteen hundred-and-froze-to-death"

that many New England farmers, who had eked out a marginal existence for some time, finally decided to leave their rock-bound ancestral homesteads for the more promising lands along the Genesee and Mohawk rivers, as well as the Ohio country. The Joseph Smith, Sr., family was part of this migration.[1]

Like many of their fellow migrants, the families of Joseph and his wife Lucy had strong roots in New England. The forebears of both sides of the family had migrated to Massachusetts in the seventeenth century. The elder Smith's parents had farmed in Topsfield, where they were full members of the Congregational church. In the language of Puritan New England, "they owned the covenant." Lucy's father, Solomon Mack, was a son of the Congregational minister at Lyme, Connecticut. In 1796, on a visit to Tunbridge, Vermont, Lucy met and married Joseph Smith whose father had left the family farm at Topsfield for better opportunities in Vermont. For the newlyweds, farming the rocky soil of Vermont yielded little profit. Failing in a number of ill-fated ventures, the Smiths were finally forced to sell their farm. In 1804 they moved to Sharon, Vermont, where Joseph, Jr., was born on December 23, 1805, the third of nine children.

The boy grew up in an environment of struggle and economic deprivation. In 1811 the family grasped at yet another chance for improving their lot when they moved to Lebanon, New Hampshire. Two years later, Vermont and New Hampshire were ravaged by a typhus epidemic. Though all the Smiths survived, illness plagued them for nearly a year and wiped out any economic gains they had made. Another attempt at farming in Norwich, Vermont, proved no more successful. In the infamous summer of 1816, the Smiths and their eight children moved to Palmyra in western New York (a ninth child, a girl, was born after their final move). But by the time the Smiths arrived, boom times were over. The more enterprising New Englanders were already moving west, into the Ohio country.

The Smiths, however, decided to stick it out—perhaps had no other choice.[2]

Although they continued to work hard, their economic lot failed to improve. It is not surprising, therefore, that young Joseph began to think of some shortcuts to economic security. According to folk rumors and legends circulating in the area, treasure buried by Indians and Spanish pirates was waiting to be unearthed. A few lucky persons had found artifacts of stone, copper, and even silver in Indian burial mounds not far from the Smith farm. The rural folk of western New York applied methods of detection that were part of their New England background, such as rods and peepstones. It was a tradition well established among the "rodsmen" of Vermont, many of whom had migrated to western New York, and young Smith's knowledge of these beliefs and practices is therefore not at all unusual. Using a peepstone (a kind of crystal ball), Joseph acquired a reputation for being able to locate buried treasure. Although there is no evidence that he was successful in these ventures, Josiah Stowel, a farmer from Bainbridge, New York, hired Smith in October, 1825, to locate treasures supposedly hidden by the Spanish in the vicinity of the town. It was at this time that one of Stowel's neighbors, perhaps disappointed in his hope for treasure, had Smith arrested on a charge of "being a disorderly person and an impostor." According to the court record of the trial, held in March, 1826, Smith testified that

> he had a certain stone, which he had occasionally looked at to determine where hidden treasures in the bowels of the earth were; that he professed to tell in this manner where gold-mines were a distance under ground, and had looked for Mr. Stowell several times, and informed him where he could find those treasures, and Mr. Stowell had been engaged in digging for them; that at Palmyra he pretended to tell, by looking at this stone, where coined money was buried in Pennsylvania, and while at Palmyra he had frequently ascertained in that way where lost property was, of various kinds; that he occasionally had been in the habit of looking through his stone to find lost

property for three years, but of late had pretty much given up on account of its injuring his health, especially his eyes—made them sore; that he did not solicit business of this kind, and had always rather declined having anything to do with this business.

Equally remarkable was the testimony of the witnesses for the defense, three of whom testified that Smith could in fact "divine things" and had done so by looking at a "dark-colored stone" in his hat. Many years later, Smith's wife Emma reported that her husband had translated portions of the Book of Mormon by looking at a seer stone in a hat. David Whitmer, who was intimately associated with the production of the book, corroborated the account.[3]

While working for Stowel, Joseph roomed at the home of Isaac Hale, where he fell in love with Hale's spirited, dark-haired daughter Emma. Hale vigorously opposed the match because of the young man's reputation—perhaps also because Smith was somewhat younger than Emma. Quite predictably, the couple eloped and were married on January 18, 1827. Joseph returned to Palmyra with his bride, where they lived in the home of his parents.

As Smith reported later, at the very time that these events transpired, he was already being prepared for un-earthing treasures of another kind. Several years earlier, on the night of September 21, 1823, he had had a visit from a heavenly messenger in his bedroom, "standing in the air," dressed in a "loose robe of the most exquisite whiteness," and surrounded with a bright light.

He called me by name, and said unto me that he was a messenger sent from the presence of God to me, and that his name was Moroni; that God had a work for me to do . . . . He said there was a book deposited, written upon gold plates, giving an account of the former inhabitants of this continent, and the source from whence they sprang. He also said that the fulness of the everlasting Gospel was contained in it, as delivered by the Savior to the ancient inhabitants; also, that there were two stones in silver bows—and these stones, fastened to a breastplate, constituted what is called the Urim and Thummim—deposited with the plates, and the possession and use of these stones were what constituted "seers" in ancient or former times; and that God had prepared them for the purpose of translating the book.

After giving numerous instructions, including the location of the records, the messenger left, but reappeared two more times during the night, repeating his message verbatim. The following day, Smith located the plates at the exact spot revealed to him by the messenger, on the side of a hill in the vicinity of the village of Manchester. "Not far from the top, under a stone of considerable size, lay the plates, deposited in a stone box," together with the Urim and Thummim and the breastplate. His attempt to remove the treasures was interrupted by the divine messenger of the night before, who instructed young Joseph "that the time for bringing them forth had not yet arrived, neither would it, until four years from that time; but he told me that I should come to that place precisely in one year from that time, and that he would there meet with me, and that I should continue to do so until the time should come for obtaining the plates." Smith did as instructed, and finally, on September 22, 1827, was permitted to remove the plates and their accompanying paraphernalia, being under strict instruction "not to show them to any person" except "those to whom I should be commanded to show them."[4]

Nevertheless, rumors of the "golden bible" spread in the neighborhood, and Joseph found it increasingly difficult to obey this instruction. Skeptics suggest that Joseph himself may have started these rumors. In any case, several people became convinced that he did in fact possess a golden treasure, and hatched schemes to wrest the plates from him. In order to escape these machinations, Joseph and Emma finally moved to Harmony, Pennsylvania, to live with Emma's family, who had by now become reconciled to the marriage. Martin Harris, a well-to-do-farmer, gave the impoverished couple fifty dollars to facilitate the move.

Joseph immediately proceeded with the translation, with Emma serving as his scribe. In the meantime, Harris had become convinced of the authenticity of the record, and of Smith's translation. In February, 1828, he moved to

Harmony and became Smith's secretary, taking dictation from the future prophet, who was separated from his amanuensis by a blanket hung across the room. By June, 116 pages of foolscap were completed. Anxious to convince his doubting wife, Harris took the manuscript home and promptly lost it. For a while it seemed that the translation might never reach the public. When a chagrined Harris asked Joseph why he could not retranslate the same section, he was told that designing enemies were only waiting for that chance, would make changes in the original, and then challenge his gift of translation. Apparently it did not occur to Harris that such changes would be easily detected, since the manuscript was in his own handwriting, and Emma's. The solution to the problem came in a revelation, which told Smith to translate from another section of the plates that happened to cover the same ground as the missing 116 pages, but from a more spiritual perspective.[5]

During the winter of 1828/29, work on the translation proceeded at a snail's pace, with Emma once again serving as scribe. In the meantime, a young schoolteacher named Oliver Cowdery had heard of Smith's work while boarding with his parents in Palmyra. Convinced of the divine nature of Smith's mission, Cowdery left for Harmony immediately after the end of school in April, 1829, where he became the prophet's new scribe. As one commentator has observed, "if Smith were composing instead of translating the book, he had had a year in which to . . . develop his style."[6] Be that as it may, with the help of Cowdery the work now proceeded rapidly, and was completed in June. Publication, however, was temporarily delayed by lack of finances, and because of public pressures on the prospective printer. When Martin Harris guaranteed payment of $3,000, printer Egbert B. Grandin delivered five thousand copies in March, 1830. Harris had amply redeemed himself for his earlier indiscretion—in fact at the cost of selling his farm to raise the money. On March 26, a local advertisement announced the publication of the Book of Mormon, with Joseph Smith as "author and proprietor."[7]

Though Joseph never elaborated on precisely how he produced the book, he insisted that "through the medium of the Urim and Thummin" he "translated the record by the gift and power of God." David Whitmer, a friend of Cowdery and early convert to Mormonism, recalled many years later that

> Joseph Smith would put the seer stone into a hat, and put his face in the hat, drawing it closely around his face to exclude the light; and in the darkness the spiritual light would shine. A piece of something resembling parchment would appear, and on that appeared the writing. One character at a time would appear, and under it was the interpretation in English. Brother Joseph would read off the English to Oliver Cowdery, who was his principal scribe, and when it was written down and repeated to Brother Joseph to see if it was correct, then it would disappear, and another character with the interpretation would appear. Thus the Book of Mormon was translated by the gift and power and God, and not by any power of man.[8]

It was by that same power that three witnesses were permitted to see the plates. These were Martin Harris, Oliver Cowdery, and Cowdery's friend David Whitmer, at whose home in Fayette, New York, the translation had been completed. Retiring into the woods, Smith and his three companions united in prayer. An angel appeared with the plates and turned the pages so that the witnesses could discern the engravings. Although all three later became disaffected from Mormonism, none of them denied his testimony. When questioned about this experience in later years, Harris replied: "I did not see them as I do that pencil-case, yet I saw them with the eye of faith; I saw them just as distinctly as I see anything around me—although at the time they were covered with a cloth." Later on another eight witnesses testified that they had "seen and hefted" the plates. These included two of Smith's brothers, his father, four members of the Whitmer family, as well as one of Whitmer's sons-in-law. After the completion of the translation, Joseph returned the plates to the custody of the angel.[9]

Faithful Mormons believe that the plates were returned because their presence would have presented a continuing temptation to thieves and robbers, and perhaps to Joseph himself, whose family lost title to their farm in Palmyra. Furthermore, Smith reported that a major portion of the plates was sealed and that he had received strict instructions by the angel not to break the seal. The time, however, would come when the plates would be returned and the rest of its contents made known to the world.

To nonbelievers, of course, it was obvious that Smith had to fabricate a story explaining the disappearance of plates they were convinced had existed only as a figment of his imagination. In their opinion he had appealed to the credulity of his contemporaries in a scheme to make money by concocting a story that would have wide appeal among a population eager to find an explanation for the origin of the Indians, and who were already familiar with stories that they were Israelites, quite possibly members of the Lost Ten Tribes. Capitalizing on these legends, skeptics argue, Smith, who had a vivid and creative imagination, spun out in considerable detail the history of a group of Israelites in the New World.

The central story of the Book of Mormon is a history of Lehi, a Hebrew prophet, and his family, whom the Lord ordered to flee Jerusalem around 600 B.C. in order to escape the impending Babylonian captivity of the Jews. Guided by the hand of God, the refugees traversed the Arabian desert, built ships, and sailed to a new continent, a promised land, known to the modern world as America. Here Lehi's descendants became a mighty people, building cities and temples, supported by an agricultural economy. As Israelites they obeyed the Law of Moses and adhered to the prophetic tradition of their forefathers, which included belief in the coming of a Messiah. After his death and resurrection in Palestine, Christ appeared to the inhabitants of the New World, preached and performed miracles, and laid the foundation of a church, just as he had done in Palestine. Before his departure he ordained twelve disciples who were to preach the Gospel to their fellow Americans. This church flourished for several centuries, bringing peace and prosperity to the land. But as the people became wealthy, they departed from the ways of the Lord, reviving an ancient struggle between the descendants of two of Lehi's sons, Nephi and Laman. The Nephites had been the primary bearers of an advanced Hebrew civilization, while the Lamanites, having departed from the God of their fathers, had given up agriculture and city-building for a nomadic life of hunting, and of making war against the Nephites. As punishment, God had cursed them with a dark skin. In a fratricidal war, these rough barbarians destroyed the now effete and materialistic Nephites, who had departed from the ways of the Lord.

The Nephites had kept records engraved on metal plates, containing a detailed history of their people. Mormon, one of the last Nephite prophets and generals, wrote an abbreviated historical account, based on these records, on gold plates, and passed them on to his son Moroni, who buried them in the Hill Cumorah in order to prevent them from falling into the hands of the Lamanites, and to allow their future discovery in preparation for the restoration of the Gospel in America. In the last pages of the Book of Mormon, in a postscript to his father's account, Moroni reported that he was but one of a few a Nephites left, and one of the even fewer who had kept the faith. He was hiding from the Lamanites who, he believed, would kill him if they found him.

The surviving Lamanites were none other than ancestors of the American Indians who, when they were discovered by Columbus, had forgotten their true identity and heritage. Through the Book of Mormon they would come to a knowledge of their origins. The records had been buried by the same Moroni who, in his postmortal state as an "angel," had revealed the location of the plates to Joseph Smith.

However fanciful this story may appear to many modern readers, about four million Mormons accept it as a divinely inspired history of ancient America. It has been translated

into all major languages, as well as some esoteric ones. It
is also available in Braille. Inexpensive missionary editions
sell for a dollar. A leatherbound edition, printed on India
paper, imitates the format of fine Bibles. It is divided into
books, chapter and verse. Though it lacks the stately gran-
deur of the King James version, its style has a biblical,
archaic flavor, liberally sprinkled with *thees* and *thous, be-
holds, wherefores,* and *th* endings. Nevertheless, in spite of
some lengthy quotations from Isaiah, the book is clearly
not—as some of its more careless critics have thought—
merely a pastiche of thinly disguished biblical stories and
homilies. When Mark Twain (never one to throw away a
line) called it "chloroform in print," it was because one of
the books in Smith's work had the title "Ether." Yet the
book has remained a puzzle to scholars.

II

In order to strengthen the argument for divine inspiration,
Smith and his early followers emphasized the notion that
he was an unlearned lad who could not possibly have
written the book on his own, thus ironically providing
critics with a convenient handle. If Smith wasn't the author, who was? One of the most persistent theories, advanced by a Mormon aspostate named Philastus Hurlbut,
pointed to Sidney Rigdon, a Campbellite minister who
became one of the most prominent early converts to
Mormonism. An orator and preacher with a capacity for
holding large audiences spellbound for hours, Rigdon was
not an implausible candidate for having written a work of
over five hundred pages filled with sermons. The historical
framework, according to Hurlbut, had been plagiarized
from an unpublished novel by Solomon Spaulding, which
had as its theme the Israelite origins of the Indians. The
Spaulding-Rigdon theory was much in vogue until discovery of the Spaulding mauscript made it quite clear that
both in style and subject matter Spaulding's florid romance
and the Book of Mormon had virtually nothing in com-

mon. A few diehards, however, have continued to advance
the possibility that Spaulding had produced yet another
undiscovered manuscript. Recently, four California re-
searchers have attempted to link Spaulding's handwriting
to that of twelve pages of original Book of Mormon manuscript in the possession of the archives of the Mormon
Church in Salt Lake City. While there are some similarities
between Spaulding's handwriting and those twelve manuscript pages, several other technicalities make the testimony of handwriting experts far from convincing.
Moreover, the massive circumstantial, stylistic, and historical evidence marshalled by scholars such as Fawn
Brodie (who can hardly be acccused of being an apologist
for Mormonism) provide formidable obstacles to any attempt to revive the Spaulding-Rigdon theory.[10]
Somewhat more plausible, yet equally difficult to prove
positively, is a theory suggesting that Joseph plagiarized a
manuscript written by the Reverend Ethan Smith, a Congregational minister of Poultney, Vermont. In 1823, Ethan
Smith had published a book *Views of the Hebrews; or, The
Ten Tribes of Israel in America,* which popularized the notion that the American Indians were of Israelite origin. It
has been suggested that Ethan Smith may have been
working on a second volume which somehow got into the
hands of the Mormon prophet, who then used it as the
primary source for the Book of Mormon. It is of course
quite possible, even likely, that Joseph was familiar with
Views of the Hebrews. Indeed, there are important parallels
between ideas in the Book of Mormon and Ethan Smith's
work. Yet the stories of the two books are far too dis-
similar to suggest plagiarism. Moreover, notions of the
Israelite origins of the American Indians were so widespread that parallels do not necessarily suggest direct influence.[11]
As a matter of fact, in the nineteenth century, Mormon
missionaries could effectively use the "red sons of Israel"
theory was empirical "proof" of the authenticity of the
Book of Mormon. It is only in the twentieth century that

these historical and anthropological claims have made the work vulnerable on those grounds. Nevertheless, modern Latter-day Saints follow with avid interest archaeological discoveries in South and Central America, hoping that these may be linked to the Nephites and Lamanites. In fact, the wish has become the father of the thought, and in Mormon folklore the ancient ruins of the Incas and the Maya, the Aztecs and the Toltecs (never mind vast cultural and chronological differences) have become so much proof of the veracity of the Book of Mormon. Handsome coffee-table books of American antiquities find a ready market among the faithful, and the more credulous continue to repeat a story according to which the Smithsonian Institution in Washington, D.C., uses the Book of Mormon as a guide for its excavations. Professional archaeologists at Brigham Young University, of course, are more sophisticated and cautious in interpreting findings, some of them from expeditions of their own. Yet one of their obvious purposes is to find scientific confirmation for the claims of Joseph Smith.

Unfortunately, these have been very hard to come by. So far the anthropological and archaeological establishment has not found any confirmation of the claims of the Book of Mormon, although some evidence of American migrations from the ancient Near East is beginning to accumulate.[12] In the face of modern scholarship, the "red sons of Israel" doctrine is particularly difficult to sustain, although modern Mormon scholars have avoided a head-on confrontation with science by accepting the prevailing opinion that most native Americans probably migrated from Asia across the Bering Strait and by arguing that the Book of Mormon is merely a history of *some* particular migrants. Other Mormon scholars have attempted to link the Book of Mormon to the cultural milieu of the ancient Near East and to deny its affinity to antebellum American culture. These efforts, however, have found credence only among the already-converted. Retreating to the higher ground of faith, modern Mormons have been

forced to argue that scientific proof would undermine the
essential requirement of religious belief, thus reversing
the nineteenth-century emphasis on "empiricism." They
are nevertheless confident that in His own due time God
will allow the scientific and historical vindication of the
Book of Mormon.[13]

What both skeptics and believers, however, have long
ago come to agree on is that whether by divine revelation
or under his own power, it was indeed Joseph Smith who
wrote the Book of Mormon, though it took the skeptics
some time to accept it as the product of a rational mind.
Until then, the most popular explanation was that Smith
suffered from psychological delusions. Sociologist Kimball
Young, none other than a grandson of Brigham, called
Smith a "parapath." Bernard De Voto, in his characteristi-
cally pungent language, attacked the book as "a yeasty
fermentation, formless, aimless, and inconceivably
absurd—at once a parody of all American religious thought
and something more than a parody, a disintegration. The
oestrus of a paranoiac projected it into a new Bible." A
facile "explanation" that really explains very little, it tell us
more about De Voto than about Smith.[14] A more serious
attempt at a psychological interpretation is Fawn Brodie's
(Smith's most influential biographer); she suggests in the
second edition of her magisterial *No Man Knows My History* that recent clinical studies of a personality type described as "impostor" may provide a clue to Smith's personality and behavior. The fact that Joseph produced the
Book of Mormon and a number of other religious works
and revelations, she says, does not necessarily imply "deliberate swindling and fraud." In a study of a number of
impostors, for example, psychiatrist Dr. Phyllis Greenacre
"concludes that they were not ordinary liars but men of
extraordinary conflicts" who are tormented by "a struggle
between two dominant identities, . . . the temporarily focused and strongly assertive imposturous one, and the frequently amazingly crude and poorly knit one from which
the impostor has emerged." Under strong compulsion to

live out his fantasy, the impostor nevertheless has a "formal" awareness of the falsity of his claims. "The sense of reality is characterized by a peculiarly sharp, quick perceptiveness, extraordinarily immediate keenness and responsiveness, especially in the area of the imposture. The over-all sense of reality is, however, impaired." Great impostors, says Greenacre, have fantasies of omnipotence which are excluded from "reality testing." "The imposture cannot be sustained unless there is emotional support from someone who especially believes in and nourishes it . . . . It is the demand for an audience in which the (false) self is reflected that causes impostures often to become of social significance." It is quite possible to fit Smith into this pattern, although Brodie admits the difficulty of imposing the clinical definitions of 1970 "on the social and political realities of 1840," and of "diagnosing a man long since dead."[15] In any case, the model may explain why Smith wrote the Book of Mormon, but not how.

For a historian, this is perhaps the more important question. The most influential explanation, popularized also by Fawn Brodie, ties the origin of Mormonism to the cultural milieu of early nineteenth-century America. Brodie took her cue from Alexander Campbell, famous contemporary of Smith and a founder of the Disciples of Christ, one of whose most prominent associates, Sidney Rigdon, became a Mormon. In a bitter attack on his competitor he charged that the Book of Mormon was a hodgepodge addressing itself to all the major theological questions of the times: "infant baptism, ordination, the trinity, regeneration, repentance, justification, the fall of man, the atonement, transubstantiation, fasting, penance, church government, religious experience, the call to the ministry, the general resurrection, eternal punishment, who may baptize, and even the question of freemasonry, republican government and the rights of man."[16] Brodie has shown that there is some truth in Campbell's charge. The virtually innumerable parallels between the historical climate and Smith's own ideas are simply too strong to allow them to be dismissed as being coincidental. The Book of Mormon and subsequent writings and revelations of Smith, she says, "can best be explained, not by Joseph's ignorance nor by his delusions, but by his responsiveness to the provincial opinions of his time. . . . His mind was open to all intellectual influences, from whatever province they might blow."[17]

Coupled with this receptivity was a vivid imagination. Lucy Mack Smith, Joseph's mother, recalled that "During our evening conversations, Joseph could occasionally give us some of the most amusing recitals that could be imagined. He would describe the ancient inhabitants of this continent, their dress, mode of traveling, their buildings, with every particular; their mode of warfare; and also their religious worship. This he would do with as much ease, seemingly, as if he had spent his whole life among them." What makes Lucy's account particularly significant is that Joseph spun out these stories some time before he produced the Book of Mormon.[18]

Yet even a cursory examination of Joseph Smith's contribution to the history of American religion makes it clear that his life and work cannot be explained merely by his penchant for tall tales and an unusual sensitivity to his environment. Even the explanation of Thomas F. O'Dea, one of the most respected scholars of Mormonism, has something bland and unsatisfactory about it: "There is a simple common-sense explanation which states that Joseph Smith was a normal person living in an atmosphere of religious excitement that influenced his behavior as it had that of so many thousands of others and, through a unique concomitance of circumstances, influences and pressures, led him from necromancy into revelation, from revelation to prophecy, and from prophecy to leadership of an important religious movement . . . ."[19] Smith may not have been a paranoiac, a "parapath," or an impostor, but "a normal person" he was not. In the opinion of some non-Mormon scholars, in fact, his religious imagination may well have lifted him into the realm of genius.[20] According

to Professor Jan Shipps, Smith's creativity may perhaps
best be explained on the same basis on which we attempt
to explain the creative genius of a Mozart or a Beethoven.
Unquestionably, environmental influences were crucial in
the development of these composers. And as in the case of
Joseph Smith, it is these necessary causes that find a ready
explanation. It is the sufficient causes that in both instances
prove to be so elusive. How do you explain "genius"? The
modi operandi of both Mozart and Smith provide at least
some clues. According to a standard cliché, genius is 90
percent perspiration, and 10 percent inspiration. Mozart
astounded his contemporaries innumerable times because
his compositions seemed to flow from his pen so ef-
fortlessly, as if dictated by some unseen power. His famous *Linz* symphony is a good example. He was able to
produce it in record time because he had in fact worked on
the composition for a number of years—in his head. When
the occasion demanded, he merely had to write the music
down.

The major portion of the Book of Mormon, likewise,
was produced in an astoundingly short time, being completed ninety days after Oliver Cowdery started taking
dictation from the prophet. This amounts to a production
of about three thousand words a day, leading I. Woodbridge Riley to the speculation that the Book of Mormon
was the result of automatic writing induced by epilepsy.
Any suggestion, however, that Smith may have suffered
from such a disease has been discredited. As the experiments by William Butler Yeats and others suggest, however, epilepsy is no necessary precondition for automatic
writing. Nevertheless, the length of the work, requiring a
consistent and sustained effort over three months, di-
minishes the plausibility of the automatic writing hypothesis.[21]

The story of Cowdery's unsuccessful attempt at translation may have some bearing on how the book was produced. After persistently requesting permission to try his
hand at translating, Oliver was finally allowed to do so, but

was unsuccessful in the attempt. In a revelation, Joseph explained Oliver's failure. Cowdery had misunderstood the gift of translation, had supposed that it would be given to him without any effort on his part. "But, behold," he was told, "you must study it out in your mind," an injunction Smith himself apparently followed.[22]

The analogy to musical genius is particularly instructive in the light of some recent speculations by psychologist Julian Jaynes, who has suggested that divine revelations are a product of the right hemisphere of the human brain, the same area of the brain that governs musical ability. Jaynes has also advanced some interesting ideas about the nature of genius. Modern men, says Jaynes, are governed by "consciousness" and reason, qualities controlled by the left hemisphere of the brain. In most of us, qualities controlled by the right hemisphere have become atrophied, but less so in certain highly creative individuals. Contrary to popular opinion, the highest processes of thought are governed as much by intuition as by reason. In the abstract sciences, especially, many of the world's greatest contributors to knowledge have reported a "sudden flooding of insights." A close friend of Einstein reported "that many of the physicist's greatest ideas came to him so suddenly while he was shaving that he had to move the blade of the straight razor very carefully each morning, lest he cut himself with surprise. And a well-known physicist in Britain once told Wolfgang Köhler, 'We often talk about the three B's, the Bus, the Bath, and the Bed. That is where the great discoveries are made in our science.'" "The essential point here is," Jaynes continues, "that there are several stages of creative thought: first, a stage of preparation in which the problem is consciously worked over; then a period of incubation without any conscious concentration upon the problem; and then the illumination which is later justified by logic."[23] Interestingly enough, Smith claimed that much of his work followed this kind of pattern.

That same kind of pattern can be identified in the work of great innovators such as Darwin and Marx. Like them,

Smith cast a vast body of knowledge and belief into a new
mold. In the words of Fawn Brodie, Mormonism "was
a real religious creation, one intended to be to Christianity
as Christianity was to Judaism: that is a reform and a consummation." Much the same, in a different context, of
course, can be said of Marx's contribution to political economy, and of Darwin's to biology. What all three have in
common are tremendous powers of synthesis and an unusual ability to transcend the confines of their "discipline,"
addressing themselves to human problems of universal
significance. All three have been accused of being charla-
tans who, far from being original, merely appropriated the
ideas of others for their own purposes. Yet at the same
time, it must, of course, be conceded that since neither
Marx nor Darwin claimed divine or miraculous assistance
in the creation of their work, they do not present the
interpretative difficulties facing us in the case of Smith.
Indeed, confronted with a multiplicity of interpretations of
varying plausibility and complexity—and all lacking absolute certainty—one of our classical ancestors, conversant
with the law of parsimony, might well have opted for divine revelation as the simplest and therefore correct explanation.[24]

As an alternative, modern secular students of Mormonism have recourse to a repertory of explanations
allowing for the plausibility of revelation without the
necessity of giving up their secular orientation. I want to
elaborate a bit further on Julian Jaynes's recent, controversial study, *The Origin of Consciousness in the Breakdown of the Bicameral Mind,* in which he develops a theory
of language and consciousness that also serves as an attempt to explain the origins of religion. According to
Jaynes, though humans developed language about 100,000
years ago (the conventionally accepted theory), they did
not evolve an inner life, or "consciousness," until about
2,000 B.C. Prior to that time, life was guided mostly by
habit, as for example in ancient Egypt or pre-Homeric
Greece. Humans lacked introspection, independent will,

or the ability to perceive a past and a future. Gradually, as life became more complex and stressful, man responded through the development of inner voices which enabled him to gain control over a hostile world. The human brain evolved to accommodate these voices, assigning them to its right hemisphere, while reserving the left hemisphere to language. In a sense, the right hemisphere was giving instructions to the left. Jayne believes he has discovered an explanation for the role of religion in the development of ordered, structured societies.

"Bicamerality," however, began to break down some-time between the second and the first millennium B.C., as society became too intricate and complex to be governed by the relatively simple command of the "voices." More and more, man began to rely exclusively on the left hemis-phere of the brain, with its highly developed potential for analytical language and rationality—or, in Jaynes's words, consciousness. "Man," says Jaynes, "became modern." Nevertheless, the transition has not been an absolute one. Stress, apparently, can work in opposite directions. While it played a significant part in breaking down bicamerality, it can also trigger its restoration. In a stressful world such as ours, "most of us," says Jaynes, "spontaneously slip back into something approaching the actual bicameral mind at some part of our lives." Others, less able to handle stress, relapse permanently, or for long periods, into the bicam-eral mind. In our society we label these people schizo-phrenics. Because auditory hallucinations are very com-mon among schizophrenics, it has in fact been suggested that Joseph Smith may have suffered from this mental dis-order. Yet Smith clearly did not exhibit any of the other symptoms of schizophrenia. Nevertheless, it is possible to fit him into the conceptual framework of Jaynes, who sees the transition from bicamerality to consciousness as far from complete. "All about us," he says, "lie the remnants of our recent bicameral past," in spite of the profound impact of Christianity, which began "as a necessarily new religion for conscious men rather than bicameral men" with its emphasis on an internalized ethic rather than a morality imposed by external authority. Yet he also points out that the history of Christianity has been a permanent struggle between a "longing for bicameral absolutes . . . [and] the difficult inner kingdoms of *agape*," with "an external hierarchy reaching through a cloud of miracle and infallibility to an archaic authorization in an extended heaven."[25]

Mormonism appeared on the American religious scene at precisely that moment when external religious authority, both intellectually and institutionally, was in headlong retreat before the forces of individual responsibility and internal consciousness. For many Americans, accustomed to an older order of hierarchy and deference, the world was literally falling apart. In the words of Mario De Pillis, they began a "search for religious authority" or, in the words of Jaynes, for "archaic authorization." It was a time when many Americans began to ask: "Why are the gods no longer heard and seen?" Some of them demanded more assurances "than the relics of history or the paid insistences of priests. Something palpable, something direct, something immediate! Some sensible assurance that we are not alone, that the gods are just silent, not dead, that behind all this hesitant subjective groping about for signs of certainty, there is a certainty to be had."[26] And it was in western New York, in the 1820s, that in the words of a famous Mormon hymn, "An angel from on high / The long, long silence broke." Thus, in Jaynes's hypothesis Joseph Smith—and people like him, who have visions, hear voices, and have dreams—can be explained as premodern individuals whose ability to use the right hemisphere of the brain far exceeds that of their more analytical and more modern contemporaries.

Jaynes's theory, admittedly, is highly controversial. Indeed, many academic psychologists, biologists, and religious scholars have expressed grave reservations about its validity. Nevertheless, even if we do not accept its physiological basis for psychological phenomena, we can use the concept of bicamerality as a metaphor that provides an imaginative and suggestive alternative framework for explaining the visions and revelations of Joseph Smith to those who cannot accept him as a "true" prophet in any objective sense, yet who do not wish to condemn him as an impostor, a charlatan, or a deluded fanatic. Even if it may be possible to dismiss Smith in these terms, there remains the puzzling question of how he was able to fool his closest associates who, likewise, had visions and heard voices. The three witnesses, for example, though all of them fell out with Smith and left his church, affirmed their supernatural experiences to their dying day. One of them, Oliver Cowdery, had also been present at an appearance of John the Baptist. After leaving Smith in disillusionment, he nevertheless wrote: "the angel was John the Baptist, which I doubt not and deny not." To explain such phenomena with the bland statement—as the otherwise brilliant Fawn Brodie does—that Smith had a "talent for making men see visions" is about as satisfactory as the medieval practice of explaining the powers of opium by its "dormitive faculties."[27]

Whatever power Smith may have had over other men, he emphatically insisted that he had the ability to see visions from his early youth. In 1838 he claimed in his official autobiography (later canonized) that as early as 1820, when he was a mere boy of fourteen, he had suffered from a severe religious anxiety regarding the truthfulness of various competing sects who vied for followers in western New York—an area well known among contemporaries as the "burned-over district" because of the fires of revivalist enthusiasms perennially sweeping the countryside in the early nineteenth century. In his confusion, he retreated into a grove behind his father's farm, where he poured out his heart to God in quest of religious security and certainty. He related that in answer to his fervent prayer he had a vision in which none other than

God the Father and Jesus Christ appeared to him in person. In reply to his question which of the various competing religious denominations were true, he was told to

> join none of them for they were all wrong; and the Personage who addressed me said that all their creeds were an abomination in his sight; that those professors were all corrupt; that: "they draw near to me with their lips, but their hearts are far from me, they teach for doctrines the commandments of men, having a form of godliness, but they deny the power thereof." He again forbade me to join with any of them; and many other things did he say unto me, which I cannot write at this time. When I came to myself again, I found myself lying on my back, looking up into heaven. When the light had departed, I had no strength; but soon recovering in some degree, I went home.[28]

To believing Latter-day Saints this first vision has become the central event of Mormonism. And it is this particular version that has been canonized as a part of Mormon scripture, and is proclaimed by missionaries across the world to sometimes believing but often skeptical audiences.

The reasons for this skepticism are of course as obvious as in the case of the Book of Mormon. Because of their very nature, religious experiences generally are beyond empirical verification. As William James said, "The attempt to demonstrate by purely intellectual processes the truth of the deliverances of direct religious experiences is absolutely hopeless."[29] Smith himself reported that when he recounted his story to friends and neighbors they believed him to be either dishonest or mad. A Methodist minister in whom he confided seemed at least to accept the reality of the vision, but proclaimed it to be "all of the devil." For a long time scholars dismissed Smith's vision in the same manner in which they had dismissed the Book of Mormon—as the product of a charlatan or of someone suffering from delusions. It is only recently that non-Mormon scholars have begun to consider seriously the possibility that Smith may have had a religious experience that should be judged by the same criteria as the experiences of other historical religious figures. Unfortunately, Smith made things difficult for himself by waiting eighteen years before setting down what was to become the official, authorized account of events that purportedly occurred in 1820. Even if he was sincere in his belief that he had "beheld a vision," by 1838 he would inevitably see those events in the light of the intervening history of Mormonism. Though in recent years Mormon historians have assembled fragments of earlier accounts, none can be traced back to the year 1820. Moreover, the versions differ in some of their details. While Latter-day Saint scholars tend to regard these earlier accounts as confirmation of Smith's veracity, some non-Mormon scholars have come to exactly the opposite conclusion, seeing them as evidence of the evolution of his fertile imagination. Because of their fragmentary nature, these accounts do not support firm conclusions for either side. Circumstantial evidence, likewise, has not helped to close the case. One scholar, who has challenged Smith's claim that the community where he lived experienced a revival in 1820, has himself been challenged by Mormon historians who, while they cannot prove that a revival did indeed occur in Palmyra in 1820, have raised valid objections to the contention that there is conclusive evidence that it did not occur.[30]

Another difficulty is raised by Smith's claim that the "telling of the story . . . excited a great deal of prejudice against me among professors of religion, and was the cause of great persecution, which continued to increase . . ." and that "men of high standing would take notice sufficiently to excite the public mind against me, and create bitter persecution; and this was common among all the sects—all united to persecute me."[31] So far Smith's words have not been corroborated by any contemporary source. That he experienced the most harrowing persecutions in his later career is a matter of record. These, however, did not begin until he inaugurated steps to launch a new religion in the late 1820s.

Joseph and his associates, nevertheless, continued to insist on the reality of their visions. The emphatic, uncompromising nature of these testimonies fits well into Jaynes's hypothesis. "Bicameral men," he says "did not imagine; they experienced." Certainly, that was the burden of Joseph Smith's own testimony. Unbelievers might scoff, he said. "However, it was nevertheless a fact that I had beheld a vision." He then likened his experience to that of Paul before King Agrippa. Few believed the ancient apostle, who insisted that he had seen a light and heard a voice. "But all this did not destroy the reality of his vision . . . and all the world could not make him think or believe otherwise." "So," continued Smith, "it was with me . . . I have actually seen a vision; and who am I that I can withstand God, or why does the world think to make me deny what I have actually seen? For I had seen a vision; I knew it, and I knew that God knew it, and I could not deny it, neither dared I do it; at least I knew that by so doing I would offend God, and come under condemnation."[32] Certainly, Jaynes's hypothesis provides a more plausible explanation for Smith's claims than Brodie's impostor thesis.

Jaynes's hypothesis is, of course, only one among a number of possible explanatory frameworks for getting a handle on Smith's revelations. T. L. Brink (a non-Mormon) has summarized four possible alternative explanations, derived from the insights of "depth psychology," in support of his assumption that "Joseph Smith was a man who was of sound mind and sincere religious convictions."[33] According to ego psychology, for example, the Freudian concept of regression with its pathological connotations can have positive significance as well, particularly in highly creative individuals, such as poets and artists, whose work can be described as a kind of adaptive regression. "According to Ego Psychology," says Brink, "Smith must be considered as a healthy, creative individual who effectively utilized adaptive regression."

Brink regards a Jungian version as even more illuminating, since it can be regarded as a kind of in-depth extension of ego psychology. From a Jungian perspective, Smith had tapped "the vast reservoir of creative energies within the collective unconscious" that he communicated to the world through symbols—such as the Urim and Thummim and the golden plates. How did Smith gain access to the collective unconscious? Possibly through daytime fantasizing or through dreams. Significantly, Smith recalled in his account of the First Vision that "When I came to myself again, I found myself lying on my back, looking up into heaven." It has been suggested that anyone capable of believing in the "collective unconscious" should have no difficulty believing in Smith's visions.

The school of individual psychology of Alfred Adler is also supportive of the serious intentions behind Smith's endeavor. "Adler felt that religion was basically an aid for healthy striving inasmuch as it called upon man to turn away from his self-boundedness . . . . all true religion had taught social interest." If this yardstick of truth is applied to Smith, he measures up very well. Several of the following chapters of this book will illustrate Smith's "healthy striving" as leader of religion and a community.

Finally, an Eriksonian approach to Smith's prophetic role gives insight into specific stages of his development. Because the record of Joseph's childhood is extremely fragmentary, and because the prophet was killed at the age of thirty-nine, only three of Erikson's eight stages are applicable: adolescence, young adulthood, and middle adulthood. Of these the first is the most significant because it was at that stage that Joseph claims to have had his first vision. According to Erikson, it is during adolescence that individuals establish their identities and firm loyalties, or "fidelity." For Joseph, the First Vision was the catalyst that helped him attain both identity and fidelity. He now knew that he was not to join any of the traditional churches, but, in refusing to do so, he was "being loyal to God's word."[34]

Joseph Kett has linked the general problem of adolescent identity to the specific historical problem of growing up in rural New England in the early nineteenth century. One of the most common pressures was the need to make a choice—especially regarding occupation and religion. Many adolescents found themselves in "a kind of moral pressure cooker." Joseph resolved this pressure by making a religious choice, a choice that in his case was absolute: ". . . it was the choice to end all choices in a society in which young people were subjected to an apparently endless sequence of role changes."[35]

Conspicuously absent from our discussion thus far has been Freud, the (often rejected) father of all the schools scrutinized by Brink. He avers that "no one has attempted to thoroughly and consistently study Joseph Smith from a psycho-analytic perspective" and regards the theories of Riley, De Voto, and Brodie as "unacceptable because they unfairly portray Joseph Smith pathologically, as an epileptic, paranoid, or psychopath." He is doubtful that a sophisticated application of psychoanalytic methods to a study of Smith would produce results helpful to a religious understanding of the Mormon prophet, since in the mind of Freud "neurosis and religion were to be considered products of infantile fantasy life." Brink believes that the disastrous consequences of Freud's method are illustrated in his psychoanalytic study of Woodrow Wilson.

The most successful psychoanalytic approach to Smith, Fawn Brodie's, nevertheless raises some hard questions because the Book of Mormon lays claim to being a work of history. Challenges to Smith's prophetic integrity, therefore, are more difficult to refute than challenges to the integrity of other prophets whose authority is based on personal revelation, such as Mohammed's or Ellen G. White's, or Mary Baker Eddy's (or even Smith's own vision). What makes Joseph unique, but also more vulnerable, is the Book of Mormon. Brodie, admittedly, makes the most of this problem. Yet her insistence that Mormonism must be either "true" or false" may be a result of her need to come to terms with her own Mormon background. It is in fact ironic that in the process of rejecting her childhood religion she became enmeshed in the very same question that had agitated Joseph Smith. From a historical perspective, however, the question whether Mormonism is "true" or "false" is simply far less important than the question of just what kind of religion it is that Smith brought into being.[36]

III

Mormonism was part of that larger early nineteenth-century American search for primitive Christianity that also impelled Alexander Campbell and his Disciples, as well as a host of other searchers for the "primitive Gospel"—a quest for simple origins, away from complexity, from sectarian competition, inspired by a hope that through the spirit of God all Christians could be returned to a unity of the faith undivided by sectarian dogmas and rituals.[37] Unlike Campbell and most other "primitivists," however, Smith did not stop at that point, but in a new scripture called the Book of Moses he insisted on going back even further in time, to a simple and Edenic past that had its beginnings with Adam and that had seen realization even after the Fall in the holy city of Enoch, which, because of its perfection, had been removed from this earth to God's glory. In the beginning, man had been pure, perfect. Yet even after the Fall the earth was peopled by a race of giants, both physically and spiritually. Their language was pure and undefiled. There were no poor among them. Their rulers were priests, governing justly, by "correct principles," and by the authority of God. When Smith spoke of the "restoration of all things" in the last days, he expressed a cyclical view of history in which the end—his own generation—would be like the beginning. Putting it differently, Smith was rejected the complex society of his own day and yearning for a return to a supposedly pure and simple premodern age—an age in which God spoke to man, something He had not done for nearly eighteen

hundred years. W. W. Phelps, in one of the most famous
and most popular of Mormon hymns, captured perfectly
the restorationist and revelatory impulse of Mormonism:
"The Spirit of God like a fire is burning! The latter-day
glory begins to come forth; The Visions and blessings of
old are returning, And angels are coming to visit the
earth."

There were of course other Protestant denominations
that believed in the gifts of the spirit. Yet none did so in
quite as literal a fashion as Mormonism. Protestant revivalism was in fact very modern in its appeal and in its
expressions, while Mormonism looked to ancient patterns
of religion not only in substance but in form. To most
modern Protestants, even those oriented toward fundamentalism, God spoke in metaphors and symbols, which
were manifested through subjective, spiritual experiences.
Mormons, however, tended to obliterate the distinction
between subject and object, between the physical and the
spiritual, between the sacred and the profane. The natural
and the supernatural world consisted of one continuum.
What needed explanation in the minds of Joseph Smith
and his followers was not why God and angels had once
again communicated directly with man, but why, for such a
long time, they hadn't.

Had God wilfully withheld his presence from his children? Not so. Quite obviously, it was the other way
around. It was his children who had ceased to listen to
Him. After the days of the apostles, a great falling away, a
great apostasy, had severed the link between God and
man, dropping the human race into the great abyss of the
Dark Ages, presided over by a great abominable church,
"the whore of all the earth," the church of the devil, whose
power was finally broken by the Protestant Reformation.
What the reformers lacked, however, was authority to act
in the name of God. Having broken with the apostolic
succession, Protestants insisted that the Bible, as the sole
and complete record of the Word of God, provided
sufficient authority for those who believed, at least in

theory, in the priesthood of all believers. Yet to Joseph
Smith and his followers it was obvious that in the absence
of a central authority and the tradition of an apostolic succession, churches and sects had proliferated, each claiming
to be sole repository of correct biblical exegesis. It was
precisely this dilemma that had sent young Joseph into his
father's woods to ask of God which of all the sects was
true.

The divine answer, that they were all false, included, of
course, that church which claimed to have a monopoly on
the apostolic succession, built on the rock of Peter, of
which none other than Christ himself had said that the
gates of hell should not prevail against it. Since according
to the understanding of Smith the gates of hell had very
much prevailed against the church of Peter, Joseph had to
find an alternative interpretation for a scripture that had
itself stood as an indestructible rock against the onslaught
of reformers. The rock that Christ had in mind, said
Joseph Smith, was not the man Peter, but the rock of revelation. And it was upon the authority of this rock that the
Mormon prophet now challenged the authority of both the
universal church and its Protestant reformers.

Thus, what made the Book of Mormon unique was not
only its story and internal message, but also the manner in
which it had been produced. It was its divine origin that
gave it, in the minds of Mormons, a status and an authority
at least equal, even superior to that of the Bible. And it was
this claim, more than any other, that so enraged contemporary Americans. Even those churches and sects that believed in a continued visible manifestation of the divine
will in visions and miracles regarded any addition to (or
subtraction from) the canon of the Bible as blasphemous,
heedful of the warning of John the Revelator in the last
book of Revelation. Not so Joseph Smith, who interpreted
John's injunction as pertaining to the book of Revelation
only, as well as in principle to any specific revelation by the
mouth of God. That the book of Revelation appeared at
the end of the Bible was merely a rather arbitrary choice of

its later compilers, a kind of historical accident. The idea that God, through the mouth of John, had suddenly closed the heavens was merely the convenient rationalization of a "sectarian" world that had closed itself off from God. Joseph Smith, who insisted that he spoke with the same authority as the prophets of old, did not claim to have made any innovative additions to the word of God. Rather, he said, he was merely restoring those old truths and principles of the gospel which had been lost or corrupted. "We believe the Bible to be word of God," he affirmed in his Eighth Article of Faith, though adding significantly, "as far as it is translated correctly," and giving his own work scriptural status by continuing: "we also believe the Book of Mormon to be the word of God." This somewhat ingenuous statement, made for public consumption, ignored the fact that Mormons believe the Book of Mormon to be more correct than the Bible, for the very simple reason that the former had been translated by the power of God and not man. Joseph, in fact, once pronounced it to be "the most correct of any book on earth."[38] (Nevertheless, Mormons hold the King James Version in high regard and prefer it to any other English translation, though Smith thought Luther's German version more correct.)

In addition to the Bible and the Book of Mormon, a third set of scriptures accepted as canonical by Mormons is the Pearl of Great Price, consisting of the Book of Moses (as revealed to Smith in 1830), the Book of Abraham (an alleged translation of an Egyptian papyrus), a small portion of an attempted "inspired" translation of the Bible, Smith's autobiographical account of the origins of Mormonism, and the Articles of Faith (thirteen succinct statements of the essential beliefs of Mormonism). In 1976, two scriptures were added to the canon of the Pearl of Great Price, one a vision of Joseph Smith pertaining to the salvation of the dead, the other a vision by President Joseph F. Smith (October 3, 1918) pertaining to the redemption of the dead.

Of these, the Book of Abraham is of special interest because of a recent controversy concerning its origins and authenticity. In the 1820s, Americans acquired a great interest in things Egyptian. In fact, the Book of Mormon may well have reflected some of this interest, for Smith claimed that the original was not written in Hebrew, but in what he called "reformed Egyptian," ostensibly because it was a kind of shorthand that took up considerably less space than Hebrew on the precious and heavy golden plates. Although Champollion had already completed his work on the Rosetta stone, the news had not yet reached America. Thus, when a Michael Chandler toured the country with an exhibit of Egyptian curiosities in 1835 he called on Joseph Smith because of his reputed competence in Egyptian and asked to his aid in translating a number of papyri. Joseph acquired these from Chandler for $2,400, in those days a princely sum. In an attempt to decipher the contents, the prophet laboriously worked out an "Egyptian alphabet and grammar," though his attempts at translation continued to be foiled until he was able to invoke "direct inspiration from Heaven." The resulting translation was published in 1842 as the Book of Abraham, named after the purported author of the document.

It is therefore understandable that Mormons have resisted a recent challenge to the authenticity of this work. Unlike the golden plates, which Smith returned to the custody of the angel Moroni, the papyri remained in the possession of the prophet until the time of his death, when they were sold by a friend of his brother William, and for a long time were thought to have perished in the great Chicago fire. Unfortunately for the Mormons, news of the incineration of the papyri was premature, for in 1967 eleven fragments were discovered in the Metropolitan Museum in New York City. A scholarly translation published in 1968 revealed the papyri as rather common funerary documents bearing absolutely no relationship to the Book of Abraham. Significantly, this translation has

caused nary a ripple among the faithful, who are secure in
the knowledge that scholarly apologists are at work rec-
onciling the seeming discrepancy. There are layers of
meaning in this text, some suggest, and "translation" may
have simply meant that the prophet's mind was "triggered"
by the papyrus to produce a work that is really the result of
revelation and that, in any case, contains "true" and inspired teachings.[39] Even should such efforts fail, it is
doubtful that the faith of many Mormons would be sha-
ken. They have found in the writings of Joseph Smith a
world view and a guide for their own lives so consistent
and satisfying that they are able to resist mere empirical
evidence, relying rather on a kind of moral and spiritual
empiricism that confirms the truths of Mormonism regardless of the caveats raised by secular scholars who,
lacking the spirit of revelation, are able to dispense only
the "learning of men."

Mormons derive much of this spiritual certainty from
the principle of continuing or modern revelation. Though
the Bible, the Book of Mormon, and even the Book of
Abraham are regarded as the word of God, and thus time-
less, in a more limited sense they are accounts of God's
dealings with specific peoples in times past. Just as God
had spoken to these ancient people, He was now speaking
to His people in these latter days. The restoration of the
gospel required specific instructions, directed to the Saints
in nineteenth-century America. In a sheaf of revelations,
Joseph Smith thus established the general principles as
well as the details of church organization and government
and the "correct principles" necessary for the establishment of a religious society, a kingdom of God, that also
encompassed principles of economics, politics, and social
relations. Moreover, the continuing and changing needs of
society required a continuous stream of revelation. In his
Ninth Article of Faith, Joseph Smith declared: "We believe all that God has revealed, all that He does now reveal, and we believe that He will yet reveal many great and
important things pertaining to the Kingdom of God." In
1833, a first collection of these revelations was published

as the Book of Commandments. At the present time, 135 of Smith's revelations and official pronouncements, as well as those of two of his successors, have been canonized in the official Doctrine and Convenants.

Most of these revelations did not occur in as dramatic a fashion as the First Vision or the visitations of the angel Moroni. Indeed, Mormons believe that the Lord speaks in numerous ways to His children through His appointed prophets. Some of Joseph's revelations came to him in dreams, others he dictated as if responding to some unseen personage, still others he issued after serious reflection on a problem, speaking by way of inspiration. The recent, dramatic revelation by the current prophet, Spencer W. Kimball, that extended the priesthood to all worthy males—especially blacks, who heretofore had been excluded form this privilege—is a striking, current example of the manner in which Mormon prophets may receive revelation. According to one apocryphal account, it was the prophet Joseph Smith himself who appeared in a vision to President Kimball. The truth is more prosaic, as Kimball reported it to *Time* magazine: "I spent a good deal of time in the temple alone, praying for guidance, and there was a gradual and general development of the whole program, in connection with the Apostles." As Jan Shipps has pointed out, it is necessary to distinguish between visionary manifestations, which in the subjective experience of the recipient originate with God, and revelations such as Kimball's, in which God responds to man's specific questions and needs.[40] Because Kimball's revelation deals with a fundamental principle of church policy, it is quite possible that it will be canonized.

Revelations received by church member without official status are in a different category, though anyone is entitled to receive them. That is, after all, what had happened to Joseph when he was a mere lad of fourteen. Very early, therefore, the prophet found it necessary to establish certain ground rules for a principle of explosive potential. Most of his followers, understandably, were anxious to try their hands at these new gifts of the spirit. I have already

mentioned that Oliver Cowdery pressed Joseph for permission to translate the Book of Mormon until the
prophet, somewhat reluctantly, gave in. When Oliver
failed at the task, he was informed that such divine gifts
required the active participation of the recipient. Another
implied message was that Joseph could not afford serious
competition for his position as prophet. Like Luther before him, he quickly realized that the doctrine of the
priesthood of all believers had a potential for anarchy.
When later in the year Hiram Page claimed to have received revelations through a seer stone, a revelation instructed the faithful that "no one shall be appointed to
receive commandments and revelations in this church ex-
cepting my servant Joseph Smith, Jun., . . . For I have given
him the keys of the mysteries, and the revelations which
are sealed, until I shall appoint unto them another in his
stead."[41]

Although the Saints, after the death of Joseph Smith,
were not quite certain for some time just whom God had
appointed to take over the keys of revelation, the majority
finally agreed that it was Brigham Young. Three years after
Young's death, the senior apostle at the time, John Taylor,
assumed the keys. This move was precedental. Ever since,
the prophetic succession has been in strict accordance with
the principle of seniority. This institutionalization of the
principle of revelation, understandably, has raised serious
doubts about its spontaneity in the minds of skeptics.

After the formal organization of the church in 1830, the
principle of revelation was incorporated into the growing
institutional framework of the young religion. As already
indicated, only the prophet, seer, and revelator can receive
commandments and revelations for the whole church.
Lesser ecclesiastical leaders are entitled to receive revelation pertaining to their specific calling and sphere of authority. Fathers may obtain the word of the Lord for their
families, and individuals for themselves. Should any of
these revelations contradict those published in the scriptures, or the authority of the prophet or respective

ecclesiastical leaders, they will be regarded as having ema-
nated from a source other than divine.

This carefully regulated, institutional approach to revelation evolved over time, to be sure. Joseph himself was at
times rather freewheeling with his own gift. As a result, his
batting average was less than perfect. Unlike the Pope two
generations later, he did not claim infallibility. For example, when the printing of the Book of Mormon was
stopped for lack of money, Joseph received a revelation
directing Oliver Cowdery and Hiram Page to travel to
Toronto, where they would find a man willing to buy the
copyright of the Book of Mormon for enough money to
ensure publication. "We did not find him," reported
Cowdery, "and had to return surprised and disappointed. . . . I well remember how hard I strove to drive
away the foreboding which seized me, that the First Elder
had made fools of us, where we thought in the simplicity of
our hearts that we were divinely commanded." Without
losing his composure, Joseph faced his disheartened emis-
saries: "Some revelations are of God: some revelations are
of man: and some revelations are of the devil. . . . When a
man enquires of the Lord concerning a matter, if he is de
ceived by his own carnal desires, and is in error, he will
receive an answer according to his erring heart, but it will
not be a revelation from the Lord."[42] This kind of disarm-
ing candor, of course, worked very much to Smith's advantage. While it is obvious that under the circumstances
there was perhaps little else he could have done, he might
well have panicked and resorted to bluff, only to have it
called.

Smith very quickly gained sufficient control over his
followers to allow him to indulge his penchant for the
playful exercise of his imagination. During an expedition
to Missouri in 1834, some members of his party encountered an Indian mound on the Illinois River, from which
they excavated a skeleton. In reply to their eager inquiries,
the prophet quickly concocted a brief biography of an Indian warrior whom he called Zelf, who "in mortal life was a

white Lamanite, a large, thick-set man, and a man of
God .... He was a warrior and chieftain under the great
prophet Onandagus, who was known from the eastern sea
to the Rocky Mountains. The curse of the red skin was
taken from him, or, at least in part." After discovering an
arrowhead lodged between two ribs, Smith launched into a
vivid and detailed description of a great battle in which
Zelf had been killed. Smith's credulous followers carried
away the arrowhead and bones as souvenirs. The account
in the *History of the Church* strongly suggests that Smith, in
this episode, was seeking relief from the burden of
prophecy at the expense of some of his literal-minded and
gullible believers.[43]

This is not to suggest, however, that for the most part the
prophet did not take his role very seriously indeed. He
instilled in his followers a clear sense of his mission and his
destiny. He impressed upon them his role as the chief
source of the word and the will of God to his church,
indeed to all mankind. Translated into more concrete
terms, it meant that the prophet believed he had been
called to restore order to a chaotic world. He would have
agreed with Alexander Pope that "order is heaven's first
law . . ." The history of the world since the great apostasy
had been a history of disorder and confusion. Now, in the
latter days, this trend would be reversed. Through the
principle of revelation, men would once again receive authority to act in the name of God, just as in the days of the
apostles. Mormons agree with Catholics that apostolic authority and succession are of crucial importance. Having
been lost, however, they could only be restored by divine
intervention.

The question of divine authority apparently first entered
Smith's mind while he was translating the Book of Mormon. On May 15, 1829, he and Cowdery inquired of God
who had the authority to baptize, a question that had agitated the minds of many restorationists. While praying in
the woods about this matter, they were visited by a
heavenly messenger who identified himself as John the
Baptist, laid his hands upon their heads, and conferred

upon them what he called the Aaronic priesthood, with the
authority to baptize. Smith and Cowdery thereupon baptized each other in the Susquehannah River. Shortly
thereafter, they were visited by three other heavenly mes-
sengers, Peter, James, and John, who conferred upon the
two the higher or Melchizedek priesthood, and with it the
apostolic succession. Smith and Cowdery now had the authority to confer the gift of the Holy Ghost, by the laying
on of hands, as well as the power and authority to organize
a church.

From these beginnings, the Mormon priesthood has
evolved into a lay organization ideally including all male
members that have reached the age of twelve. A boy is first
ordained to the office of deacon in the Aaronic priesthood,
and then advances to the offices of teacher and priest. At
about age nineteen, a young man who has moved up
through the ranks, and who is deemed worthy, is then
ordained to the office of elder in the Melchizedek priesthood. Elders form the backbone of the church, with most
male adult members retaining this rank for the rest of their
lives. Those in higher leadership positions are appointed as
high priests. The office of seventy involves a special missionary calling. The most special calling of all is that of
apostle. In emulation of their predecessors in the days of
Christ, twelve men are organized into this highest quorum
in the church. It is from their ranks that the First Presidency, consisting of the prophet and normally two coun-
selors, is appointed. Altogether, then, there are usually
fifteen apostles. It is these men who direct the affairs of the
church, assisted by a growing number of other general
authorities, the largest body of which is called the First
Quorum of the Seventy.

IV

Having thus restored the authority of the priesthood by
divine revelation and having published the Book of Mormon, Smith was now ready to organize a church. Thus it
was that on April 6, 1830, he gathered with some of his

followers at Peter Whitmer's farm in Fayette, New York, and officially launched the "Church of Christ." In order to distinguish it from other churches of Christ, the name was changed in 1834 to the Church of the Latter-day Saints, in keeping with the Mormon belief in the imminence of the Second Coming. Finally, in 1838, as a result of revelation, the name was changed to the Church of Jesus Christ of Latter-day Saints, a name that has remained official to this day—although the church has always been much better know by its unofficial name, Mormon. Originally, this name was used as a term of opprobrium and derision, to which the Saints took vigorous exception. Yet as conflict ceased, Mormons readily embraced a name that simply would not come unstuck. In fact, it has acquired a certain advertising glamour, a brand name that now sells Mormonism in the press, on TV, on radio, and even on bumper stickers.

These media, of course, did not sell Mormonism in the days of its infancy. Neither were they needed. The magnetic personality of the young prophet got the new religion off to an auspicious start among members of his family, friends, and neighbors. Within a short time, "branches" of the church formed in Colesville, Fayette, and Manchester, and in Harmony, Pennsylvania, while Smith and his converts embarked on missionary trips to spread the message of the restored gospel. The conversion of Newel K. Whitney in January, 1831, gives a clue to Smith's success. Traveling by sleigh in Ohio, he alighted in front of a general store owned by Gilbert and Whitney, dashed up the steps, and strode into the store.

"Newel K. Whitney! Thou art the man!" the prophet exclaimed dramatically as he extended his hand.

"You have the advantage of me," replied the startled co-owner of the store. "I could not call you by name as you have me."

"I am Joseph the Prophet," he replied with a smile. "You've prayed me here, now what do you want of me?"

An overwhelmed Whitney was baptized shortly thereafter and remained a loyal Mormon all his life.[44]

Less dramatic, but more momentus for the future course of the young faith, was the conversion of Sidney Rigdon some months earlier. Significantly, it was not Smith's personality but the Book of Mormon that convinced him of the truth of Mormonism. Rigdon was one of the most prominent revivalists on the Western Reserve, a convert to the Disciples of Christ, and a close associate of Alexander Campbell. In August of 1830, however, Rigdon had broken with Campbell because the leader of the Disciples opposed Rigdon's involvement in a communitarian experiment at Kirtland, in the vicinity of Cleveland. When Mormon missionaries arrived shortly after the break, Rigdon received them warmly. A Christian "primitivist" who was looking to the restoration of the ancient gospel, Rigdon saw in Mormonism the fulfillment of his expectations. The Book of Mormon, especially, was to him concrete evidence of the authenticity of the new faith. Though he had not yet met its prophet, he joined the church, bringing with him about 150 members of his flock. This was more than double the number of followers Smith had been able to convert in New York and Pennsylvania. Rigdon soon after traveled to New York to meet the author of the book that had converted him. When he was able to persuade the prophet to pull up stakes and move to Ohio with all of his eastern followers, there were those who thought that Rigdon was gaining control over Smith and the new church. This, however, was not so. Rigdon became a close confidant of Joseph. Yet the prophet always made it very clear that it was through him, and through him alone, that the Lord spoke to the church. It was a point on which Rigdon needed reminding from time to time.

Not so another convert, whose impact on the history of Mormonism was to be even more momentous. Brigham Young unquestioningly accepted the primacy of Joseph all his life, even after the prophet's death. This was one important reason why Young quickly rose to prominence in a church that almost from its beginning stressed obedience to authority—of course not just any authority, but an authority derived directly from God. And to Young, as to all those who were not converted by the personal magnetism of Joseph, it was the Book of Mormon, more than any other vehicle, that convinced him of the truthfulness of Smith's claims. What convinced seekers such as Young was not so much the story of angels, golden plates, and magic spectacles, or the historical setting and the story of the book, important as they were. Rather, it was its message of the restoration of the ancient gospel. And that message was something with which most of these seekers were thoroughly familiar. They found in the Book of Mormon confirmation of what they believed already, or what they wanted to believe. This, more than anything else, was the genius of the book. Once having accepted its message, believers found it easy to accep the manner of its origin.

The story of the conversion of Brigham Young, though perhaps not typical, nevertheless illustrates the appeal of Mormonism. Like so many of his contemporaries, he encountered on the frontier "those flaming, fiery revivals so customary with the Methodists." Yet these fires of the spirit left him cold. He later recalled that at an early age he "had but one prevailing feeling" regarding religion: "Lord, preserve me until I am old enough to have sound judgment and a discreet mind ripened upon a good solid foundation of common sense." Like many another Mormon convert, he flitted from church to church, attending meetings of Episcopalians, Freewill Baptists, Reformed Methodists, and even the Quakers. Yet none satisfied his search for truth. Even when he first encountered the Book of Mormon, he withheld judgment: "I examined the matter studiously for two years before I made up my mind to receive that book . . . . I wished time sufficient to prove all things for myself." On another occasion he recalled that "I watched to see whether good common sense was manifest; and if they had that, I wanted them to present it in accordance with the Scriptures . . . when I had ripened everything in my mind, I drank it in, and not till then."[45]

Quite clearly, the majority of those drawn to Mormonism were out of tune with the revivalistic temper of the times. And however antiintellectual Mormonism may appear to a modern citizen of the twentieth century, it was separated by an intellectual gulf from such church fathers as Tertullian, who unblushingly proclaimed, *Credo quia absurdum est,* "I believe because it is absurd." Although early Mormonism lacked the philosophical and theological subtlety that makes possible a Saint Thomas or a Paul Tillich, it had an internal consistency as well as a kind of common sense rationality that set it very much apart from much of the emotionally infused, nonintellectual emphasis of antebellum American revivalism. Most early Mormon converts had been disillusioned by Protestant evangelical religion. To many of these anxious souls the fires engendered in a revival meeting flared up briefly, only to be extinguished shortly after the seekers returned to their daily chores.

What most of those who joined the new faith seem to have needed was to reason out their relationship to God. The Book of Mormon, and later the other writings of Smith, provided ample opportunity for a confrontation with those questions that agitated their souls and minds. The New England heritage of "piety and intellect" of many early Mormons may partially explain this predilection. So may the social origins of early Mormons. Though many of them, like the Smiths, were beyond the edge of successful, genteel society, they were on the whole better educated than their social and economic position might have suggested. The reason is that many of them were displaced persons whose families had known better times. An outpouring of early Mormon diaries, journals, and letters comprise a popular subliterature pointing to a high degree of literacy of a folk who for the most part made their living as artisans and farmers.

As a class, many of these kinds of people, when they turned from established religion, had found their way to Universalism, or even Deism. Joseph Smith's own grandfather, who became a Universalist, is a good example of this trend. Both of these faiths (if Deism can be called that)

had a kind of common sense, rational appeal. Even as
Deism was dying out among the intellectual classes, it persisted among certain groups of artisans and mechanics.
Not many of these, to be sure, became Mormons. Yet
their frame of mind, or disaffection from established religions, and the search for alternatives that were not only
emotionally but also rationally satisfying were much the
same.

Perhaps it may seem self-contradictory to call people
who believed in divining treasures in the earth, in folk
magic, who believed in spirits, and accepted tales of angels,
of golden plates, and sacred spectacles—as being "rational." And yet, as we learn more about popular beliefs
and so-called superstitions, they were frequently derived
from logically consistent connections between religious
belief, a specific need, and an empirical attitude toward
nature. It must be remembered that the anthropological
and cultural context of the Book of Mormon did not contradict the scientific opinion of the day. Indeed, this can be
said for the entire cosmology of Mormonism which helps
explain the emphases on physical evidence: the golden
plates, the spectacles, the papyri of the Book of Abraham.
Moreover, these people did not tend to make the distinction that a modern, scientifically oriented world makes
between the natural and the supernatural. Rather, the two
merged into one. And the validity of experiences in both
worlds could be verified by a kind of common sense
"Baconianism"—a crude process of hypothesis verification
that was also part of such cults as Mesmerism and Spiritualism.[46]

These shrewd Yankees were also imbued with a simple
kind of pragmatism. They were not fooled very long by
gold-seekers whose treasures remained forever hidden, or
by faith healers who could do no better than ordinary
medical doctors. The fact is, of course, that in an age when
the record of academic medicine was a dismal one, many a
faith healer could compete effectively. And though
Smith's discovery of the golden plates may well have

smelled of fraud to the skeptical, his very boldness put many a skeptic on the defensive. They were asked to inquire, to test, to satisfy their questions and doubts before they accepted Smith's claims. Conversion might take days, even weeks, or, as in the case of Brigham Young, years. When it came, it is true, it could come only through the spirit. As Moroni admonished in the concluding chapter of the Book of Mormon, the truthfulness of the record would be made known only to those who asked of God, "with a sincere heart, with real intent, having faith in Christ."[47] Yet implicit in this admonition is the idea of putting one's faith to the test, of participating actively in the process.

What I have said here may appear to contradict the metaphor of "bicamerality" as applied to Joseph earlier in the chapter. This, however, is not so. It is quite clear that in the entire history of Mormonism the prophetic gifts of Joseph stand apart. A few of his early contemporaries, such as Oliver Cowdery, did have some intense spiritual experiences. Smith, however, was the only one whose mind and spirit were open to revelatory manifestations throughout his prophetic career. It was Joseph who stood as the link between "bicamerality" and "reason." His followers, for the most part, were rational individuals who had lost contact with the life of the spirit and who yearned for its return.[48] Unlike Joseph's, most of their spiritual experiences were vicarious. Brigham Young is a good example of this frame of mind. Though a number of Smith's other prophetic successors were more "spiritual" than Young, none could remotely match the founder of their church in spiritual gifts.

The kind of people who became Mormons were individuals who hungered for these gifts. If they had been familiar with a current expression, they might have agreed that, if Mormonism had not already existed, it would have had to be invented. Yet it is also true that for these seekers no one could have taken the place of Joseph, whose gifts set him apart from all competitors, both within and without Mormonism. Whatever the nature of Joseph's gift, it enabled him to speak to a substantial minority of Americans who were out of tune with the temper of the times. More than anyone else, he put into words their fears and hopes, their discontents and aspirations.

2 Mormonism and American Culture

The Mormon people teach the American religion.

Tolstoy

I

The birth of Mormonism coincided with the birth of modern America. This was an age of fundamental and dramatic change, though change was not, of course, an invention of nineteenth-century America. In a way the entire history of America, from its seventeenth-century beginnings, has been a history of change. Yet many historians are in agreement that measured against the nineteenth century, the society of colonial America was a relatively stable one. It was in the early part of the nineteenth century that physical, institutional, and psychological change accelerated to a degree unknown to previous generations. Though the population continued to grow at a rate no faster than in Benjamin Franklin's age of a "rising people," because of its sheer numbers the doubling of the population in the first quarter of the nineteenth century appeared much more dramatic than the doubling in the third quarter of the eighteenth. (In 1775, the U.S. population was 2,500,000; in 1820, it was 10,000,000.) When the Smiths, for example, arrived in New York in 1816, Rochester was little more than a clearing in the wilderness. By 1830, the year Smith founded the Mormon church, Rochester had become America's newest city, with a population of 10,000.

For most Americans, such growth continued to be a cause for optimism. Yet for an increasing number it also became a source of anxiety. As more and more people moved into the growing cities, in the eyes of patrician reformers Christian virtues were declining in favor of vice and corruption. The teeming frontier, likewise, seemed to breed bad manners at best and irreligion at worst. The necessity of feeding a growing population speeded the transformation of the economics of agriculture as more and more farmers changed their subsistence operations to market-oriented production—a necessity that explains the spectacular success of cities such as Rochester. The transportation revolution was both cause and effect of this transformation (the Smith family arrived at the beginning of the second stage of that revolution, the canal era). A secondary consequence was an increase in physical mobility, providing many Americans, like the Smiths, both with the encouragement and the means for pulling up stakes for greener pastures, while at the same time increasing in many of the migrants a sense of rootlessness and a yearning for stability.

This physical change was accompanied by a transformation, even dissolution of traditional institutions. While the Revolution had already destroyed the traditional political order, the disestablishment of the churches was completed in its wake. By the first quarter of the nineteenth century the privatization of the church, of the economy, and even the family, were well along their way. The Federalists had clung to patrician notions of government and society for the better part of a generation, but with the election of Andrew Jackson in 1828 the last vestiges of their influence were trampled under the feet of the "mob" congratulating the Old Hero as they soiled the carpets in the White House. While it is true that the government continued to play an important role in the economy, the Jacksonian ideology proclaimed the arrival of the modern, negative state, a doctrine which achieved some substance in the Maysville veto and the Charles River Bridge case. The traditional, paternalistic conceptions of the state that had motivated the Federalists were gradually making way for the principle of laissez-faire, which exchanged the visible hand of the government for the invisible hand of Adam Smith. The natural world of equality of opportunity, in the minds of most Jacksonians, was self-regulating, in distinction to the old and now presumably defunct artificial world of special privilege, deference, and monopolies. Where the Federalists had enjoyed a privileged status based on inheritance and ascription, the Jacksonians had persuaded themselves that they had risen through their own efforts. By the 1830s institutional restraints in America had loosened dramatically.

In the opinion of some scholars, this transformation was accompanied by profound psychological changes that were especially manifest in the creation of a competitive, individualistic personality type that derived from a shift in the locus of authority in government, in religion, and in the family. While "stern fathers" had presided over the individual in colonial society, both physically and metaphorically, exercising externally sanctioned authority, modern individuals were self-directed, or "inner-directed" (to use the terminology of David Riesman), having internalized the ethical and social demands imposed upon them. According to some historians, the development of this new "modal personality" was an essential element in the process of modernization—in the creation of the new capitalist, urban, competitive order.[1]

Perhaps no institution played a more formative role in this transformation than religion. According to historian William McLoughlin the modernizing influence of religion was first dramatically revealed in the Great Awakening of the eighteenth century (1725–65), which strengthened the direct relationship between the individual and God, and thus loosened the ties to the traditional authorities of state, church, and family. The climactic culmination of this separation of a younger generation from its elders was the American Revolution. Having broken with their literal fathers, the rebels were psychologically prepared to break with their king. In McLoughlin's opinion, however, the revolution was only the first stage in a long and arduous process in which Americans were attempting to establish their national identity. The First Great Awakening had resulted in the external separation between England and America. A second awakening was now required to "provide the internal ideology which every new nation needs but which America's founding fathers purposely omitted from the Constitution." According to McLoughlin, therefore, the Second Great Awakening, which convulsed the American nation in several waves between the 1790s and 1860, was "the most central, the most pivotal" event "in the formation of the American national character or culture."

In order to fully understand this search for a national identity, McLoughlin suggests that the historian should take advantage of the insights of the anthropologist:

> American society, like any other, has its customs and rituals, its totems and taboos, its initiation ceremonies and its *rites de passage.* Just as no anthropologist would consider that he had come to grips with any so-called primitive tribe in Africa and Polynesia until he thoroughly understood its religious rituals and its enculturation process for the young, so no American historian can ever understand his social system until he understands the function which revivalism has played, and is still playing, in these aspects of our culture.[2]

Because anthropological studies of American culture have been very limited (with the exception of the Indians), McLoughlin also suggests that it might be appropriate to apply the insights anthropologists have gained in their studies of other cultures to American society. In *New Heaven, New Earth,* for example, Kenelm Burridge reports on a number of prophetic, millennial movements of the Third World.[3] In spite of profound specific differences among these various cults he has discovered a remarkably similar pattern of social and cultural transformation. As the prophetic movement gains momentum, the old rules of the society are jettisoned, and there follows a period of "no rules"—a time of intense, even frenzied experimenta-

tion with new social forms and rituals. By its very nature,
the intensity of this stage soon leads to exhaustion. It does
not take long before the participants consolidate and
stabilize the rules of the "new heaven and the new earth."
The society has adopted "new rules," which in time may
well be regarded as the old rules of yet another, future,
prophetic movement. If applied to antebellum American
history, it is perhaps possible to identify the waning
Federalist era as the period of old rules, the age of romantic revivalism—of "freedom's ferment," as Alice Felt Tyler
called it—as the period of no rules, and the era of the
consolidation of corporate capitalism as the age of new
rules (John Higham wrote of a transformation "from
boundlessness to consolidation").[4]

This model, of course, is not without its difficulties.
Anthropologists, for the most part, work with rather com-
pact societies or groups over short time-spans. In the case
of antebellum American culture, millions of people, comprising a variety of racial, ethnic, and cultural groups and
subgroups were involved. In the primitive societies
studied by Burridge, the overwhelming majority of the
members were caught up in the prophetic movement. If
we can believe Professor McLoughlin, in America,
likewise, it was a significant majority that became committed to one or another of the various phases of revivalism (at least in the white culture). This was an age of
transition in which individuals were suspended between
two worlds, "between an old order and that is dying a new
order that is yet to be born."[5] It was a brief time in American history during which, to some people, "all things are
possible." It was during these years that the old, paternalistic reform impulse directed toward social control
yielded to a romantic reform movement impelled by mil-
lennialism, immediatism, and individualism. A moderate,
patrician temperance movement that had attempted to
reform the drinking habits of the lower orders was transformed into an evangelically infused, middle class crusade
for total abstinence, and a conservative, gradualist African

Colonization Society was eclipsed by a romantic and radical movement for the immediate abolition of slavery.
American feminism had its origins in these same years
(with roots in abolitionism). An articulate peace movement began to inveigh against the horrors of war. Tocqueville and Beaumont traveled to America to study re-
forms in the prison system. The treatment of the mentally
ill became the concern of a crusade by Dorothea Dix.
Sylvester Graham sought to improve the human condition
through dietary reform. Thousands regarded hydropathy
as a significant improvement over traditional medicine.
Mesmerism and phrenology enjoyed widespread respectability. Numerous communitarian experiments, such
as Robert Owen's New Harmony in Indiana and the scores
of Fourierist phalanxes under the tutelage of Albert Bris-
bane, sought to provide alternatives to the individualism of
the age.

In the opinion of Professors Perry Miller and William
McLoughlin, the Second Great Awakening was like a tidal
wave—a *tsunami*—that swept away the last vestiges of an
old order and made possible the creation of the modern,
capitalist American empire with its fundamental belief in
religious, political, and economic pluralism.[6] What is so
impressive about these high-flying and imaginative (skeptical historians said imaginary) works is that a number of
recent, down-to-earth studies have corroborated the importance of evangelical religion in the formation of the
cultural values of modern America. In a seminal study of
Rochester from 1815 to 1837, Paul E. Johnson has shown
brilliantly how the revivals of Charles Finney proved the
essential linchpin in the development of industrial
capitalism and the legitimation of free labor.[7] In his
monumental *Rockdale,* anthropologist Anthony F. C. Wallace carefully and convincingly traced the formative role of
evangelical religion in the establishment of the modern
capitalist order in the cotton mill communities along the
Delaware River in Southern Pennsylvania.[8] In their
examination of precisely how the modern order was born

Johnson and Wallace have corrected the perspective of
historical inevitability implicit in the works of Miller and
McLoughlin.

Johnson and Wallace have restored the dialectical process to history by showing how the new order was born out
of a conflict that did not make it all apparent to the participants just what the outcome would be. Not suprisingly,
these evangelical, modernizing entrepreneurs and em-
ployers encountered strong resistance from traditionally
oriented workers, who attempted to shape a separate
identity and consciousness out of their own experiences of
class and culture. That in the long run only the most
strong-willed (or recalcitrant, if you wish) were able to
resist the onslaught of the evangelical-capitalist ethos does
not deny the intensity and historical significance of a struggle in which many workers ended up on the losing side.

There were of course many other losers as well. It is
only to be expected that in a country as large and diverse
as the United States significant cultural and religious
minorities would either fail to share this general evangelical fervor or else attempt to establish revitalization movements of their own that did not necessarily reflect and in
some cases even were in opposition to the cultural values
emerging out of the evangelical revivals. The old,
Calvinist-Federalist establishment, for example, did not
give in to the emerging democratic, pluralistic middle class
society without a fight. For reasons of their own, a variegated group of outsiders who had not shared in the power
of the old order likewise opposed the atomistic individualism of a society that seemed to thrive on competition and
conflict. Catholicism is a major example. Another group of
Americans who stood outside the evangelical pale were
those who founded or joined a collection of dissenting
movements that attracted many who were physically or
psychologically uprooted by the emerging new order.
Prominent among these were the Shakers, the Oneida
Perfectionists, and the Mormons.

Of all these movements, Mormonism emerged as the

most serious threat to the evangelical empire. Catholics, of course, were far more numerous. But, to Protestant Americans their ideology was so obviously alien that it lacked the subversive potential of Mormonism, which both in its origins and doctrines insisted on the peculiarly American nature of its fundamental values. At the same time, Mormonism was not merely one more variant of American Protestant pluralism but an articulate and sophisticated counterideology that attempted to establish a "new heaven and a new earth" intended as an alternative to the Protestant evangelical millennium. Mormonism, from a cultural and ideological perspective, may well have been for nineteenth-century Americans what communism became in the twentieth century.

While it is true that a religion such as Mormonism could arise only in the relatively open, evangelically enthusiastic period of American history, Mormonism itself was clearly no enthusiastic religion. As we have seen, the kind of people who became Mormons were either confused by evangelical revivals, such as Joseph Smith, or were left cold by the fires of enthusiasm, such as Brigham Young. The intensity of anti-Mormon persecution was in its way a backhanded compliment to a movement that became the most articulate and the best organized in its opposition to the values and practices of the evangelical empire. Even more than Shakers and Oneida Perfectionists, Mormons actively attempted to change the world through their all-encompassing vision of a kingdom of God that presented a challenge not only to the religious values of the evangelical empire but also to the closely related political, economic, and social values of antebellum America.

Thus, conflict between the Mormon empire and the American empire is, of course, not at all suprising. If, to repeat Professor McLoughlin, it was the Second Great Awakening that provided the internal ideology that consolidated the American national character and culture, and was thus "the most pivotal" movement in antebellum

America, then it stands to reason that a movement such as
Mormonism, which attempted to interfere in the formation of these values, did so at the risk of persecution.
When it is further understood that this challenge occurred at a time when what was to become the dominant
ideology was still very much in the process of being
formed, at a time when the national identity was far from
secure, at a time, in fact, when the evangelical crusade, in
the opinion of scholars such as McLoughlin and Miller,
was the manifestation of a national identity crisis, then,
perhaps, the surprising thing about the anti-Mormon
crusade is not that it occurred, but that the tales of mob
violence, of arson, pillage, and murder do not fill an even
larger volume.

Yet if Professor McLoughlin is correct in his assertions
that the Founding Fathers had purposely omitted the
internal ideology of the American people from the Constitution and that this ideology was, in fact, in the process
of being formed at the very time that Mormonism attempted its own definition of the meaning of America,
then the label un-American, so freely attached to the
Mormons (and other groups), has merely propaganda
value. Nevertheless, historians have addressed themselves
at great length to the question whether or not the Mormons were "American." Those unsympathetic to the
Saints have tended to answer the question in the negative,
while the Mormons themselves have always vigorously
rejected these allegations.

In the light of the foregoing discussion it may well be
true that this question is indeed a nonquestion. It is only
from hindsight that certain historians have felt confident in
settling the question with any degree of finality, after the
evangelical empire and the pluralistic, capitalist values it
helped establish became victorious in their quest for defining the American identity. Because the Mormons, along
with other antievangelical dissenters, were on the losing
side, the propaganda of the victors has prevailed and has

become a quasi-official version of America's quest for its national identity. At least that is the main thrust of historians of the evangelical mind, such as McLoughlin. Clearly, this is an American version of what Professor Herbert Butterfield has called the Whig interpretation of history.

In all fairness to the Whig historians, it should be conceded that the very complexity of the Mormon movement may well have encouraged their version of the relationship of Mormonism to American culture. Perhaps I have been too insistent on discovering a consistency that the historical record simply will not sustain, for as the next section will show, the social and intellectual history of Mormonism does not always seem to be cut of the same cloth.

II

In order to locate Mormon beliefs within the spectrum of American intellectual history, a brief sketch outlining the transformation of American religious thought may be appropriate. The New England origins of Mormonism dictate an emphasis on the social and intellectual transformation of that region. Puritanism, of course, had never been a static religion. Born in the religious ferment of Elizabethan England, it settled into seeming orthodoxy after its transplantation to New England. Yet even here, faced with its own heterodox challenges to the central tenets of Calvinism—especially predestination—New World Puritanism had to soften the relentless logic of its position in the Federal theology of the New England way as a subtle (an unacknowledged) concession to the Arminians, those heretical followers of the Dutch theologian Arminius, who insisted on the primacy of the will. Even so, Arminianism continued as one of the great thorns in the side of Puritan divines. Accompanying this intellectual dilemma was a social one. On the one hand, the Puritan "errand into the wilderness" demanded the strong social cohesion of the community; on the other, it encouraged

the development of the strong sense of individualism
among settlers. In time, Puritans were transformed into
Yankees, a change that involved traumatic intellectual and
social adjustments. It was in the early nineteenth century
that this transformation moved into the final stage. The
death of Calvinism, at least as a potent social and intellectual force, accompanied by the triumph of an individualistic ethic and a romantic world view were the dominant themes of antebellum American religious thought
and culture.

In a superficial sense, religion had as pervasive an influence in Jacksonian America as in colonial society. In
fact, the 1820s and 1830s experienced a tremendous religious upswing from the relatively irreligious age of the
revolution. Church membership, though not a very accurate guide to the religiosity of a people, increased dramatically. Tocqueville was right when he observed that
"there is no country in the world where the Christian religion retains a great influence over the souls of men than in
America; and there can be no greater proof of its utility
and of its conformity to human nature than that its influence is powerfully felt over the most enlightened and
free nation of the earth."⁹ And yet, in a subtle way, for all
its religious fervor, romantic America had experienced a
religious decline. A shift had occurred in the hierarchy of
values. Rhetorically, religion and theology remained eminently in the saddle, in fact more so in the 1830s than in
1800. But in the new world of pluralism the boundaries of
institutions were more narrowly drawn than in colonial
days. In an age of increasing specialization, competing institutions jealously guarded their prerogatives and resisted encroachment from the outside. The clear demarca-
tion of the line between church and state is a particularly
telling example of this change.

That decline is not unrelated to the rise of denominationalism so brilliantly described and analyzed by Sidney
Mead. Denominationalism derived from the varieties of

religions, state or free, that found a home in the American colonies. After the revolution, in the wake of disestablishment, the sects or churches—and in the American environment, though not in the European, these terms could almost be used interchangeably—found themselves more or less on an equal footing. All of them, even those descended from established churches in Europe, shared a general "sectarian" tendency, that is, each church conceived of itself as conforming more closely to the primitive church than any of its rivals. Each church believed that it had been stripped of the corrupting historical influences of its European progenitor. Each church built anew in the wilderness on its own version of the true and ancient foundations of the apostolic church.[10]

In America, however, these foundations were subject to sometimes extensive shifts. Though the principle of religious toleration, even in America, evolved only slowly, geographic, political, and social realities strongly favored that trend. By the eighteenth century, clearly, most sects and churches were "free to move with the tides of history, pragmatically, experimentally." Just as economic competition grew on the expanding and increasingly open market, so did competition among churches for followers. And by the nineteenth century, in their quest for growing membership, the sects discovered that the social context and the climate of opinion served as a not so subtle lever to encourage a pragmatic approach to religion. "Hence in a sense the very freedom which they felt and acted upon, . . . served to bind them to the obvious tendencies of the moment. In all innocence they built into the life of the denomination what time and tide happened to bring to their shores."[11]

The voluntary principle underscored this tendency even more. A "necessary corollary of religious freedom," it had, of course, deprived the churches of their coercive powers. In their competition for members, the denominations therefore had to appeal to potential converts. As a result, theological debates were deemphasized in favor of a general

antiintellectualism intended to make prospective members
comfortable. This tendency was further enhanced by a
general reaction to the "rational religion" of the American
enlightenment. The old harmony between reason and revelation, which had been consummated with such skill in
the theology of Jonathan Edwards, had broken down.
This was particularly evident in that famous nineteenth-
century institution that became the chief means of attract-
ing members to the denominations—revivalism. Because
the revivals of the various denominations were conducted
along similar lines and rested on the same intellectual and
cultural assumptions, they reveal a great deal about the
nature of the intellectual transformation of Calvinism.

On the surface the Second Great Awakening, which
began in 1795 in those famous camp meetings on the
Kentucky and Tennessee frontier, convulsed western New
York in the 1820s to such an extent that it was called the
burned-over district, and finally even invaded the eastern
seaboard cities, resembled very much the Great Awakening of the eighteenth century. But where Jonathan Edwards counted his converts in the hundreds, Charles
Grandison Finney, perhaps the most famous and representative revivalist of the Second Great Awakening,
counted them in the thousands. Surely, then, Finney
seemed to have wrought greater miracles than Edwards;
and yet, in the minds of the respective protagonists, precisely the reverse was true. Edwards, in 1735, viewed "the
conversion of many hundred souls in Northampton" as the
"surprising work of God." Finney, in contrast, recorded in
his *Lectures on Revivals of Religion,* written a hundred years
later (1835), that a revival "is not a miracle, or dependent
on a miracle in any sense. It is a purely philosophical result
of the right use of the constituted means." As William
McLoughlin put it, "the difference between the medieval
and the modern temper. One saw God as the center of the
universe, the other saw man. One believed that revivals
were 'prayed down' and the other that they were 'worked
up'."[12]

The conflicting implications of these two positions were such that they could not be reconciled. To Edwards, the assumption that a revival was a miracle, no matter how much men would contribute through "the use of proper means and endeavors," was essential to his fundamental belief that man is saved not by works but by grace. This belief, in turn, followed from the axiomatic proposition that God was sovereign, and that this sovereignty implied omniscience and omnipotence. Therefore, nothing in this world could occur without the will of God. Hence all events had been predestined by the deity. All men were sinners in the hands of an angry God. Yet empirical evidence, such as revivals, demonstrated what God in fact had promised through the sacrifice of His only begotten son, Jesus Christ, that not all men were eternally damned. A few, through His infinite grace and miraculous will, had been chosen for salvation. Therefore, the notion that man could bend and influence this will in his own favor detracted from God's sovereignty.

Even in Edwards's own day, there were many who regarded such a theology as unnecessarily harsh and cruel. In fact, Edwards perceived correctly that the social and intellectual currents of New England were very much against him. In a brilliant feat of intellectual legerdemain, Edwards, veritably the last scholastic of America, seized upon the science and philosophy of his day to shore up a crumbling system. Using Sir Isaac Newton and John Locke against the very apostles of the Englightenment to whom these men were prophets, Edwards, with devastating logic, reminded the critics of his position that the reality of both the metaphysical and the natural world did not depend upon the wishes of its residents. Man could no more deplore the nature of God than he could the laws of Newton. Edwards was not talking about the world as it ought to be but as it was. Man, in his finite wisdom, might well call a God who chose some for salvation as he dropped others into the eternal pit vengeful and cruel. But by the same token, man might lament the ebb and flow of the tides or the natural consequences of the violations of the laws of nature. The Fall, in fact, could be interpreted as such a violation, and its consequences the natural results.

Logically, such a position was difficult to refute. But romantic religion, of course, did not have to rely on logic. The Second Great Awakening released quite as much emotion as the first, although, viewed superficially, it may appear paradoxical that sinners in the hands of a benevolent God should manifest as much terror as those suspended, like spiders, over Edwards' fiery pit, in the hands of an angry God. But the paradox has a rather simple explanation. Men to whom sin—original sin—was a reality did not have to talk about it as much as those for whom sin became a *means* for salvation. Therefore, hellfire-and-brimstone sermons were just as much the stock-in-trade of nineteenth-century revival preachers as they were of the eighteenth. In fact, as Sidney Mead suggested, "the revivalists' emphasis that Christ came to save sinners had the effect of encouraging the Church to nurture sinners in order that it might save them."[13]

Finney's career as a revivalist, particularly in the 1820s and 1830s, helped deliver the coup de grâce to traditional Calvinism and replace it with "the Arminianized Calvinism called evangelicalism." The intellectual assumptions of this new mode of belief had been worked out painfully and slowly in the intervening century, and the main protagonists of that struggle, though lacking the intellectual stature of an Edwards, handled these difficult theological questions with a great deal more sophistication than Finney.

But Finney's theology was the kind a rising American middle class could understand and appreciate. Moreover, the social implications of Finney's rhetoric fit hand in glove with the individualistic rhetoric of Jacksonian America, though Finney himself was no Jacksonian. Hence, the influence of his ideas extended far beyond the Presbyterian church that held his nominal allegiance. In fact, his work probably more than that of any other of his contemporaries helped to transform evangelical Protestantism into a kind of national religion, popular not only among church members but among that great number of Americans who claimed allegiance to no particular denomination. Moreover, a goodly number of the members of more orthodox churches who professed to follow in the Calvinistic "tradition of the elders" privately held opinions that were more in harmony with diffuse national religion than that disseminated by their own ministers. To an increasing number of Americans, creeds, simply, were becoming less and less important. Just as Democrats and Whigs agreed to disagree, so did Methodists and Presbyterians. A modernizing America was slowly being transformed from a nation of believers to "a nation of behavers."[14]

In harmony with this shift, Finney stressed the benevolence of God, a fundamental divine attribute manifested in an orderly, predictable universe intelligible to man. God was gradually revealing the laws of this world to those who made the effort of understanding them. These included the laws of chemistry, of physics, of geology, the laws of society, of economics and politics, the laws of the mind, and, overarching all, the moral law. Once men had truly learned to understand these, they could not help but choose to live by them and thus achieve physical, moral, and spiritual perfection. To a number of critics, this concept of perfectionism seemed dangerously close to the "antinomianism" of an earlier generation of Puritan dissenters, especially Anne Hutchinson, whose heresy had racked New England with dissension between 1636 and 1638. Nothing, however, could have been further from the truth. On the contrary, the deceptive similarity of this terminology hid a fundamental intellectual transformation that had occurred in the meaning of the word perfection within two hundred years. Anne Hutchinson, in her own mind, had merely pushed the doctrine of grace to its logi-

cal conclusion. If grace was a miracle, a free gift to God,
then the law was not an instrumental condition necessary
for its attainment. Her critics went one step further and
argued that she had in fact implied that a saint, therefore,
was beyond all and any requirements of the laws. The fact
that a person sinned did not signify that he or she was not
saved. There could not be any kind of relationship between the one condition and the other. Finney approached
perfectionism from a perspective precisely the reverse of
Mistress Hutchinson's. Though he would not go so far as
to state blatantly that perfectionism was instrumental, a
means of attaining a state of grace, the logic of his position
led subtly in that direction. At the same time Finney insisted that those who had achieved grace would "habitually
live without sin and fall into sin only at intervals so few and
far between that, in strong language, it may be said in truth
they do not sin." To a believer in original sin, such an
attainment, of course, could be only rhetorical. To an orthodox Calvinist, therefore, this kind of perfectionism
seemed an ultimate manifestation of spiritual pride and
indulgence in sin.

This was inevitably so because a Calvinist could never
get beyond the fall of Adam. Here was one of the most
profound stumbling blocks to perfection, to progress, to a
literal interpretation of the biblical injunction to the "perfect, even as your Father which is in heaven is perfect."
The metamorphosis of the doctrine of original sin thus
made it possible for a post-Calvinist romantic religion to
create an image of Adam that stood in sharp contrast to
the traditional Christian image of the father of the human
race. As Professor R. W. B. Lewis has shown, the antebellum literary imagination transformed Adam from the author of sin and corruption into a symbol of innocence and
perfection.[15] Although the literary images, however, were
developed with more sophistication and imagination than
the popular ones, the image of Adam conjured by revivalists such as Finney served as a more representative
source for the power and fascination this image exerted

over the popular imagination. As the New England primer's "In Adam's Fall We Sinned All" slowly disappeared from school and pulpit, it was being supplemented by a more hopeful message contained in Finney's doctrine that man could learn to "prefer the glory of God and the interest of his kingdom to his own selfish interests," and that "the perfect control of this preference over all the moral movements of the mind brings a man back to where Adam was previous to the fall and constitutes perfect holiness."[16]

Finney was representative of all those evangelists whose work, in the words of William McLoughlin, "did much to stabilize and unify American evangelical Protestantism and to transform it into a national religion without destroying its zeal for soul winning or its independent denominationalism." Yet their work also had an unintentional weakness, for by "institutionalizing revivalism," evangelical Protestantism was pushed "toward those inherent weaknesses of any national religion: a propensity for empty formalism, bland uniformity, social conformity, and political conservatism."[17] Perhaps the sharpest indictment of the evangelical denominational empire that resulted from the ministry of Finney and his contemporaries has come from Martin Marty, who has changed that

> the success with which Protestants developed denominations, local churches, Sunday schools, revivals, and benevolent agencies, came at a high price. These institutions grew larger and larger, but their goals encompassed ever narrower portions of life. Something of a division of labor went with the birth of these forms. In order for them to live their own lives, to be supported, and to be effective within a limited sphere, church leaders had to abandon involvement in area after area of men's lives.... By the time they discovered the implications of this institutionalized divorce between faith and the surrounding world, they found that society at large was eager to honor the new informal contract. In effect, church leaders were told: "You stay within your narrowed sphere, and we will sanction you. Step out of it to discuss society's discontents; involve yourselves in the grand issues of slavery or oppose our wars or call into question our ways of arranging society, and we will destroy you."[18]

What the churches had done was to follow Tocqueville's prescription that "religions ought . . . to confine themselves within their own precincts; for in seeking to extend their power beyond religious matters, they incur a risk of not being believed at all. The circle within which they seek to restrict the human intellect ought therefore to be carefully traced, and, beyond its verge, the mind should be left entirely free to its own guidance."[19] In other words, religion was becoming modern.

III

Of all the religious and social movements spawned in antebellum America, Mormonism may well have been the most controversial and paradoxical. Emerson, with some justification, called it "an after-clap of Puritanism." At the same time, Mormon theology represented the most extreme repudiation of Calvinism in North America, possibly going even beyond transcendentalism in its negation of original sin and predestination and in its apotheosis of the free agency of man and his inherent divine potential. The chief paradox of Mormonism is that theologically it was too liberal even for the seemingly most extreme "Arminians," while socially it repudiated the denominational contract, thus clashing with an egalitarian, individualistic, laissez-faire Jacksonian creed.

If Mormonism had been merely another religion, competing for its share in the open market of nineteenth-century American religious pluralism, it is doubtful that it would have aroused such deep-seated hostility, especially since its professed Americanism seemed to fit so well into the antebellum national ethos, for which John Adams had provided so apt a text when he said that "I always consider the settlement of America with reverence and wonder, as the opening of a grand scene and design in providence for the illumination of the ignorant and the emancipation of the slavish part of mankind all over the earth," and to which Thomas Jefferson gave assent when he wrote to Joseph Priestley: "we feel we are acting under obligations not confined to the limits of our own society. It is impossible not to be sensible that we are acting for all mankind."[20]

It is therefore unlikely that the majority of Americans who believed in the divine mission of their country could have objected strenuously to that message as it found expression in the Book of Mormon. From its very beginning, it taught, America was destined to be a land of freedom. The first immigrants to the New World were told that God was sending them to a "land of promise, which was choice above all other lands, which the Lord God had preserved for a righteous people ... and whatsoever nation shall possess it, shall be so free from bondage, and from captivity, and from all other nations under heaven, if they but serve the God of the land, who is Jesus Christ."[21] Because the Nephites had failed to obey this injunction they were destroyed. Here was a cautionary tale for antebellum Americans whose fate would be the same if they followed in the footsteps of the Nephites—if, indeed, they had been in need of one more such warning. As it was, the idea that the republic faced a grave internal moral crisis was a common one. Certainly it was the kind of moral implicit in the ministry of Lyman Beecher, who almost singlehandedly attempted to save the West from infidelity. Lincoln, almost a generation later, insisted that the destruction of the republic by outside enemies would be possible only if the American people had suffered moral decay.

This was the theme expressed by Thomas Cole in a five-panel painting series titled "The Course of Empire" (1836), which was intended to show "the history of a natural scene ... showing the natural changes of landscape, and those effected by man in his progress from barbarism to civilization." The first picture, representing the wilderness state, showed a cragged, rocky landscape that dwarfed a few hunters, tepees, and some canoes on a distant river. The second picture, which Cole called the *Arcadian or*

Pastoral, appears to be an idealized portrait of America in
the 1830s. The wildness of the landscape has been tamed,
but by no means obliterated. Serene and happy men,
women, and children appear to be in harmony with nature.
In the middle distance, smoke arises from a simple temple.
The third panel, titled *The Course of Empire*, reveals a glit-
tering and luxurious, overcivilized urban society from
which nature has been all but banned. A mere hint of
rocks, and trees remains in the distance. That the fourth
picture, therefore, depicts the inevitable destruction of
empire should not be surprising to those familiar with the
nineteenth-century American philosophy of nature. The
final picture, according to Cole, portrayed "the funeral
knell of departed greatness, and may be called the state of
desolation." Americans flocked in large numbers to these
massive canvases, which today can be seen in the New-
York Historical Society in New York City. If Cole had
chosen pre-Columbian architecture as a model for his
paintings instead of the conventional Roman one, a pub-
lisher looking for illustrations to the Book of Mormon
depicting the rise and decline of the Nephites might have
been hard put to find any that are more apt, graphic, and
convincing.[22]

If the rather terrifying message of Cole's art was all but
inescapable, he presented no overt remedy. The message
of the Book of Mormon, however, was intended as a
warning for the avoidance of such catastrophes. Moreover,
God had singled out the American continent as the state
for the restoration of the gospel because of His great faith
in the moral potential of the American people. It was
through His providence that the New World had been
settled by a people capable of living up to the challenge of
its millennial destiny. Here was another sentiment with
which Protestant Americans could agree. None other than
James Fenimore Cooper, who had pronounced Cole's
paintings "the work of the highest genius this country has
ever produced," let it be known in 1832 that "so vast a
portion of the earth as America" had been so long and so

mysteriously concealed from the rest of the world in order
to fulfill God's plan for His people.[23]

It is another message that could have come straight out
of the Book of Mormon. When the time for the fulfillment
of God's purposes had come, He prevailed upon Columbus to venture across the seas to the Promised Land, to
open it to a new race of free men, who would "prosper in
the land" as long as they served its God, and would be
"lifted up by the power of God above all other nations,
upon the face of the land which is choice above all other
lands." America was to be "a land of liberty . . ., and there
shall be no king upon the land . . . For it is wisdom in the
father that they should be established in this land and be
set up as a free people by the power of the Father." Thus,
the American Revolution was part of a plan decreed by
God to achieve political and religious liberty in the New
World, to be preserved through a constitution framed by
"wise men" whom God had "raised up into this very purpose."[24]

Mormonism was to be the culmination of this grand
design. "The United States of America," wrote Apostle
Parley P. Pratt, "was the favored nation raised up, with
institutions adapted to the protection and free development of the necessary truths, and their practical results.
And that Great Prophet, Apostle, and Martyr—JOSEPH
SMITH was the Eilas, the Restorer, the presiding Messenger, holding the keys of the 'Dispensation of the fulness of time.'" Without the United States, continued Pratt,
this consummation would not have been possible. For the
"grain of mustard seed" needed "a land of free institutions,
where such organizations could be legally developed and
claim constitutional protection. No other country in
the world provided the necessary conditions for the
establishment of the Kingdom of God."[25] Thus, when it
came to the rhetoric of American destiny, the voices of
Mormonism blended readily into the national consensus.
Indeed, in comparison with the ambitious historical background that Mormonism provided for the mission of

America, the Protestants appeared virtually un-American. For by modifying the Judaeo-Christian heritage and providing American church history with pre-Columbian native roots through the Book of Mormon, Smith, in a sense, had produced America's religious declaration of independence.

Later on he expanded this historical conception of America through a revelation in the Doctrine and Covenants, where he gave expression to the Edenic myth in its most literal form by placing the Garden of Eden in the New World. After Adam and Eve were cast out of Paradise, they had dwelt in the land of Adam-ondi-Ahman, located in the Mississippi Valley in Daviess County, only a short distance from Independence, Missouri—the very heartland of America. The presence of the patriarchial Old Testament cultures in the Near East found a very simple explanation in the Flood. After forty days of rain, Noah and his family had drifted on the waters until the flood subsided. Quite obviously, they would not land at the same spot where they had embarked. Winds and waves had driven them far away from their original habitation.[26]

Thus, Smith assigned the entire antediluvian history of the Old Testament to the New World. The term "New World" was in fact a misnomer because America was really the cradle of man and civilization. The American search for the new Adam, in the understanding of Smith, was but a quest for a return of the Old Adam, another corollary of the restorationist theme. The historical reconstruction of Joseph Smith thus made it possible to conjure from the bones of an American Adam and his pre-Columbian descendants an image of America that could motivate those who believed in this past to recreate the Garden of Eden in its literal, original setting. It was no accident, then, that Joseph Smith dreamed of building the New Jerusalem in Missouri. Even today, nearly a century and half after the expulsion of the first Mormon settlers from their future Zion, faithful Latter-day Saints still believe that the day will come when they will return to claim an inheritance in

Zion and will build a temple that will receive Christ at His Second Coming. To the Mormons, the search for a usable past is thus inseparably connected to the quest for an American paradise to be established in the future. Yet however bizarre this quest may have appeared in its Mormon guise to Jacksonian Americans, they, too, were engaged in a quest for their version of an American paradise.

IV

Yet much of this agreement was clearly rhetorical. The similarity in the contents of the imagery masked profound cultural differences between Mormons and Gentiles, as I shall continue to point out in this book, such as their respective attitude toward the physical world and nature. Though Cole's "Course of Empire" might have served as an effective general illustration for the major moral lesson of the Book of Mormon, the specific Mormon solution to the problems of the ills of society was quite different from that of its evangelical adversaries. A major reason, of course, was that the two saw both society and nature in very different terms. As Mormon theology and doctrine evolved, it became clear that a careful examination of Cole's paintings revealed some profound differences between romanticism and the cosmology of Mormonism. For example, as Marjorie Hope Nicolson has pointed out in *Mountain Gloom and Mountain Glory*,[27] a changing attitude toward nature, especially mountains, provides significant clues to an understanding of that profound intellectual transformation of the modern world from the aesthetic sensibilities of neoclassicism to romanticism. The men of the Enlightenment loved order, harmony, a society in which the community took precedence over individualism. Men of the seventeenth and early eighteenth century laid out their gardens with care and precision and built symmetrical houses. If they felt they had to paint mountains, these were as carefully manicured as their gardens. Mountains in raw nature represented disorder and chaos—nature beyond the control of man.

The romantics, however, gloried in the wildness of the
mountain scene. Here nature was untouched by human
hands. Here man could communicate directly, if not with
God, then with His unspoiled handiwork. A man that
climbed mountains had separated himself from his fellow
men. He stood alone, above the herd, a solitary individual.
Unsupported by his fellow man, he encountered both the
full beauty but also the terror of nature. Romantics dis-
tilled this mixture into the concept of the sublime.
Thoreau, for example, experienced it on his expedition to
Mt. Katahdin in Maine.[28]

American romantic painters conveyed this romantic experience of the sublime with the same immediacy as
American writers. The romantic landscapes of someone
like Thomas Cole clearly revel in the beauty of unspoiled
nature. It is instructive, for example, that in the second
panel of "The Course of Empire," depicting the arcadian
or pastoral stage, a high range of mountains is visible in the
distance. Significantly, they are obscured in the other four
panels. Neither in the savage nor the overcivilized stage
does man have the time or inclination to raise his sights to
the lofty peaks.

It should not be surprising, however, that Mormonism,
representing as it does a quest for order, did not share this
enthusiasm for unspoiled nature and for mountains. In the
mind of Joseph Smith, the Garden of Eden looked very
much like a manicured version of the sight that greets
visitors today who make the trip to Adam-ondi-Ahman,
northeast of Independence. What they encounter is a lush,
green countryside of gently rolling hills, sloping down to
the river. Smith taught his followers that before the Fall
the entire earth looked very much like those Missouri
hills. At that time, also, the earth was in one piece, surrounded by water—a theory not completely incompatible
with modern scientific concepts of continental drift. As for
rivers and oceans, another favorite element of the romantics, Joseph instructed the Saints that the Lord had cursed
them in the last days: "I, the Lord, have decreed, and the
destroyer rideth upon the face thereof, and I revoke not

the decree." It was only after the expulsion of Adam and
Eve from the Garden of Eden that the earth acquired its
contemporary topography. In keeping with the idea of the
restoration of all things, however, at the Second Coming
of Christ "the earth will be renewed and receive its
paradisiacal glory." In physical terms this mean that the
Mormons believed—borrowing the imagery of Isaiah—
that "the crooked will be made straight, and the rough
places plain." Valleys and mountains would be flattened
out into a gently rolling countryside, to the chagrin of
romantics and mountain climbers.[29]

Neither would have felt very comfortable in the ideal
society Joseph envisioned as he dedicated a site near Independence as the Center Place of Zion in August 1831.
Two years later he completed plans for an ideal city "one
mile square, with ten-acre blocks, divided into one-half-
acre lots, one house to the lot." Two blocks were reserved
for the construction of a temple complex. A city such as
this would contain a population of about ten thousand.
After it was filled up, another would be built in the vicinity. A highway, planted with shade trees, would connect
the two cities. Additional cities would be built as the need
arose, until the entire world was thus populated. Because
each city was laid out in a grid pattern, a formerly crooked
world would be made very straight indeed.[30]

These ambitious plans for the City of Zion had to be
deferred, however, because of persecution. They were revived, to some extent, in the building of Nauvoo in Illinois. Later on, in Utah, most Mormon cities and towns
were laid out on a modified pattern of Smith's original
plan. Even today, the wide streets of Salt Lake City point
straight north and south, east and west. Mormons, of
course, had no monopoly on the straight line. The survey
of the United States Land Office, certainly, had set the
pattern with its own unromantic parceling of the land.

The pattern imposed upon the land was the reflection of
a pattern etched into the Mormon mind. Unlike the
romantics, who believed that reality was shaped by the
consciousness of the individual, Mormons believed in an

objective reality "out there." Joseph's account of the First
Vision establishes this very clearly. One of the most important aspects of the story is the very question in Joseph's
mind, "which of all the sects was right." Most American
Protestants had been sufficiently influenced by the romantic mood so that the question simply never occurred to
them. Conversion was an individual experience that could
happen to a Baptist as well as a Methodist or a Presbyterian. All of them had a pathway to heaven; as long as they
got there, it did not matter very much how. In the literal
mind of Joseph, however, there had to be one church that
was objectively true.

The First Vision, significantly, occurred within the
framework of Joseph's question and confirmed it. The idea
of the one true church became a cornerstone of Mormonism. The vision also provided the basis for an extremely anthropomorphic definition of God. The entire
Christian world had proclaimed God to be a spirit.
Moreover, Catholics and Protestants alike (Unitarians ex-
cepted) agreed on the nature of the Trinity as established
in the Nicene Creed. Joseph, however, insisted that God
and Christ were separated personages of flesh and
bone—though not of blood, which was an attribute of
mortality. The Holy Ghost, though invisible to mortal
eyes, likewise possessed a body, albeit a spiritual one. Yet
even spirit was comprised of a kind of matter. "There is no
such thing as immaterial matter," proclaimed Smith. "All
spirit is matter, but it is more fine or pure, and can only be
discerned by purer eyes; we cannot see it; but when our
bodies are purified we shall see that all is matter."[31] In an
even stronger expression of this same idea, the Mormon
Millennial Star quoted the prophet as saying that "God the
father is material, Jesus Christ is material. Angels are material. Space is full of materiality. Nothing exists which is
not material." In a reductio ab absurdum, one Mormon
writer went so far as to accuse the established Christian
churches of atheism because they worshiped an immaterial
God.[32]

The Christian churches, in contrast were outraged by

what they regarded as the crude anthropomorphism of the
Mormon conception of God. They were even more
shocked by the corollary of this belief that matter therefore must be eternal, cannot have been created, thus
negating the Christian concept of the creation ex nihilo.
Thus, what God did in the "beginning" was merely to
organize the earth out of already existing matter. It followed further that God was not the author of the laws of
nature but the one who had learned to understand and
control them. Miracles were merely the application of natural laws beyond the understanding of man. Yet the time
would come when they would be as understandable as the
laws of Newton. In the meantime, the world continued in
a process of cosmic evolution from which no part of the
universe was exempt. It followed that if God evolved there
must have been a time—beyond human comprehension to
be sure—when God was less than He is now. Likewise, it
was conceivable that at some future point in time some
humans might evolve to that stage where God is at the
present. This line of reasoning has led to that famous
Mormon phrase: "As man is God once was: as God is man
may become."[33] The final step in this logical procession is
the belief in the plurality of Gods, though Mormons hasten to add that the only God they *worship* is God the
Father, in the name of His only begotten son, Jesus Christ.
Unlike the God of Paul Tillich or Karl Barth, the Mormon
God, clearly, is not "wholly Other." Yet to the charge that
this philosophy pulls God down to the level of man, and in
fact destroys the very cocept of God, Mormons, in a curi-
ously Barthian twist, reply that God is who He is, regardless of our preconceived notions who He should be.[34]

However heretical such ideas may have appeared to the
majority of antebellum Americans, their progressive optimism is nevertheless compatible with the general cultural
climate of the period. Mormon philosopher Sterling
McMurrin, of the University of Utah, has provided a
somewhat oversimplified and yet convenient map that will
help us locate Mormonism within the spectrum of the

western intellectual tradition. According to McMurrin, this tradition has concerned itself with the proximate and ultimate condition and fate of man from either an optimistic or a pessimistic perspective. Traditional Christianity tends to combine a proximate pessimism—this life is a vale of tears—with an ultimate optimism through a belief in the atoning sacrifice of Christ. The apostle Paul expressed this idea most succinctly when he said that "even as in Adam all men die, so in Christ shall all be made alive." With the rise of a liberal, secular humanism the proximate pessim of Christianity gave way to an optimism regarding the possibilities of life on earth, while negation of the reality of life after death resulted in an ultimate pessimism. With modern disillusionment in the idea of progress, and increasing recognition of the destructive potential of science, men have become proximate as well as ultimate pessimists—a position perhaps most widely articulated in existentialism. Finally, there are those who have been able to devise a philosophy optimistic both in proximate and ultimate terms. Much of antebellum American Protestantism fits into this category. So, of course, does Mormonism.[35]

This kind of optimism, clearly, is incompatible with earlier American beliefs in original sin and predestination. I have already outlined the decline of these beliefs in antebellum America—a process Perry Miller called the "binding of God." Perhaps no religious source of the period documents this frame of mind more powerfully than the Book of Mormon. Although it contains vestiges of traditional Calvinist notions of human depravity and sin, its main thrust is clearly Arminian. In an almost Manichean fashion, the Book of Mormon argues that evil is a necessary corollary of good, existing independently of God: "For it must needs be, that there is an opposition in all things . . . . If ye shall say there is no sin, ye shall also say there is no righteousness. And if there be no righteousness nor happiness there be no punishment nor misery. And if these things are not there is no God." These opposing forces are essential for the moral conduct of man: "Wherefore, man could not act for himself save it should be that he was enticed by the one or the other." These eternal principles were in operation when Adam had to make his fateful decision to eat of the forbidden fruit: "And now, behold, if Adam had not transgressed they would have had no children; wherefore they would have remained in a state of innocence, having no joy, for they knew no misery; doing no good, for they knew no sin." Therefore, God in His widsom had allowed Adam to be placed in a condition resulting in a fall more fortunate than any Milton ever could have imagined: "Adam fell that men might be; and men are, that they might have joy. And the Messiah cometh in the fulness of time, that he may redeem the children of men from the fall. And because that they are redeemed from the fall they have become free forever, knowing good from evil; to act for themselves and not be acted upon, . . ."[36]

In later writings and revelations, the prophet expanded on these ideas and incorporated them into a drama of cosmic proportions. Before the creation of the earth humans had existed in a spiritual state in the "preexistence," in the presence of God, as His children. In keeping with the law of eternal progression it was necessary that these spirits should acquire mortal bodies and live on the earth. In a gigantic council in heaven, which all spirits attended, Lucifer, one of the great spirits of the preexistence, presented a no-risk plan for this earthly venture. At the end of their sojourn, all souls, without exception, would be returned to the presence of the Father—but at the cost of their free agency. Christ, however, presented a plan fraught with danger: only those who obeyed the commandments of the Father would be allowed to return to His presence—that is only those who had exercised their free agency in resistance of temptation and evil. The majority accepted Christ's plan, while a furious Lucifer rebelled and was cast out, along with his adherents. Having kept their "first estate," all those who accepted Christ's

plan were thus allowed to move on to their "second estate"
of mortality on earth. "And they who keep their second
estate shall have glory added upon their heads for ever and
ever."[37]

Thus, if the risks were high, so were the rewards. At the
same time, the venture was not quite as risky as Lucifer
and his hosts apparently seemed to think. God and Christ
had worked out a very detailed map, a "plan of salvation,"
that would guarantee all those who followed it a safe return to their celestial home. It was this plan of salvation
that God had revealed to Adam and the patriarchs of old;
to Abraham, Isaac, and Jacob, and to Moses; through
Christ himself and the apostles to the Jews and Gentiles in
the "meridian of time"; and to Joseph Smith in the "latter
days."

The mission of Christ was central to this plan. While
Adam's transgression was essential so he could have a
posterity, and thus in fact make the plan operative, he had
broken a divine law and thus brought death into the world.
As Mormons see it, Adam, faced with a dilemma, deliberately broke a lesser law in order to fulfill a higher one.
Realizing that this would happen, God had planned the
mission of Christ to undo the consequences of the Fall.
These were both physical and spiritual. All men would die
in the flesh and were prevented from returning to the
Father. As a result of the atoning sacrifice of Christ, however, all men would eventually be redeemed from physical
death—that is, like Christ himself, the bodies of all men,
saints and sinners alike, would be resurrected to immortality. An immortal body, then, was a reward not for
having kept the second estate, but the first. This was a
privilege denied Lucifer and his followers. Realizing that
they had missed this opportunity, they were now desper-
ately anxious to enter the bodies of humans. Biblical accounts of the possession of evil spirits are explained in this
fashion. So eager are some of these spirits to posess a
body that they will even enter animals. That is how Mormons account for the story in the New Testament where

evil spirits, driven out of some men, entered a herd of
swine.

The mere possession of an immortal body, however, did
not guarantee that its owner would return to the presence
of God. This would be possible only through redemption
from the spiritual consequences of the Fall. Through his
transgression Adam had introduced sin into the world,
although this did not mean that his posterity would be
punished for what the Christian world called original sin.
Joseph Smith taught that "men will be punished for their
own sins, and not for Adam's transgression." Still, it was
through Adam that they had become *capable* of sinning.
And inevitably, all humans did sin and were thus subject to
the punishment of God. It was the atoning sacrifice of
Christ that had the potential of releasing all mankind from
the bonds of sin and spiritual death, "by obedience to the
laws and ordinances of the Gospel." The first step on the
road back to God was "Faith in the Lord Jesus Christ;
second, Repentance; third, Baptism by immersion for the
remission of sins; fourth, Laying on of hands for the gift of
the Holy Ghost." As I have already suggested, these ordinances could be performed only by those who had the
proper authority to act in the name of God.[38]

According to Joseph Smith, this authority had disappeared from the earth shortly after the death of the
ancient apostles, not to be restored until the visitation of
John the Baptist on May 15, 1829. Did this mean that all
those who had lived and died in the intervening years had
missed their chance of redemption through no fault of
their own? It was a question that agitated Joseph for
some time, especially because his brother Alvin had died
at the age of 24 in 1823, prior to the restoration of the
gospel. In fact, a Calvinist minister had caused profound
agitation in the Smith family by insisting that Alvin resided
in hell. In 1836, in a revelation, the prophet received divine assurance that his deceased brother had been saved
"because he would have accepted Mormonism with his full
heart if he had lived." Mormons, understandably, ex-

tended this reassuring principle to their deceased ancestors in general.[39]

In time, however, they regarded this reassurance as insufficient. According to one of Joseph's revelations, "there
is a law, irrevocably decreed in heaven before the foundations of this world, upon which all blessings are predi-
cated."[40] Baptism was one of these irrevocable laws. The
solution to the problem was the doctrine of baptism for
the dead, to be performed vicariously in this world. This is
one major reason why Mormons diligently seek out the
genealogies of their ancestors, for whom they are then
baptized in specially consecrated temples. In keeping with
the principle of free agency the deceased spirits are free
either to accept or reject the work done in their behalf—to
be either saved or damned.

This simple division, however, did not fit very well into
the concept of free agency and eternal progression. While
revising the gospel of John for an "inspired" retranslation
of the Bible, Smith speculated "that if God rewards every
one according to his deeds done in the body, the term
'Heaven' must include more kingdoms than one."[41] In response to this question, Joseph and Sidney Rigdon had a vision revealing the future state of man in the afterlife. Those
who had submitted to the ordinances of the gospel and
kept its commandments returned to the presence of God
the Father in the "celestial glory," "whose glory is that of the
sun." Those who had not accepted the testimony of Jesus
in the flesh, who had allowed themselves to be "blinded by
the craftiness of men," but were nevertheless "honorable
men of the earth," were assigned to the "terrestrial glory,"
where they would "receive of the presence of the Son, but
not the fulness of the Father." A third group, that "received not the gospel of Christ, neither the testimony of
Jesus," went to their eternal reward in the "telestial
glory." Lacking direct access to the Father and the Son,
they had to be content with the administration of the Holy
Spirit. These were the sinners who would be delivered
over to Satan until the day of their resurrection—an obvi-

ous parallel to the Catholic doctrine of purgatory. "These
are they who are liars, and sorcerers, and adulterers, and
whoremongers, and whosoever loves and makes a lie."
Nevertheless, even the "glory of the telestial . . . surpasses
all understanding." The only ones who would meet the
kind of fate Calvinist ministers had graphically portrayed
to generations of sinners—"who shall go away into the lake
of fire and brimstone, with the devil and his angels," were
those who had received the gospel and then rejected it,
who had committed the sin against the Holy Ghost. These
were the "sons of perdition, of whom I say that it had been
better for them never to have been born."[42] In the early
days of Mormonism, such language was clearly intended as
a deterrent to potential apostates. Modern Mormons, however, are much more reluctant to charge defectors with the
sin against the Holy Ghost. The enormity of the sin is
such, they believe, that few mortals are capable of com-
mitting it. They are certain that Judas Iscariot is one of
them. Joseph Smith, if he had denied his testimony of
Christ, would have been a likely candidate. Altogether,
those who have become sons of perdition may well be
numbered on the fingers of one hand.

The question arises how anyone can be persuaded to
subject himself to a religion as rigorous and demanding as
Mormonism if even adulterers and whoremongers will
achieve a degree of glory that "surpasses all understanding." Might not such a belief lead to the same kind of
excesses that the opponents of antinomianism saw as the
inevitable consequences of that heresy? The righteous
lives of most Mormons as they strive to achieve the highest
degree of glory are perhaps the most effective answer to
that question. Still, why do they strive? Mormons reply
that salvation is as much a state of mind as a physical condition. All those who have failed to attain the celestial
glory will know that it is only their own, deliberate wrong-
doing, against their better knowledge, that has prevented
them from returning to the presence of their Father: "For
they shall be judged according to their works, and every

man shall receive according to his own works, his own
dominion, in the mansions which are prepared; And they
shall be servants of the Most High; but where God and
Christ dwell they cannot come, worlds without end."[43]
This realization of an opportunity irrevocably lost can
torment the soul as much as any lake of fire.

Joseph may well have derived this notion of lost opportunity from the social and economic realities of Jacksonian
America, where this was an everyday occurrence. According to the reigning ideology, men were rewarded according to their works—though in reality the cards were
heavily stacked in favor of those who had inherited wealth
and social position. Mormons, clearly, were not among
these. Realizing the glaring discrepany between Jacksonian
rhetoric and reality, the Mormon prophet may have projected the Jacksonian credo into an afterlife where social
position and rank counted for nothing, and where men
were truly "judged according to their works," just as the
official ideology professed.

The progressive aspect of Smith's theology, as well as its
cosmology, while in a general way compatible with antebellum thought, bears some remarkable resemblances to
Thomas Dick's *Philosophy of a Future State,* a second edition of which had been published in 1830.[44] Though we
have no conclusive evidence that Smith was aware of the
book prior to 1836, when Sidney Rigdon quoted from
Dick in the *Latter-Day Saints Messenger and Advocate,* some
very striking parallels to Smith's theology suggest that the
similarities between the two may be more than coincidental. Dick's lengthy book, an ambitious treatise on astronomy and metaphysics, proposed the idea that matter is
eternal and indestructible and rejected the notion of a
creation ex nihilo. Much of the book dealt with the infinity
of the universe, made up of innumerable stars spread out
over immeasurable distances. Dick speculated that many
of these stars were "peopled by 'various orders of intelligences,' and that these intelligences were *'progressive* beings' in various stages of evolution toward perfection." In

the Book of Abraham, part of which consists of a treatise
on astronomy and cosmology, eternal beings of various
orders and stages of development likewise populate
numerous stars. They, too, are called "intelligences." Dick
speculated that "the systems of the universe revolve
around a common centre . . . the throne of God." In the
Book of Abraham, one star, named Kolob, "was nearest
unto the throne of God." Other stars, in ever diminishing
order, were placed in increasing distances from this center.[45]

As Mormon ideology evolved, these ideas provided
the metaphysical underpinning for the prophet's expanding conception of man's role in the universe. At the same
time, they formed a basis for Joseph's enlarged vision of
man's social role. It is within this context that Mormonism's most notorious institution, polygamy, must be
understood. Because I will discuss its social theory and
practice in relation to American culture in another chapter, I will here merely attempt to place it within the
framework of Joseph's theology and cosmology.

In keeping with the evolutionary cosmology of the
Book of Abraham, the idea of the three kingdoms of glory,
clearly, could bear further refinement. The concept of the
infinity of worlds and intelligences suggested to the
prophet that God's primary function was the creation and
peopling of such worlds. The drama of the creation of the
earth and its ultimate redemption, no doubt, had been
enacted many times before and would be repeated innumerable times in the future. The idea that man, on this
earth, was evolving toward godhood suggested that other
men in other worlds had already arrived at this exalted
state. The highest purpose of life, then, was not merely
salvation in the celestial kingdom, but the achievement of
godhood, or "exaltation"—that is the power to create and
people worlds according to the same pattern as it was un-
folding on this earth.[46]

According to Joseph Smith, we are not only the children
of our physical parents in the flesh, but also the spirit

children of our heavenly father in the most literal sense.
Spiritual procreation, like physical procreation, requires a
union of the sexes—that is we have a heavenly mother as
well as a heavenly father. And because of the immense
number of spirits required for the peopling of just one
single world, God in fact has several wives to accomplish
his purposes.

On its highest level, then, this earth is a testing ground
to single out those who will be chosen to follow in the
footsteps of their heavenly father. It goes without saying
that they must obey his commandments without exception. In addition to the first principles of the gospel—faith,
repentance, baptism, and the gift of the Holy Ghost—they
must obey the "new and everlasting convenant of marriage—that is, they must be "sealed" by proper priesthood authority to a partner of the opposite sex not only for
time but all eternity. This kind of marriage can be performed only on this earth. And only those who have entered into this covenant will be able to achieve the highest
state of progress in the world to come, or exaltation. Because of the immensity of the task facing those who have
achieved this highest degree of glory, the men among
them are permitted—even encouraged— to marry more
than one wife. (In response to pressures from the U.S.
government, plural marriage was outlawed in 1890.) In
fact, the degree of exaltation in the next world is directly
related to the number of spirit children an individual will
be able to sire. And the physical family of a person in this
life is the beginning of an eternal family in the next—but
only if they were sealed by proper priesthood authority.
All those who remained single in this life, or who were not
married under the "new and everlasting covenant" would
be unmarried in the life to come. If they obeyed all other
principles and ordinances of the gospel, and lived righteous lives, they would attain the celestial glory, "but are
appointed angels in heaven; which angels are ministering
servants, to minister for those who are worthy of a far
more and an exceeding, and an eternal weight of glory."

Those who have entered into the new and everlasting
covenant "shall inherit thrones, kingdoms, principalities,
and powers, dominions all heights and depths—" "and
they shall pass . . . to their exaltation and glory in all things,
as hath been sealed upon their heads, which glory shall be
a fulness and a continuation of the seeds forever and ever.
Then shall they be gods, because they have no end; therefore shall they be from everlasting to everlasting, because
they continue; then shall they be above all, because all
things are subject unto them. Then shall they be gods, because they have all power, and the angels are subject unto
them"[47]

However heretical—even blasphemous—such ideas
may have appeared to contemporaries of Smith, I am inclined to agree with Professor A. Leland Jamison that
Mormonism is "at once an irreconcilable Christian heresy
and the most typical American theology yet formulated on
this continent."[48] The American locale and historical
framework of the Book of Mormon is perhaps the most
obvious and yet the least important reason why this is so.
More typically American is the optimistic, progressive,
"materialistic" nature of Mormon theology; its denial of
original sin and its Arminian thrust. But perhaps most
typical of all is its practical, nonutopian emphasis—not
only in its social thought, as we shall later see, but also in
its metaphysics. Mormon cosmology fits readily into the
framework of nineteenth-century American science—at
least as it was perceived in the popular mind. The expan-
sive ideas of Smith were thus entirely plausible to those
who accepted them. More than that, they were capable of
being realized by most ordinary human beings. It is
therefore possible to argue that the Mormon cosmology
represented, on a metaphysical level, a quest for power by
ordinary people to whom that quest had been denied in
the Jacksonian world of individualism and competition. At
the same time, this quest was no mere escape. By defining
the next world in terms of this, and by devising a "plan of
salvation," Smith put his followers on the road to godhood

not via utopianism or mysticism, but via a clearly defined
set of beliefs and practices. Anyone willing to accept these
could achieve "exaltation." Andrew Jackson may have
professed belief that the common man could hold public
office, but Joseph Smith out-Jacksoned the Jacksonians by
proclaiming that the common man could become a god.

3

The Mormon Rationalization of Death

The celestial order is an order of eternal life; it knows no death, and consequently makes no provisions for any.

Parley P. Pratt

I

For most Mormons the promise of godhood was indeed a heady prospect. Yet however magnificent such a belief system may have appeared in theory, its real test was its ability to deal with the vicissitudes of life. Among these death, as in most cultures, has been a profound source of fear and apprehension. Indeed, it has been suggested that one of the major purposes of religion is to explain or at least to rationalize the inescapable and universal reality of death. The Mormon response to death, then, may well provide us with a fundamental insight into the Mormon belief system.

Mormons have always emphatically insisted (and not without a considerable sense of grievance) that they are indeed Christians. In any case, they share the general Christian perspective on life and death—that the resurrection of Christ was a model for the resurrection of all mankind. They, like their fellow Christians, accept the apostle Paul's succinct affirmation that "as in Adam all die, even so in Christ shall all be made alive."[1] It was through sin that Adam had introduced death. It was through the defeat of sin by his death that Christ had reinstituted the possibility of eternal life.

This point of view, which dominated the thinking of Christianity for nearly a millennium and a half—Saint Au-

gustine to the contrary notwithstanding—was revised by
some of the thinkers of the Protestant Reformation. According to John Calvin, as a result of the Fall all men
deserved eternal damnation by a just God. But because of
His infinite and inscrutable mercy, God had chosen some
few, His Saints, to become heirs of the atoning sacrifice of
Christ. As for the majority of mankind, they would indeed
be resurrected, but only to their eternal doom—to a life
that was worse than death.

No Calvinists followed this doctrine more consistently
to its inexorable and terrifying conclusion that the New
England Puritans, whose visions of hell fire and brimstone
were conjured with such frightening reality that some lis-
teners to Puritan sermons sustained real blisters from
imaginary fires. Because the Puritans were never quite
sure if and when they were saved, and were thus compelled perpetually to monitor the state of their endangered
souls, death for them held a terror matched in few other
human cultures. Thus even the Saints—or particularly the
Saints—faced the prospects of a terrifying afterlife, com-
forted only by the thought that no matter how awful the
agony, it was merely the richly deserved retribution meted
out by a God of infinite justice and—if the promise of
Sainthood might indeed be fulfilled—mercy.[2]

In spite of these tensions, however, religion in
seventeenth- and eighteenth-century America does not
appear to have been dysfunctional. Calvinism sustained a
stable social order and was, in turn, sustained by it. However, as Puritans, through a subtle process of accommoda-
tion and transformation, turned into Yankees, traditional
Calvinism became increasingly incapable of maintaining a
sense of community that was fast disappearing from the
world of work and family. In colonial America the terrors
of death were mitigated by the sustaining spirit of the
community. Both life and death were shared experiences.
By the nineteenth century, however, the rapid pace of
modernization severed an increasing number of individuals from their ties with family and community. If

seventeenth- and eighteenth-century Calvinists, anchored
with reasonable security in their society, found the prospect of death terrifying, how much more those of the
nineteenth century who increasingly perceived society as
being disruptive and isolating.[3]

In the seventeenth and eighteenth centuries, moreover,
death, paradoxically, may have been accepted because of
its very ubiquity. Even by the middle of the eighteenth
century, when Benjamin Franklin could optimistically
project the demographic curve of a "rising people," death
in its many forms continued to claim not only the old and
the infirm. Epidemics such as smallpox periodically ravaged the populations of major American cities. Women
continued to die in childbirth in relatively large numbers,
Infant mortality remained high. Even though medicine in
the eighteenth century made notable advances, most
Americans had no choice but to accept death at any time
and any age as one of the facts of life. As with salvation, so
with life: God would allow whom He chose to live out the
biblical age of threescore years and ten. As for those whom
he recalled at an earlier age, it was His will, not to be
questioned. The Calvinist world view merely reflected an
inexorable reality. If belief in a just God was axiomatic,
Calvinism can be seen as a kind of empiricism sustaining
that belief. To question God's way of life and death would
be to question God Himself. Thus, however much psychological anxiety was generated by the Puritan concept of
death, its intellectual consistency could not help but re-
affirm the existence of a just God. The Puritans were thus
caught in a double bind. The very source of their anxieties
was an essential part of their identity.

The Calvinists, of course, perceived this paradox only
dimly, if at all. The same was true of that generation of
post-Puritan divines who bravely attempted to have the
best of both worlds when they dismantled the edifice of
Calvin by modifying the doctrine of original sin, of the
Fall, of divine grace, of determinism, in their effort to

create a world of free men who would be punished for
their own sins only, and who would inherit life or death
not because of the inscrutable will of God but because of
their own freely chosen actions. What they failed to understand, of course, was that, as Erich Fromm has pointed out,
a great many individuals find that much freedom unbear-
able. Therefore they should not have been surprised and
disappointed to find that for a significant number of
Americans life and death in this brave new post-Calvinist world were as terrifying as in the old world of
determinism.

Moreover, the dismantlers of Calvinism also failed to
understand that even as the social stability of colonial
American society diminished the terror of Calvinist theology, for some Americans the hopeful Arminianism of the
nineteenth century failed to fill the spiritual vacuum
created by the social disruptions resulting from rapid
modernization. On the contrary, by shifting the burden for
life and death from God to man, the new theology further
increased the potential for anxieties. Nineteenth-century
Americans increasingly became responsible for their souls
as well as their bodies. Thus, even as they banished the hell
of Calvin from their minds, they reinvented a hell of their
own, consisting less of the terrors of spiritual death in the
next life than of the tribulations of the flesh in this, which
foreshadowed physical death.

It is perhaps true that from a materialistic perspective of
"progress" in the long run this transformation was all to the
good, leading to the harnessing of science in behalf of
man's welfare, to a more empirical approach to medicine,
and to the great strides in public health that by the end of
the nineteenth century banned the scourges of smallpox,
cholera, and yellow fever from American society. In the
antebellum period, however, these developments were
still very much in the future. In the meantime, while the
new individualism undoubtedly fulfilled the needs of millions of venturesome and ambitious Americans, in others

it only increased anxieties produced by a socially disruptive environment. The Calvinist ideology had at least reflected an empirical reality. But for many Americans the
new Arminianism did not.

If anything, life was becoming more precarious. For
many complex reasons mortality in the first half of the
nineteenth century was higher than in the last quarter of
the eighteenth. And beginning in 1832, the great cholera
epidemics of the period confirmed dramatically what most
Americans knew already: that life continued to be unpredictable and could be terminated at any moment. It is
true that demographically the impact of cholera was minimal. But its psychological effect was not. As many women
died in childbirth as in the previous century. Mortality
among children remained "staggering." "In more than the
ultimate sense," writes Lewis Saum, "death was inescapable. People knew it by its existential proximity as well as
by its actuarial prevalence." Hence their attitude toward
life remained tentative. A young man recorded in his diary:
"Tomorrow I'm twenty-three if I live . . . ."[4]

Perhaps to a majority of beleaguered American Calvinists these uncertainties provided the much needed reassurance that if the world was falling apart, God, at least,
was still in His heaven, ruling the world according to His
will. Not that a great many antebellum Americans of whatever persuasion failed to pay at least lip-service to the
existence of God. But a growing number of those who had
been swayed by the appeals of the new Arminianism could
not help but accept the logic of their position: that the
state of their bodies and their souls was as much in their
own hands as that of God. Hence, if someone became ill or
died it might well be his or her own fault.

This, perhaps, is one reason why nineteenth-century
Americans were less willing than their predecessors to accept the inevitability of death. We begin to encounter,
more and more, the notion that for some death was "premature." In ages past, when life expectancy was not only
short but regarded as being in the hands of God, death was

generally met with a stoical acceptance of its inevitability,
whenever it occurred. As David Stannard has suggested,
Puritan children, for example, were as much indoctrinated
in the reality of death as their elders. But as more and
more of the mysteries of nature were being unravelled in
the nineteenth century and as this process increasingly
captured the popular imagination, the idea began to grow
that nature, both physical and human, could be controlled.
It is not surprising, therefore, that an age of emerging
science and technology would lead to rising expectations
about the quality of life, or at least its duration.[5]

The same social and intellectual forces, however, which
stimulated these expectations, ironically, prevented, at
least for the time being, their fulfillment. The American
Revolution had disrupted the activities of a rising scientific
community. Its reestablishment foundered temporarily on
the shoals of a growing democratic individualism. It is true
that by the time of Jackson science once again found institutional support. But its fruits did not mature until
about the middle of the century. In the meantime, much of
what went for science exhausted itself in the democratic
amateur rambles amid America's flora and fauna.

Perhaps no profession suffered more grievously from
the modern spirit than medicine, which, for many of its
practitioners, had deteriorated into the pursuit of quackery.
Public confidence in American medicine reached an all-
time low at precisely that moment at which Americans
were anxiously attempting to gain control over their own
bodies, if not over life and death. If this, at first, may seem
ironic, on further reflection those two currents may well
be related. Medicine, like law and the ministry, was one of
the ancient professions, deriving its authority as much
from its social and cultural eminence as from any intrinsic
value inherent in its presumed ability to cure the ills of
humankind. As a traditional, stable colonial social order
crumbled, the authority of the minister, the lawyer, and
the doctor were greatly diminished. The individualizing
democratic ethos of the nineteenth century demanded that

like the butcher, the baker, the candlestickmaker they
"deliver the goods," so to speak, without any resource to
social eminence.[6] Not that the Jacksonians were radical
egalitarians. But where the eighteenth century, in the
words of the *United States Magazine and Democratic Review,*
had fostered an aristocracy of "artificial distinctions," the
"free democratic system" of the nineteenth century rested
on "a natural charter of privilege" which was conferred
upon those of "superior knowledge and talent."[7] In the
free-for-all of Jacksonian individualism it took some time
to identify that new elite. In the meantime, most Americans had to fend for themselves in their struggle against
disease and death.

Existence was made more precarious by some of the
very technological improvements that were raising American expectations about the quality of life. Like cholera and
yellow fever, the nineteenth-century steamboat was an in-
discriminate and unpredictable mass killer. According to
Fred Somkin, most Americans willingly accepted the risks.
"Not simply as a matter of rhetoric," he wrote, "but in
frightening actuality, Americans seemed strangely able to
accept the possibility of violent death on a mass scale."[8] If
all of them had been good Calvinists, it would have been
surprising had they reacted otherwise. But, in fact, fewer
and fewer of them were. Somkin's appraisal, in my opinion,
is but half the story. Many antebellum Americans, in fact,
made increasingly frantic efforts to avert disease and
death. If they may have been stoical about steamboat explosions, it was perhaps because technology had disappointed them and appeared to be no more of an ally
against death than establishment medical science. For
many antebellum Americans, therefore, salvation lay
elsewhere. If establishment science and religion were no
help, perhaps popular science and sectarian religion were.
It may be worthwhile to pursue the hypothesis that as the
antebellum apotheosis of the freedom of the will com-
bined with a profound terror of death, it produced all those

innumerable phenomena and movements—from medical
messiahs pushing magic pills to religious messiahs preaching the impending millennium—that would enable Americans to save their bodies and their souls.

If this theory is perhaps too simplistic to account solely
for the popularity of mesmerism, phrenology, and spirit
rapping, or for the origins of temperance and purity
crusades, as well as for the increasing numbers of those
who sought salvation in hydropathy or the dietary rules of
Sylvester Graham, it nevertheless provides motivations
that in my opinion cannot be ignored. Certainly Shakers,
Oneida perfectionists, and Mormons had their origins in
complex social and intellectual conditions. Yet these
movements particularly—and most profoundly—addressed themselves to the problem of vindicating disease and death. Mother Ann Lee, the founder of the Shakers, had a vision in which Christ revealed to her that
human misery and sin had its origins in the sexual transgression of Adam and Eve. Because Eve had tempted
Adam, woman became subservient to man. A celibate
Christ redeemed mankind from the Fall. As a result of
apostasy, however, Antichrist gained temporary ascen-
dancy until the Second Coming of Christ in the female
incarnation of Mother Ann Lee, who restored the Edenic
condition of men and women in equality. Celibacy would
result in—among other things—the conquest of physical
disease. Propagation became unnecessary because in the
millennium men and women would live forever. To those
only superficially familiar with the supposed sexual liber-
tinism of John Humphrey Noyes, it may seem surprising
that the Shaker philosophy had a powerful appeal for the
founder of the Oneida community. Yet Noyes, too,
sought to achieve victory over disease and death through
sexual control. Complex marriage was far from libertin-
ism. According to Ernest Sandeen, Noyes believed that
through his sexual innovations he was on the verge of
discovering the secret of eternal life. In fact, Noyes found

his life-giving power confirmed by some rather spectacular manifestations of faith healing.[9]

II

When it came to dealing with the problems of disease and death, however it is doubtful that Ann Lee or Noyes could compete with the Mormons, who insisted that healing was one of the essential "gifts of the spirit" identifying a true religion. The promise that at least some of the faithful should not taste death was given scriptural support by the Book of Mormon, according to which three of Christ's Nephite disciples had not died and were to remain in mortality until the Second Coming, at which time they would be changed from mortality to immortality without suffering the agony of death. This same change would be experienced by all righteous Saints at the time of the Savior's return, an event the Mormons anticipated at an unspecified yet early date. The language of the Book of Mormon is reflected in numerous patriarchal blessings, which promise their recipients escape from the terrors of death that will overtake the wicked, who will be "burned as stubble," while the righteous will be "changed in the twinkling of an eye."[10]

Such beliefs found their strongest expressions in the early years of Mormonism, particularly in the 1830s, when millenarian expectations generally ran high. To what extent such hopes and fears were a motivating factor in conversion is difficult to tell, although some converts, such as Millen Atwood, acknowledged that prior to their conversion to Mormonism they had been obsessed with the "terror" of death. Religious conversion for some was clearly motivated by its promise of salvation for the body as well as the soul. The reverse, of course, was also true. Elizabeth Haven, in a letter to a friend, wrote of a man who had a vision in which he was being chastized for not being faithful in doing the work of the Lord. He died shortly thereafter, interpreting his death as punishment by the Lord for

his sins.[11] The simplistic formula for certain literal-minded
Saints clearly was: the sinners must die; the Saints shall
live. It was a formula that none other than Joseph Smith
himself exploited during the abortive Zion's Camp adventure (a paramilitary relief expedition to Missouri) in
order to enforce discipline. The ravages of cholera, which
had killed fourteen members of the "camp," he implied,
were God's punishment for unfaithfulness and dis-
obedience.[12]

It was at Zion's Camp, also, that Joseph gave one of the
most dramatic demonstrations of the power of healing.
After chastizing his followers for their unfaithfulness, he
administered to the sick and the dying and promised that
all still living would recover if they obeyed the will of the
Lord. His word was fulfilled, and no other members of the
expedition died.

Such promises of health and life seem to have enhanced
the appeal of Mormonism. Early missionary journals reveal numerous accounts of miraculous healings of new
converts, although the missionaries generally stressed the
idea that the signs followed those who believed, and not
vice versa. William Appleby, for example, does not in-
dicate that escape from disease and possible death was a
motivating factor in his conversion. Still, his health had
been a major concern for many years, during which he had
"paid dollars upon dollars" for medicines. Not even "a Box
of Golden Magnetic Pills," for which he had paid ten dollars, had relieved his sufferings. But after he became a
Mormon, he records, "I threw aside nearly all medicines
that I had been in the habit of taking for years, . . . trusting
in the Lord for health and strength . . . My health increased
and from the time I was baptized up to the present (July
1848) I have not had a Physician attend me, or any of my
family, except once or twice to my wife and child, then not
by her request but by others in my absence."[13]

Appleby's faith was further strengthened the following
year, 1849, when he and his family survived the second of
the great cholera epidemics sweeping across the United

States in the nineteenth century. Appleby did not believe
that his survival was accidental. He had put his "trust,"
confidence, and repose" in the Lord: "I dedicated myself
and family to his care and protection, and exercised faith in
the promises and blessings sealed upon my head from time
to time in days that are gone, by the servants of God. And
my prayers were answered."[14]

But what about the testimony of those whose prayers
were not answered? Inevitably, they are silent, leaving the
accounts of death to the living, who are caught in a sur-
vivor's psychology so perceptively explored by Freud, who
wrote that "it is indeed impossible to imagine our own
death, and whenever we attempt to do so we can perceive
that we are in fact still present as spectators. Hence . . . at
bottom no one believes in his own death, or, to put the
same thing in another way . . . in the unconscious every one
of us is convinced of his own immortality."[15] The early
Mormon millenarian "in the twinkling of an eye" psychology seems to be one expression of this state of mind.
Appleby's seems to be another. "Indeed I hope if it is the
will of him who reigns on high," he wrote, "I may never
witness such a scene again. My Brethren, Sisters and
friends, falling by the shaft of death around me on ever
side." His language, of course, is inspired by that of the
Psalmist David rather than Freud, who wrote that "A
thousand shall fall at thy side, and ten thousand at thy right
hand, but it shall not come nigh thee."[16]

By why not? Had Appleby been saved by the inscrutable mercy of a benevolent God, in the same fashion in
which the Puritans believed Saints were sifted from the
sinners? As a faithful Mormon, clearly, Appleby could not
believe this. Man, Mormonism taught, could be instrumental in the salvation of the body as well as the soul.
Those who obeyed the dietary rules of the Word of Wisdom, for example, had been given "a promise, that the
destroying angel shall pass by them, as the children of
Israel, and not slay them." Appleby's escape from cholera
was in fulfillment of a promise to the Saints that if they

lived in purity, "the destroying angel will pass by your
dwelling—the desolating scourages from the Almighty
shall not find you out—your virtue shall be unto you as a
cloak from the open pestilence that stalks abroad . . . and
which [was] every day sweeping off mankind by the
thousands to a premature grave."[17]

Such a doctrine, however, was fraught with both logical
and empirical difficulties. The belief that God would slay
the wicked and save the righteous could be promulgated in
a flash of millenarian enthusiasm, but it could hardly sustain the church in space and time. True, it seemed to have
worked well enough as news of the first cholera epidemic
of 1832 reached the Saints, when the *Star* editorialized:

> the destroying angel goes waving the banner of death over all; and
> who shall escape his pointed arrow? Not he that could brave death at
> the cannon's mouth, but shrinks at the sound of the cholera; not he
> that worshiped his God in some stately chapel, every Sabbath till the
> cholera comes, and then flees for his life; no; none but he that trust
> in God, shall be able to stand when a thousand shall fall at his side,
> and ten thousand at his right hand by the noisome pestilence.[18]

But at Zion's Camp, where the cholera ravaged the
Saints, the explanatory response left something to be desired. An insert in the *History of the Church* impugned the
faith of at least one of those who died. Of Algernon Sidney
Gilbert, "the keeper of the Lord's storehouse," the *History*
recorded that "He had been called to preach the Gospel,
but had been known to say that he 'would rather die than
go forth to preach the Gospel to the Gentiles.'" Heber C.
Kimball recorded in his journal: "The Lord took him at his
word." Such crude exegeses prompted historian B. H.
Roberts, editor of the *History,* to rehabilitate the reputation of Gilbert by pointing out that he had indeed been a
most faithful Saint whose diffidence regarding missionary
work derived not from a lack of testimony, but from innate
shyness. Though the *History* has nothing specific to say
about the faith of the other thirteen who died at Zion's
Camp, Joseph's innuendos seemed to suggest that they
died because of lack of obedience, humility, and faith. The

whole incident points to the inability of the prophet and his followers to cope with so threatening an incident of disconfirmation.[19]

As time went on, explanations of this kind clearly did not suffice. Yet some years later Brigham Young attested to their popularity among the Saints when he recorded that "some of the brethren thought that our sickness was owing to some great wickedness we had been guilty of."[20] In time, the prophet became aware that he had encouraged the opening of a Pandora's box that needed closing. In 1839, when the Saints were ravaged by disease and death after their expulsion from Missouri, he made the following statement:

> it is a false idea that the Saints will escape all the judgments, whilst the wicked suffer; for all flesh is subject to suffer, and "the righteous shall hardly escape;" still many of the Saints will escape, for the just shall live by faith; yet many of the righteous shall fall a prey to disease, to pestilence, etc., by reason of the weakness of the flesh, and yet be saved in the Kingdom of God. So that it is an unhallowed principle to say that such and such have transgressed because they have been preyed upon by disease or death, for all flesh is subject to death; and the Savior has said, "Judge not, lest ye be judged."[21]

This statement bespeaks a pragmatic response to reality. For if any nineteenth-century Americans were ravaged by disease and death, it was the Mormons. A continued persistence in the early millenarian hopes pertaining to disease and death could only have cast the most severe doubts upon the validity of Mormonism, for if these were a test of the truth, the Saints failed miserably. The personal history of the Saints that emerges from letters, diaries, and journals is an almost continual and finally numbing story of disease and death.

Five of Emma Smith's nine children died. The death of Don Carlos, for whom the Smiths had held high hopes, was particularly traumatic. Shortly after Brigham Young joined the church his first wife died, leaving him with two young daughters. In a period of five monts, Hosea Stout lost his wife and three children. Many families lost their

fathers in skirmishes with the Gentiles: at Crooked River,
at Haun's Mill, at Carthage. But most of the deaths resulted from fevers, epidemics, and other diseases to which
a people continually on the move was particularly vulnerable. Elizabeth Haven has written of the trying times after
the expulsion from Missouri. The place is Quincy, Illinois,
September, 1839:

> Death has made its greatest havoc among the Saints here. Some
> families 2 and 3 members have been cut off by death. Br. Godead
> family who lives across the street from us, 3 weeks ago to day his
> wife died, a week this day his eldest daughter aged 16, died. To day
> he has followed them to the world of spirits. He left 5 children, 4 of
> them sick on their beds, one of them not expected to recover,
> neither does he wish to get well, but desires to depart also.

In another passage she writes: "I have not been to meeting
since last June have watched over the *sick, dying,* and *dead*
night and day."[22] If the health of the Saints improved
under the relatively settled circumstances prevailing in
Nauvoo, disease and death nevertheless continued at a
staggering rate. After the expulsion from Nauvoo, mortality further increased. Several hundred Mormon graves
were dug at Winter Quarters. The exodus to Utah took a
further toll. So did life on the Mormon frontier.[23]

Thus, to an objective observer it might well appear that
it was upon the Saints and not the Gentiles that the predicted plagues of Babylon were visited. It is therefore not
surprising that not a few of the Saints defected, having
become disillusioned in their millenarian expectations.
What is surprising is the large number of those who persisted in their new faith. Disconfirmation only seemed to
strengthen their testimony. Commenting on the scenes of
disease and death in the summer of 1839, Elizabeth Haven
recorded: "It is a time of mourning, yet not of mourning
either, they all died rejoicing in the fulness of the glorious
gospel."[24] At the death of his first wife, Brigham Young
recalled that "in her expiring moments she clapped her
hands and praised the Lord, and called upon brother Kimball and all around to praise the Lord."[25]

To the first generation of Saints, clearly, Lehi's statement that "men are, that they might have joy," had a
meaning encompassing few of the pleasures and comforts
of this life. "Prosperity never fitted any soul for the celestial kingdom, but adversity." wrote Elizabeth Haven.[26]
Thus, those Saints who endured knew they did so for a
purpose. Unlike Calvin's flock, or that of Jonathan Edwards, they were not merely sinners in the hands of an
angry God. What was it that made them not only endure
but prevail?

III

It appears that while Mormonism, in the long run, was
unable to do away with the reality of physical disease and
death, it was capable of alleviating the anxieties of those
concerned with the prospects of a Calvinist hell. Millen
Atwood, on the one hand, recorded in his diary that he was
"always desirous to serve the Lord aright, but not being
able to reconcile the Bible and my feelings to any of the
sects of the day my mind became troubled with regard to
the future state of man, and death became a terror to me."
William Appleby, on the other hand, rejected "the terrors . . . of that dreadful hell, fire and brimstone" taught
him by his mother. "I will here candidly state, I could
never believe it, . . . to burn there in 'fire and Brimstone' for
ever and ever I could not comprehend any reason, Justice
or satisfaction in it the way it was explained to me."[27]
Mormonism provided an answer for both, the one to
escape the terrors of a Calvinist hell, the other to confirm
and support that escape. According to Mormonism only
those few who had committed the unpardonable sins of
shedding innocent blood, or of denying the Holy Ghost,
would suffer the kind of tortures that Puritans believed
would be meted out to most mortals as their just deserts.
As for most sinners, after having been delivered from the
"buffetings of Satan," they would be rewarded with an
eternal "degree of glory," if a lesser one than that awaiting
the faithful Saints. Joseph Smith had worked out an in-

genious exegesis for the term "eternal punishment." According to the prophet's interpretation, "eternal" was a
synonym for "God." Eternal punishment was God's
punishment, and, however dreadful, not endless.[28] Divine
justice, moreover, was meted out only for sins personally
committed by an individual. Smith insisted emphatically
that "men will be punished for their own sins, and not for
Adam's transgression."[29] Likewise, each Saint had to work
out his or her own salvation.

Such a doctrine, of course, could also place an undue
burden on the individual conscience in the free-for-all of
Jacksonian individualism. Like the Puritan community
before it, however, the supportive system of the Mormon
community seems to have mitigated the possibility of such
stress. In a way, Mormonism may well have embodied
the best of both worlds: the optimistic theology of the
nineteenth century with the social cohesion of the seventeenth.

This is not to say, however, that Mormonism denied the
reality of evil any more than that it denied the reality of
death. It is true that the philosophical optimism of Mormonism seems entirely compatible with much of the optimistic thought of the nineteenth century. Nevertheless,
we must be cautious to see in early Mormonism the beginnings of that "unremarked shift in prudery" that has led to
the virtual denial of the reality of sin and death in the
twentieth century, and that Geoffrey Gorer has called "the
pornography of death."[30] The intellectual antecedents of
the modern "American way of death," to use the term
popularized by Jessica Mitford's critique, must rather be
sought in the philosophy of transcendentalism, particularly
in the thought of Ralph Waldo Emerson, who insisted that
death and evil were but shadows on the walls of Plato's
mythical cave with such unrelenting single-mindedness
that one cannot, in fact, suppress the suspicion that he was
whistling in the dark.[31]

But William Appleby, like his fellow Mormons, and indeed like many of his fellow Americans, was not. Perhaps
he could not, as Freud would later insist, truly imagine his

own death. But this does not mean that to him death was
not very real. Like sin, it was everywhere and could be
defeated only by accepting its reality. The Book of Mormon had posited a dialectic of good and evil, of life and
death. The two forces were locked in a gigantic, interdependent cosmic struggle. Righteousness had meaning
only through defeat of sin; life only through defeat of
death:

> For it must needs be, that there is an opposition in all things. If not
> so, . . . righteousness could not be brought to pass, neither wicked-
> ness, neither holiness nor misery, neither good nor bad. Wherefore,
> all things must needs to be a compound in one; wherefore, if it
> should be one body it must needs remain as dead, having no life
> neither death, nor corruption nor incorruption, happiness nor mis-
> ery, neither sense nor insensibility.[32]

Yet however much the Book of Mormon had thus
established the necessity of evil and death as a prerequisite
for the appreciation of righteousness and life, at the end of
the first decade of Mormonism it may well have appeared
to many a Saint that if opposition was the key to joy, there
was so much of the former that the latter, surely, would at
some future date burst in such abundance that the Saints
would scarce be able to contain it. In the meantime, however, the Saints needed all the help they could get to sustain their faith. The power of the priesthood in healing the
sick and, on occasion, even raising the dead, was a great
comfort to most of the Saints in their affliction. But the
grim statistics of disease and death, in their objectivity,
could not help but imply that from an actuarial perspective, the Gentiles did not fare any worse, to say the least.
In the light of the early millenarian hopes for triumph over
disease and death, the prophet's statement of 1839 can be
viewed as an implicit concession of defeat.

With the benefit of hindsight, however, it is possible to
interpret it, rather, as a tactical retreat. That the prophet
had always stressed salvation of the soul as more important
than salvation of the body goes without saying. Still, Mormon theology tended to obliterate the distinction between

the two. Matters physical and spiritual blended into one
another. God had a body of flesh and bone. The Holy
Ghost, to be sure, was a spirit, but even spirit consisted of
matter. No particle of the universe could be destroyed.
Death was merely the transformation from one state of
existence to another. Theoretically, therefore, death could
hold no terror for the Saints, whose bodies would not only
be resurrected—like those of all men, even sinners—but
would dwell in eternal glory with the Father. Surely, the
Saints knew this, or should have. Still, as the Mormon
prophet began to build his kingdom of God in Nauvoo, he
seems to have realized that he had to do better than to
admonish his followers that "all flesh is subject to death."
So it was indeed. What, then, could be done about it?

The Book of Mormon and the revelations of the
prophet had attempted to give an answer to that question.
But to many of the Saints these scriptures may well have
appeared highly theoretical, especially in the wake of the
continuing disasters of the 1830s. Something more,
something tangible and concrete was needed to reassure
the Saints of the reality of eternal life. Joseph's answer—
the summation and culmination of all that he had taught
before—was the "new and everlasting covenant," recorded
on July 12, 1843.[33] Because plural marriage was the socially most explosive aspect of the covenant, it has generally received the most attention by scholars—and perhaps
properly so. But from a theological perspective the novel
idea that the marriage covenant was not only for time but
for eternity if sealed by the proper priesthood authorities
was of equal if not of greater long-range significance. This
idea, more than any other, placed the idea of eternity in
concrete human terms. Death was thus placed in an entirely new perspective, as Parley P. Pratt pointed out
shortly after the promulgation of the new doctrine:
". . . the celestial order is an order of eternal life; it knows
no death, and consequently makes no provisions for
any . . . we must leave death entirely out of the consideration, and look at men and families just as we would look at

them if there was no death. This we can do with the greatest propriety because the time was when there was no death, and the time will be again, in which there will be no death."[34] Mormons, of course, had believed for some time that life on earth was merely a very temporary probationary state sandwiched between the two vast expanses of time of the preexistence and life after death. To use a modern analogy, for the Saints life on earth was like existence in a room with one-way mirrors on two opposing sides. Those on the outside could look in, but the occupants of the room could not look out. Because faith was one of the essential ingredients of what Mormons called the "plan of salvation," the one-way mirror set-up was a fundamental condition of life on earth. At the same time, those who had already exercised a certain degree of faith, such as the Saints, might be permitted temporary glimpses into those other worlds to sustain them in their probationary travails. It was partly for this reason that Joseph Smith devised the temple as a sacred edifice in which the Saints would participate in a symbolic drama that took them from the preexistence through this life to immortality. The culmination of the drama was the "passing through the veil," dramatizing the transition from earth life through "death" to eternal life. To this day, devout Mormons can be heard referring to a particularly close relative who has died—especially a wife or husband—as "having passed beyond the veil." Mormon folklore does not lack accounts of how, within the sacred precincts of the temple, the veil between this world and the next was lifted, not only symbolically but literally, allowing temporary communication between the living and the dead.[35]

Such communications, the participants believed, were primarily intended to facilitate the salvation of the dead. As I have indicated in chapter 2, certain ordinances believed to be essential to salvation, such as baptism and eternal marriage, can be performed only by mortals on this earth. Throughout much of history—because of apostasy from true principles—humans lacked the priesthood au-

thority to perform these essential ordinances. Therefore, a
great portion of the human race had died without the opportunity for participating in these saving ordinances.
After the restoration of the Gospel it became the sacred
duty of those who had accepted its principles to perform
these ordinances vicariously for the dead in temples
specifically constructed for this purpose, thus linking the
living and the dead in one gigantic chain of family and
kinship that would ultimately bind together the entire
human race. This is one of the major reasons why Mormons are such avid keepers and collectors of records, for
these are regarded as essential for documenting the existence of a person before his or her temple work can be
performed vicariously.

It is difficult to prove conclusively whether or not such
ideas were in part prompted by the sense of crisis that
gripped large segments of antebellum American society.
As I have suggested earlier, a declining sense of community
and an accelerating decline of ties of family and kinship
may well have heightened anxieties about death. If this is
the case, then Mormonism may be seen as one response to
these anxieties, and the vast Mormon genealogical ap-
paratus, which in the eyes of many critics appears as a
bizarre exercise in ancestor worship and antiquarianism,
acquires a plausible historical rationale. Faithful Mormons
could thus become active participants in the vast drama of
existence they called "eternal progression," thus placing
life on earth under the aspect of eternity while at the same
time diminishing the terrors of death through a life of
constant work for their salvation and that of others.

Of related interest to this response is the Mormon relationship to their children. Because marriages concluded
in the temple continued beyond the grave, children born
"under the covenant" belonged to the parents forever,
even should they die before the age of accountability,
which began as a child reached its eighth birthday. According to the Book of Mormon, baptism prior to that age
was a "solemn mockery before God," since children were

innocent and pure, contrary to prevalent Protestant beliefs, and were saved in the celestial kingdom.[36]

The antebellum period continued to be a period of relatively high mortality for children. To many Americans,
therefore, children were a grim reminder of the ubiquity
of death. Many parents, fearful of forming too great an
attachment to their children lest they lose them, affected an
outward coldness and distance. In a letter to a bereaved
couple, a writer reminded the recipients of the comforts of
the children still living, but then went on to warn: "But do
not O do not I beseech you lean too much on this fond
hope lest in a moment you least suspect it shall be torn
away *forever* . . . O how heart-rending it is for us to be told
that we must call off our affections from these second
selves and yet if we do not in some degree turn our affections away from them we sharpen the Arrow that is to
pierce our vitals." According to Lewis Saum, "a situation
incorporating 'little strangers' and involving the self-
preservation need to 'in some degree turn our affections
away from them' tells much about childhood, life and
death in pre–Civil War America."[37]

It is only possible to speculate what psychic scars those
children who survived derived from such a physical and
emotional environment. David Stannard has suggested
that among Puritan children the possibility of separation
anxiety—a fear of death "generally rooted in the anticipa-
tion of separation from their parent"—was very high,
especially since one of the most common defenses—
"expectation of reunion in death"—'was a defense denied
the Puritan child." It appears, however, that even in the
nineteenth century this defense was far from common.[38]
Whether Shaker celibacy or Noyes's male continence were
at least in part and perhaps unconsciously motivated by
such considerations will most likely remain a speculation.
But the fact that the unborn were spared much potential
psychological scars will not. This may have significance for
the declining birth rate in the first half of the nineteenth
century, which was the result not only of postponement of
marriage, but of fewer children by married couples. Mor-

mons, of course, were a notable exception to this trend.[39]

It is to these anxieties, among others, that Joseph Smith may well have addressed himself in a revelation that had as its text a passage from the biblical prophet Malachi: "Behold, I will send you Elijah the prophet before the coming of the great and dreadful day of the Lord: And he shall turn the heart of the fathers to the children, and the heart of the children to their fathers, lest I come and smite the earth with a curse."[40] Because the temple ordinances were believed to be binding in eternity, they had a real and pragmatic effect on this life. The testimony of the Saints suggests that they grieved as much as other parents for their deceased children. But because of their assurance that family ties were eternal, they had no need to call their children "little strangers," or to withhold their affections from them as a means of self-protection. They were able to turn their hearts freely to their children. And the children were able to reciprocate.

Thus, at a crucial time in its history, the Mormon leader was able to counter the destructive and demoralizing impact of death by a brilliantly conceived ritualization of its meaning that addressed itself not only to the solution of an internal crisis, but to the larger crisis confronting American society as well. To those familiar with the ideas and aspirations of the Mormon prophet, this is not surprising, for almost from the inception of the new religion he envisioned it not merely as another sect, but as a comprehensive religious and social movement that addressed itself to the fundamental problems confronting mankind. Although even the Mormons seem to have perceived this larger legacy only dimly, there can be no doubt that the vitality of Mormonism derived to a large extent from its unique confrontation of that seemingly greatest enemy of mankind, death.

IV

This assessment, of course, derives much of its force from the benefits of hindsight. For Joseph Smith barely had a

chance to implement some of his innovative ideas pertaining to the "new and everlasting covenant" before he
was killed. In fact, some of these ideas, as we shall see,
were indirectly responsible for his murder. At the
prophet's death, many of these concepts were still too ex-
perimental to be of immediate help to the Saints in a crisis
far exceeding their private sufferings and deaths. One of
the favorite hymns of the Saints started with the lines: "A
Church without a Prophet is not the Church for me; It has
no head to guide it; in it I would not be." Now a new hymn
was added to the collection started by Emma, Joseph wife:
"O give me back my Prophet dear!"[41] Joseph had given
only cursory consideration to the possibility of a successor.
The Saints even less so. In their millenarian expectations,
they do not seem to have contemplated the need for one.
In any case, who could take the place of Joseph?

To his people he had been a father, and his sudden death
had the potential of triggering a kind of mass separation
anxiety. The fact that even the prophet was not immune to
death, furthermore, might well have been a poignant reminder to the Saints of their own mortality. Not a few of
Joseph's erstwhile followers seem to have been incapable
of coping with this traumatic shattering of their sense of
belonging and security. Having, as it were, been "deserted" by their prophet, they deserted him. The majority
of Saints, however, responded differently. Joseph, they
rationalized, was still the head of the Church under Christ
in the Latter Days. The Lord had merely called him and his
brother Hyrum on a more important mission in order to
speed the building of the kingdom. According to one
commentator, the murderers of Joseph and Hyrum "did
not realize that they were removing [them] to a sphere of
far more extended usefulness, where they could more effectively help . . . to roll forward the designs to God in
relation to this latter dispensation."[42] Thus Joseph remained the father of his Saints.

At the same time, someone else had to take his place on
earth. As a result of their inability to agree on that ques-

tion, the Saints have divided into a surprisingly large
number of sects, each of which claims to be carrying out
the true intentions of its founder, who is believed to lead it
in the world beyond. At this juncture I have chosen to
follow the ideas of Brigham Young and those who joined
him in the exodus to Utah, not because they are theologically or intellectually more interesting or important than
those of his competitors, but simply because the
significantly larger number of Utah Mormons gives their
ideas greater social weight.

Young's success in uniting the largest number of Saints
behind his leadership was perhaps primarily a result of his
pivotal position in the church hierarchy as president of the
Quorum of the Twelve. Accession to that rank, of course,
had not been accidental and was a tribute to Young's
forceful personality as well as to his loyalty to the prophet.
But on that historic day in Nauvoo, on August 8, 1844,
when the assembled Saints accepted the leadership of the
Quorum of the Twelve with Young as president against
the claims of Sidney Rigdon, something else seems to have
been at work that Joseph had had in abundance, but the
Brigham normally lacked—charisma. For as Young presented the case for leadership by the Twelve many of those
in attendance suddenly thought that they heard the voice
of Joseph and saw the face of the deceased prophet instead. To the believing Saints it was a miracle. Joseph has
personally placed his mantle on Brigham.[43]

Though Young, in time, became a father of his people in
his own right, he correctly assessed this significance of the
miracle of August 8 and shrewdly insisted on the primacy
of Joseph's spiritual leadership as long as he presided over
the Saints. Even as Brigham transformed Mormonism in a
necessary adaptation to the Great Basin kingdom, he
merely claimed that he was carrying out the intentions of
Joseph. In a very real sense, then, it can be said that for the
Saints Joseph never died. And as much as anything, he
lived on in the institutionalized if modified concepts of the
"new and everlasting covenant," which helped sustain the

Saints through the travails of their exodus from Nauvoo and continued to provide a focus for the meaning of life as they carved an empire from a hostile environment, where death remained an everpresent threat.

Realizing the sustaining potential of Smith's grandiose vision, Young pushed for the completion of the Nauvoo Temple although he knew that the Saints would be able to enjoy the fruits of their labors for only a short season. As a result of feverish construction activity, the building advanced to the point where most of the Saints were able to receive their "endowments" before embarking on their uncertain journey to yet another promised land, where, they hoped, they would finally be able to live unmolested in order to achieve salvation for themselves and their dead. One of their first tasks upon arrival in the Great Salt Lake Valley was the survey of a temple lot. It was fittingly symbolic that the Salt Lake Temple, which took over forty years to build, was the most ambitious Mormon architectural project of the nineteenth century. That it has become Mormonism's most popular iconographic symbol reflects not only its architectural significance, but the importance of the ideas it represents.

While the Salt Lake Temple was under construction, the sacred ceremonies were performed in a temporary building called the Endowment House. As the Mormon empire expanded, temples arose in St. George, Logan, and Manti, along the so-called Mormon corridor. While most of the ceremonies in the Endowment House were for the living, with the completion of the first temple in St. George in 1877, the Saints earnestly began their work for the dead. Although the saving ordinances had to be performed vicariously in this life, the beneficiaries of these rituals would first have to be presented with the principles of the Gospel so that they could use their free agency either to accept or to reject them. Because of the vast multitude of those who had died without knowledge of the Gospel, the world of the "spirits in prison" provided opportunities for missionary work far exceeding those of this life. Christ himself

had initiated this work in the three days between his death
and resurrection. But many others were needed to perform this monumental task. The departed Saints were of
course the most logical candidates.[44] This belief provided a
convenient and comforting rationale to explain death, especially that of a young missionary, who would merely
continue his labors in the world beyond, or of a young
father suddenly plucked from this mourning wife and children, or for many a death that otherwise seemed merely
accidental.

Because for Mormons existence consisted of a progressive continuum, the next life had many of the characteristics of this. As a result, they drastically modified the traditional concept of heaven or the world of spirits as a place
of rest, a notion that the early Mormons had shared with
Protestants and Catholics. In 1840, after the death of his
daughter Mary Elizabeth, William Appleby had recorded
in his journal: "Her loss affected me considerably at the
time. But on reflection I considered that she was better
off; that she was at rest and in peace with her Saviour."
Even the the Book of Mormon had referred to death as "a
state of rest."[45] But as the Saints, subsequent to the introduction of the new and everlasting covenant, conceived of immense labors to be performed in the next
world, this image naturally changed. Brigham Young
taught that the departed Saints were "just as busy in the
spirit world as you and I are here. They are preaching,
preaching all the time, and preparing the way for us to
hasten our work in building temples here and
everywhere." Wilford Woodruff corroborated this concept of the afterlife in a vision in which he saw Joseph and
a number of other prominent departed Saints, all moving
about in a great hurry. In reply to Woodruff's inquiry why
heaven did not seem to be a place of rest, Joseph remarked: "We are the last dispensation, and so much work
has to be done and we need to be in a hurry in order to
accomplish it."[46] Whatever such notions may tell those
who believe in them about the world of the dead, they

reflect significantly upon the values of the world of the living. Building the kingdom of God in nineteenth-century America required Herculean labors. The belief that heaven was a place of work rather than rest could not help but have a practical influence on an already strong Mormon work ethic that, by comparison, made even the Protestant ethic a virtual guide for laggards. For most Protestants, as indeed for most Christians, death after all signified the end of human effort, for at the point of death time ceased to be.

Mormons, however, while freely using the term "eternity," seem to see it as an endless progression of time. According to the Book of Abraham, the patriarch had a knowledge of the times of various planets, "until thou come nigh unto Kolob which Kolob is after the reckoning of the Lord's time; which Kolob is set nigh unto the throne of God, to govern all those planets which belong to the same order as that upon which thou standest." One revolution of Kolob "was a day unto the Lord, after his manner of reckoning, it being one thousand years according to the time appointed unto that whereon thou standest. This is the reckoning of the Lord's time, according to the reckoning of Kolob."[47] God's time thus conformed perfectly to the laws of Galilean relativity and Newtonian mechanics.

For traditional Christianity, such a concept placed virtually insurmountable obstacles in the way of its ideas concerning immortality and eternal life, which are inoperable in space and time. Physical death is one of the logical consequences of the passage of time. The process of aging follows as inexorably as the revolutions of the earth, the ticking of a clock. In the next life, there will be no clocks. But for the Mormons the clocks keep on ticking.

Does this mean, then, that for Mormons there will be a form of death in the next life as well? Yes and no. There will be continued "progress," and therefore change. But that, after all, is what death represents in this life. For believing Mormons, therefore, death has lost a great deal of the mystery it has for most Christian religions, and

many non-Chrisitan ones besides. It has also lost a great
deal of its terror, at least for people belonging to a culture
stressing ego-identity and individual achievement, such as
North American and Western European culture in the
nineteenth and early twentieth century, or the modernizing Japanese and Latin American cultures of the third
quarter of the twentieth century as they attempt to adapt
to the work ethic of industrial society. Significantly, it is in
societies that are moving into a postindustrial order, such
as Sweden, West Germany, and certain sections of the
United States, that modern Mormonism is least successful
in its appeal.

V

Rationalizations of death in particular and belief systems in
general are, of course, intended for the living. Their primary purpose is to provide meaning for the mystery of
existence. If we measure the success of Mormonism by its
institutional vitality, its belief system seems to have served
it well. At the same time, there comes a moment when
indeed all those living will face death not as an abstraction,
or as a belief system, but as a personal reality. How did the
Mormon concept of death serve the dying and their kin?
Based on my impressionistic survey of diaries, journals,
family histories, and obituaries, I feel reasonably safe in
asserting that for most, it was a great help and comfort.
The death of Dudley Leavitt, pioneer of southern Utah, in
1908, seems representative of the death of many Mormons. One evening, a few days before he passed away, he
sat down in his chair and began to sing the old popular
hymn "Come, Let Us Anew Our Journey Pursue." According to Juanita Brooks, one of his granddaughters, his
family—his four wives, his children, and his grandchil-
dren—assembled for his departure to the world beyond:
"There was something dignified about his passing. No
hysterical weeping, no shaking him and calling him back,
no nurses punching needles into him or poking oxygen

tubes up to his nose. His family accepted the inevitable calmly, as he would have wished." Before his death he spoke of it as a release "or, as he said, a promotion." He remarked that "there are so many things I want to do, if I were not chained to this old worn out body. I'll be glad to lay it down. Maybe then I can accomplish something again."[48] As a devout Mormon Dudley Leavitt believed that heaven was no rest for the weary.But that is how he wanted it to be. And that, after all, is what heaven is about.

4

The Kingdom of God: Its Economy and Politics

I calculate to be one of the instruments of setting up the kingdom of Daniel by the word of the Lord, and I intend to lay a foundation that will revolutionize the whole world.

Joseph Smith

I

Few Jacksonian Americans were interested in Smith's elaborate conceptualization of relations between the living and the dead. Like the prophet's road to godhood, his plan for the reconciliation of fathers and children strained the credulity of most of his contemporaries and, in any case, required too much effort for a people who had their eyes on the main chance. Still, as emerging capitalists, they had some appreciation of the principle of deferred compensation even if they wanted to cash in their chips in this world and not the next. What they did not appreciate was that Smith also had very specific and elaborate plans for this life that directly threatened all those who had stock in the future of antebellum America. As I have indicated earlier, the philosophical optimism of Mormonism was not only ultimate but proximate. Smith and his followers may have given up on the hope of achieving social, economic, and perhaps even psychological security within the pluralistic world of Jacksonian individualism and competition; and they may have staked their *ultimate* hopes on the realization of the promises of the celestial kingdom in the world to come. But they also firmly believed that Book of Mormon prophet Lehi's promise—that "men are that they might have joy"—applied to this life as well. Therefore, if

the political, social, and economic arrangements of Jacksonian America were an obstacle to the fulfillment of that
promise, then those arrangements would simply have to be
changed. Joseph Smith thus emphatically rejected
Tocqueville's proposition that "religions . . . ought to
confine themselves within their own precincts." On the
contrary, the Mormon prophet refused to honor the unwritten contract that the denominations had entered into
with American society to mind their own business and not
to question the social and political arrangements of the
powers that be. Smith questioned those arrangements very
much, indeed. More than that, he attempted to supplant
them with an organization that included all conceivable
facets of human existence. This total institution, designed
to sever the ties of men and women from the old world of
religious, political, economic, and social competition, was
intended as a new reality—a new heaven and earth in-
habited by the Saints of God. Not surprisingly, it was
called the kingdom of God. Its ultimate purpose on earth
was to usher in the millennial reign of Christ.

This millennial aspiration, in and of itself, was nothing
new. Indeed, the pursuit of the millennium, in antebellum
America, was the major passion of nearly every sect or
church, every religious or secular reform movement.[1]
Establishment Protestants, Evangelicals, Perfectionists,
Transcendentalists, New Light Calvinists, Campbellites,
Millerites, Freesoilers, Abolitionists, secular utopians and
communitarians, all pursued their own version of the millennium. In an attempt to get some order out of confusion,
historians have traditionally divided these various groups
into pre- and post-millennialists. Some postmillennialists
believed that Christ's thousand-year reign on earth had
begun with the Emperor Constantine and was to be understood spiritually. Others, such as nineteenth-century
American main-line Protestants (including the Evangelicals), interpreted it as meaning the gradual moral and
physical perfection of society through an outpouring of the
spirit of God and the binding of Satan in the hearts of men.

Theirs was an optimistic faith, a religious version of the
idea of progress that provided the intellectual underpinning for the individualistic ethos of antebellum America. It
was a faith of successful men whose hopes and dreams
were being realized in the age of egalitarianism."

The premillennialists, however, were literal believers in
Christ's reappearance in the clouds, to be accompanied by
catastrophes of nature that would destroy the wicked while
the Saints would reign on earth with their redeemer for a
thousand years. These literal believers in the millennium
generally rejected the existing social order because the
Jacksonian rhetoric of individualism, egalitarianism, and
progress had left the hopes of these people unfulfilled, or
raised the specter of social and economic dislocation,
threatening an established, traditional social order.

One of the most typical movements deriving from such
frustrations was Millerism. William Miller, a sometime
soldier, deist, and preacher from northern New York, appealed to a variegated group of followers, including not
only those on the margin of society but also substantial
members of the community. What bound these disparate
enthusiasts together was their inability to find within
themselves the hope for regeneration, which presupposes
an outlook on life essentially optimistic and based on a
progressive ideology. Unlike the postmillennialists, who
believed that the world was on the threshold of un-
parallelled improvement, the millenarian or premillennial
Millerites held out no hope for this world. They were the
kind of people unable to envision a realistic escape from
what they regarded as a corrupt and evil society richly
deserving its impending destruction. At the same time
they were not merely irrational visionaries. Miller's calculations for the end of the world were based on years of
painstaking research into biblical chronology that he
matched up with major events in secular history. When the
predicted end of the world failed to materialize in 1843,
Miller blamed it on an error in his calculations. But after
the revised date for the day of doom in 1844, likewise

passed without catastrophe, many of the disappointed followers denounced Miller as a deluded fanatic, a charlatan,
and a false prophet. Miller and a hard core of true believers, however, steadfastly clung to their premillennial
beliefs, being careful not to commit themselves to another
precise date for the Second Coming. In later years, some
of these millenarians formed the nucleus for the Seventh-
day Adventist faith.[2]

Miller was the most prominent of numerous antebellum
millenarians. What all of them lacked was an ideology of
power, or at least the kind of ideology that could operate
in space and time. And yet, paradoxically, this vision of the
millennium held out to those who saw no hope in the
progressive, individualistic society of Jacksonian America—who could not conceive of attaining or regaining social and political power through human agency—the
achievement of an ultimate kind of power that would totally destroy the existing world, with the exception of the
small band of true believers. In their mind, Christ's kingdom was neither of this world nor in this world.

Some millenarians were responding to the destruction
of an old, established social order. Others were reacting to
the growing discrepancy between the democratic rhetoric
and reality. The revivalists, in the words of William Warren Sweet, had "placed stress on the doctrine that all men
are equal in the sight of God."[3] This rhetoric had led Professor Sweet to rather too optimistic a conclusion about
the impact this idea would have on "the common man."
"When this doctrine is preached to humble people, it *inevitably* develops self-respect and a desire to have a part in
the management of their own affairs" (my italics). Professor Sweet based his reasoning on the assumption that
the "common man" had in fact succeeded in his quest for
power in the age of Jackson. A number of recent historians, however, have presented evidence that raises serious
questions about his assumption. Social and economic mobility in this period, they argue, declined. Their evidence,
however, is incomplete and thus cannot sustain the full

weight of their argument. What Sweet on the one side and
the revisionists on the other have failed to take sufficiently
into account is the psychological impact of modernization.
According to some recent studies, the social fabric of
American society was subjected to serious strain in the
first half of the nineteenth century, leading to consequences more complex than those alluded to in the studies
of Sweet and the revisionists.[4]

According to current studies of economic growth, there
was a significant increase from the Federalist period to the
age of Jackson.[5] In fact, without some empirical evidence
of this kind, it is doubtful that the progressive millen-
nialism of the nineteenth century could have been sustained for any length of time. In contrast, we have to account for the obvious fact that contrary to Professor Sweet
a significant minority of Americans did not develop the
kind of "self-respect and desire to have a part in the management of their own affairs." The surge of millenarianism,
certainly, is evidence of this. Quite possibly, many of these
people simply were left out entirely of the race for the
main chance. But even if some of them may have experienced an objective improvement in their social and economic position relative to the preceding generation, the
millennialist rhetoric of progress triggered an acceleration
in expectations that far outdistanced any objective gain in
position. Therefore, in spite of a possible improvement in
their condition, some of these people, unable to live up to
the accelerating rhetoric of rising expectations, may have
found their frustrations increased. Unlike the *millennialists,* who represented the upwardly mobile segment of
society, many of the *millenarians* were either on the fringe
of social and economic progress, or else belonged to a
displaced elite that was losing out to the rising self-made
men of Jacksonian America. Millennialists and millenarians, clearly, were diametrically opposed in their assessment of the present and future state of antebellum American society and religion.

II

Although the Mormons, likewise, rejected the established order, they do not fit conveniently into the millenarian framework. True, in his Tenth Article of Faith, Smith held to a millenarian vision: "We believe in the literal gathering of Israel and in the restoration of the Ten Tribes; that Zion will be built on this [the American] continent; that Christ will reign personally upon the earth; and that the earth will be renewed and receive its paradisiacal glory."[6] Disagreeing with Miller's timetable, Smith nevertheless believed in a literal apocalypse and made some attempts to determine precisely when the Lord would appear like "a thief in the night." Martin Harris, one of the three witnesses of the Book of Mormon, predicted in 1831 that the faithful would see Christ in fifteen years while the nonbelievers would be damned.[7] Mormon publications, led by the *Millennial Star,* recorded the "signs of the times," such as earthquakes and other natural catastrophes, epidemics, wars, railroad accidents, steamboat explosions, and signs in the heavens. Every calamity was looked upon as a signpost of and contribution to the end of the world: "One and all are, to the Saint, so many cheering confirmations of his faith."[8]

Yet if this had been the essence of Mormonism, if it had been merely another millenarian cult, its end, in all probability, would have been as inevitable as that of the Millerites. Much of the millenarian language of the period merely expresses a general rhetorical style quite prevalent in 1830s and 1840s among both millenarians and millennialists, and thus had a certain propaganda value. It is quite instructive, for example, that one of the most popular and most fervent of Millerite hymns, "The Alarm," which some historians have regarded as an example of Millerite extremism, was composed by an Episcopalian. If we want to understand Mormon millenarian aspirations, we must therefore look more closely at the social background as well as some of the more specific millenarian doctrines that

set the Mormons apart from the Millerites and other protagonists of millenarian enthusiasm.

  Professor Robert Flanders has called Joseph Smith "an
alienated youth, the product of an alienated family."[10]
Smith clearly started out with less education than Miller.
Those writers who have emphasized the poverty and the
cultural crudeness of the Smiths probably are not far off
the mark; but they are misguided in their efforts to use
such evidence to "denigrate and discredit Smith's
achievements." We lack an entirely satisfactory explanation
for the obvious differences between the millenarianism of
Smith and Miller. We may never know precisely why the
two responded in such strikingly different fashions to the
dislocations of nineteenth-century America, but we do
know that these differences had historically significant
consequences. The Smiths belonged "to the large company of Americans who were beyond the edge of successful, genteel society and the institutional Establishment of
their time. And they were generally inclined to distrust the
Establishment, whether its manifestations be theological,
ecclesiological, political, or economic. Like many Americans descended from forebears in the backwoods of New
England . . . they tended to be 'agin the government,'
whether in or out of church." But in spite of their alienation the Mormons continued to believe not only in divine
providence, but in the "promises of mythic America, and
their own ingenuity," while the Millerites had given up on
these beliefs. Where Miller directed all his efforts toward
determining the precise date of the end of history, Smith
constructed a complex religious, social, economic, and
political system that would usher in the "fulness of times,"
to be sure, but one that also required the continuation of
human effort. In order to accomplish such an ambitious
goal, Smith forged an ideology of power that differed radically from Miller's. The message of Mormonism was to all
the world, "and there is none to escape, and there is no eye
that shall not see, neither ear that shall not hear, neither
heart that shall not be penetrated . . . and the voice of

warning shall be unto all people, by the mouths of my
disciples, whom I have chosen in these last days, and they
shall go forth and none shall stay them, for I the Lord have
commanded them."[10]

That is not to say, of course, that all those who heard the
message would accept it. Indeed, one of the main obstacles
to acceptance was the all-inclusiveness of the message.
Those who became Mormons did not merely exchange
one religion for another, such as exchanging Baptism for
Prebyterianism, but entered into a new and all-encompassing world that, like Islam, regulated the lives of
its members both spiritually and temporally. Mormonism,
like Millerism, may not have been of the world, but unlike
Millerism, it was very much in it. The establishment of the
Mormon kingdom thus required a revolutionary ideology
that may not have been as hard-hitting and ruthless as
Cromwell's, or Lenin's, or Mao's; yet the Mormon kingdom was perhaps the closest antebellum Ameica came to
the realization of a disciplined, tightly knit, quasi-totali-
tarian society.

An important difference was that Mormons were not
able to capture the state for the revolution. Their movement, therefore, always remained a voluntary one, thus
being spared the totalitarian excesses of the other movements. Still, there are important parallels, especially to
Puritanism. In *The Revolution of the Saints,* Michael Walzer
has presented a Puritan model for revolution that may be
more appropriately applied to Jacobins, Leninists, and
Maoists, and yet, certain features of Walzer's Puritans can
be transferred to Mormons with almost uncanny accuracy:
"the historical role of the chosen band is twofold. Externally, as it were, the band of the saints is a political movement aiming at social reconstruction. It is the saints who
lead the final attack upon the old order and their de-
structiveness is all the more total because they have a total
view of the world. Internally, godliness and predestination
are creative responses to the pains of social change. Discipline is the cure for freedom and "unsettledness'."[11]

No nineteenth-century American movement had a more total view of the world, and none was more disciplined than Mormonism. The Saints, like other nineteenth-century millennialists did not, of course, believe in predestination. But as John William Ward has pointed out, the antebellum American mind had as its "structural underpinnings" contradictory expressions of the concepts of nature, providence, and will.[12] And an examination of a revelation given to Smith at Hiram, Ohio, in 1831, reveals some of these same inherent tensions. For here the Mormon rhetoric of free will was countered by the historical logic of the juggernaut of progress, to be achieved through the power of God in the hands of His servants, a power men would not be able to oppose: "And they shall go forth and none shall stay them, for I the Lord have commanded them . . . . What I the Lord have spoken, I have spoken, . . . and though the heavens and the earth pass away, my word shall not pass away, but shall be fulfilled."[13]

The Mormons, like their American ancestors, believed that the fulfillment of the Lord's words depended very much on them. In order to build the kingdom of God on earth, they had to organize, had to plan. To accomplish the establishment of a new social and political order, Smith organized a cadre of the most dedicated and loyal followers into a secret central committee of about fifty members called the Council of Fifty that acted as the executive political and temporary arm of the kingdom. These were also the men who would enforce the discipline necessary to achieve victory over the old order.

The kingdom of God provided those people who were alienated from the American social order with a social order of their own. The problem of equality, after all, is a very complex one. Professor Sweet's approach, certainly, is almost meaningless. Christianity had, of course, always stressed "the doctrine that all men are equal in the sight of God." But historically this argument has been used more often in support of social inequality than equality. Social distinctions were considered mere temporal and temporary ephemera as man contemplated eternity. Because the church rules in the city of God, not the city of man, the Millerites, clearly, saw no hope of achieving equality on earth. Mormonism, in contrast created such a hope by creating a city of God on earth. A man who could not achieve self-respect in society of Jacksonian America could achieve it in the society of the Mormon kingdom of God. Through an elaborate system of interlocking political, social, and ecclesiastical organizations, a hierarchy of offices and positions in the Mormon priesthood provided a prestige ladder for those who may not have been even on the bottom rung of that other American ladder of upward mobility and progress, thus providing an outlet for a search of recognition that was being stifled in a large number of common people. In America this search had led to the formation of numerous voluntary and fraternal organizations that sprang up like mushrooms in this period. Though these organizations were themselves subject to a pecking order of their own, a member could feel important as a mason, or an imperial primate or potentate of some lodge or other. Yet all but the most literal-minded and naive must have known in their hearts that they were playing a game, that in the real world outside their worth was not measured by fancy titles and fancy uniforms.[14]

To Mormons, however, the kingdom of God was the real world. When Joseph Smith called the members of the Council of Fifty princes of the kingdom of God, the language itself may have been metaphorical, but the power of these "princes" was social and political, and Smith's promise that they would ultimately rule the world was an inevitable expression of the millennial program of Mormonism which made these men feel absolutely certain they would achieve this end. Mormonism provided the essential ingredients for a potentially successful movement of revolutionary dimensions in this world—a realistic means for achieving not only a religious but a social, economic, and political millennium.

III

That Mormonism was to be more than just one more church within the colorful spectrum of American religious pluralism became obvious very soon after its inception. The precise nature of this departure from the accepted Protestant norm, however, evolved only gradually over time. The first Mormon congregations in New York and Pennsylvania, in 1830, however separate they may have conceived themselves as being from the world, operated in a manner not altogether different from those of other churches. It was not until 1831, after Smith had persuaded the majority of his followers to pull up stakes and move to Ohio to join Sidney Rigdon and his flock that a major change in relations to the world occurred. Here, for the first time, the Mormons organized as a distinct and separate community. Indeed, not all the Saints were convinced of the desirability of the move, even after the considerable urgings of the prophet. Some were reluctant to dispose of their property at possibly considerable loss. Others seem to have rejected the major implication behind the move—that Mormonism was to become more than a religious belief, was to become a kingdom of God separate from the world in its totality. It is here that we have the origins of a long and sometimes bloody conflict between those—both within and without the church—who preferred to see Mormonism as part of the religious pluralism of Protestant America and those, like Smith himself, who envisioned it as a new and separate reality both spiritually and temporally.

About 190 of the New York and Pennsylvania Saints accepted this latter vision of Mormonism, buoyed up by the prophet's promise that after their arrival in Ohio the Lord would "give unto you my law, and there you shall be endowed with power from on high."[15] More specifically, it meant that they would acquire land in and around Kirtland, and would establish a communitarian society in accordance with the law of the church as revealed to Smith on February 9. The opportunity for this new economic order, also called the "law of consecration and stewardship," arose directly out of the conversion of Rigdon and some of his followers. One of these, Isaac Morley, had organized a "family" that held all things in common, in emulation of the primitive Saints of the New Testament. But because "they considered from reading the scriptures that what belonged to one brother, belonged to any of the brethren," Morley's family was on the verge of breaking up. At just that moment, their conversion to Mormonism gave them the opportunity for a fresh start, especially when Smith's revelation replaced the family system with "the more perfect law of the Lord."

To the biblical precedents for this economic order Smith had already added that of the Book of Mormon, which described the Nephites as living in ideal Christian communities, with no poor among them. The same conditions, according to the prophet, had prevailed in the ancient city of Enoch, which was caught up into Heaven because of the righteousness of its inhabitants. Thus, the establishment of a Mormon communitarian society was clearly an essential part of the restorationist impulse. The system was intended to work as follows: those entering the order were asked to "consecrate" their property and belongings to the church "with a covenant and a deed which cannot be broken." Every member, in return, would then be made "a steward over his own property, or that which he has received by consecration, as much as is sufficient for himself and his family." Any surplus would then "be kept to administer to those who have not, from time to time, that every man who has need may be amply supplied and receive according to his wants"—or, as Marx would put it not too many years later: "from each according to his abilities, to each according to his needs."

A recent, authoritative history of Mormonism has effectively summarized the major objectives of the law of consecration and stewardship:

First, it would eliminate poverty and create an economic equality tempered by individual needs, circumstances, and capacities. Second, through the continuing consecration of excess production into the storehouse, there would be sharing of surplus, creating capital for business expansion and for church programs. Third, the system relied heavily on individual initiative. Each steward operated under a system of free enterprise in the management of property. He was subject to profits and losses, the laws of supply and demand, and the price system. But despite this involvement in the capitalistic system, the stewards were part of a united community working toward a fourth objective, group economic self-sufficiency.

Once this had been achieved, the Saints would extricate themselves from the capitalistic system as a major step toward separation from the world.[16]

Certainly, as economic historian Jonathan Hughes has pointed out, Mormon economic ideals were a radical departure from classic American economic practices. The concept of consecration was incompatible with American fee simple law. Altogether, "the Mormons appeared to be recreating a feudal landownership chain, with tenure given for services, and the heirs barred from direct inheritance. Alternately, one might imagine in his deed the transformation of Zion's entire domain into a 'use,' except that the trustee did not agree to support the heirs of the original owner." Other throwbacks to a more traditional society involved controls on the freedom of movement. A bishop's "recommend" was required if a Saint wished to move from one Mormon "ward" to another. "This practice," says Hughes, "is similar to the seventeenth century English laws of settlement. When the early Mormon villages farmed with common fields and herd boys, the outsider might have thought he was seeing a European medieval village reincarnate."[17]

The Mormon village thus represented an attempt to return to a more traditional economic as well as social order—strongly reminiscent of the early settlements of New England, where houses were clustered in relatively close proximity and strip farming served the purpose of dividing the land equitably. The Mormons were thus deliberately attempting to reverse a trend that had resulted in the virtual disappearance of the old New England village in favor of autonomous farmsteads. One result of this nucleization process had been the breakdown of the social ties of these individual farm families to the larger community. By the nineteenth century, the old, cohesive village communities that had provided "the entire range of social, economic, and political services" was at best a mere memory. Quite obviously, the majority of American farmers in the nineteenth century preferred "familial autonomy to the demands of corporate existence."[18] The Mormons, however, wished to restore a more traditional society in which the economy was regulated in behalf of the larger interests of the group even if this entailed individual sacrifice. Such attempts, inevitably, would bring the Mormons in conflict with their neighbors, who not only had very little sympathy for communal solidarity but more often than not perceived it as a threat to their own economic ambitions. On the indvidualistic Missouri frontier, especially, Mormons were regarded as clannish, as not belonging.

As a result of successive failures in Ohio, Missouri, and Illinois, such practices, to any extent, were implemented only after the Saints had removed themselves from the American market economy after their trek to the Great Basin under the leadership of Brigham Young. Joseph Smith, the originator these ideas, soon discovered, like Marx after him, that it was as easy to commit them to paper as it was difficult for fallible humans to follow them. Early attempts to put these economic principles into operation quickly faltered, as much because of the imperfections of the practitioners as because of flaws in the principles themselves. Changes and adjustments, however, did little to alleviate the problems generated by these heroic attempts to repudiate the Jacksonian doctrine of equality of opportunity in favor of the more radical principle of equality of condition. It was soon obvious to the prophet that the realization of such ideals would have to be deferred until the Saints had removed themselves more effectively from the world, both physically and spiritually. In meantime Smith instituted the law of tithing as a kind of schoolmaster and means of obtaining funds. Under this principle, still in operation, faithful Mormons are expected to donate 10 percent of their annual net income to the church.

After their western migration the Saints renewed their efforts at establishing a cooperative economic system. One of Brigham Young's major goals was independence for the kingdom of God, economic as well as political. Under a plan of economic self-sufficiency the Saints attempted to develop local industries thtrough a system of cooperation rather than private enterprise. In order to finance these and other ventures Young attempted in 1854 and 1855 to revive the law of consecration and stewardship, but failed because the federal government did not see fit to institute procedures for the legal ownership of land. Young therefore had to fall back on tithing as a major source of capital. Because cash was extremely scarce, however, most tithing was paid in kind or in labor on work projects. In this way the church became "thoroughly involved in the economic life of its members."

Nevertheless, after a quarter of a century in the Great Basin, and after many significant economic accomplishments in building the kingdom of God, Young and his associates felt strongly that the Saints were becoming ever more entangled in the market economy of the United States. This process accelerated significantly after the completion of the transcontinental railroad in 1869. Just how thoroughly the Mormon economy had become enmeshed with that of the outside world came to the painful attention of the Saints in the wake of the financial depression of 1873. As a result, Young redoubled his efforts to promote a cooperative movement that had been initiated in 1867 in response to the anticipated completion of the transcontinental railroad. Now, more than ever, the Saints felt they had to stand together against the outside world.

In a speech in 1869, Young declared that "this cooperative movement is only a stepping stone to what is called the Order of Enoch, but which is in reality the order of Heaven." In 1873, the Mormon leader believed the time had come to take that next step. A major impetus to the establishment of the United Order of Enoch was the spectacular success of the cooperative in Brigham City. Owned by about four hundred shareholders from nearly every family in the community, the cooperative survived the depression of 1873 without difficulty because its links with the outside economy were minimal. Spurred by this example, Young preached the doctrine of cooperation, and organized the first United Order in the southern settlement of St. George during the winter of 1873/74, followed by the establishment of about twenty such orders throughout southern Utah. The following spring, most of the other settlements in the territory were organized along the same economic principles. Altogether, about 150 United Orders were established. Many of these followed the model of St. George, where the majority of adults

> pledged their time, energy, ability, and property to the order and became subject to the direction of an elected board of management. In return for property, each person received a commensurate amount of stock. Stockholders pledged themselves to boost local manufacturing, stop importing goods, and deal only with members of the order. The order was also to be a spiritual union, and a long list of rules for Christian living was drawn up. Each person entered the order by being rebaptized and pledging to obey all the rules.[19]

Three other types of order were established, depending on the needs and size of the community. Although the United Order of the 1870s, on the whole, was more successful than Smith's communitarian attempts in the 1830s, by 1877 most of the orders were disbanded both for internal and external reasons. A growing number of Mormons found the perceived benefits of joining the larger American economy too attractive to resist. At the same time, the Saints found it increasingly difficult to keep out Gentiles eager to explore the economic opportunities of the territory, especially mining. By 1890, it was apparent that the

inland empire of the kingdom of God was no match for the
American empire.

The economic transformation of the kingdom, however,
was not the result merely of external pressures. Many of
the Saints had never been totally immune to the lures of
the market economy. Certainly, these inclinations had
contributed to the failures of the economy in Kirtland and
had ensured that Nauvoo was something less than a
cooperative commonwealth. Even in Utah, the leaders had
to exert considerable pressure and persuasion to keep
those Saints in line who were forever being lured away by
the promises of capitalist Babylon. These pressures increased measurably after the completion of the transcontinental railroad in 1869.

It is nevertheless surprising how quickly even the leaders became converted to the ethics of capitalism. Heber J.
Grant, who was born in 1856 and became president of the
church in 1918, was a close friend of Henry Ford and
shared the economic philosophy of the automobile magnate. Those Mormons who have become conspicuously
successful in the world of business and industry, such as
automobile executive George Romney and hotel magnate
T. Willard Marriott, have generally attributed their
achievement to the teachings and philosophy of Mormonism. I shall attempt to speculate on the reasons for this
remarkable transformation in chapter 7.

Although modern Mormons are thoroughly in tune with
the American business ethos they revere the law of consecration and stewardship as an ideal that they believe will
be restored in preparation for the millennium—an event
to occur at an unspecified future date. In the meantime,
the Saints are enjoined to pay their tithing in preparation for the higher law of sacrifice and cooperation. Today
tithing is the chief source of revenue for the church. The
cooperative spirit is also kept alive through a large-scale
welfare program, started in the 1930s in response to the
relief and recovery programs of the New Deal. Unsympathetic to the ideas of the welfare state, Mormons
decided to take care of their own needy through a program

of self-help. Though the Saints long ago accepted the in-evitability of federal social programs, they have continued to expand their own welfare activities, largely supported by volunteer labor. Bishops' storehouses in various parts of the world are equipped to handle not only the long-term needs of the economically deprived, but also the im-mediate needs of the community and region in times of natural disasters and emergencies.

These impressive achievements, however, do not negate the fact that the majority of Mormons, at least in the United States, are fully committed to the pluralistic American economy. The welfare plan, in fact, serves as an effective safety valve to maintain the economic individu-alism of the Saints. As long as "the more perfect law of the Lord" remains an ideal, it will not threaten an economic way of life that the majority of Mormons find eminently satisfactory and desirable. Those few Mormon intellectuals and idealists who are dreaming of making the economic ideas of the kingdom of God once more relevant to Mor-mon thought and practice have found little response among their fellow believers, and unless the economic system of the United States is headed for a major collapse, it is not very likely that they will.[20]

This same attachment to economic individualism is not always evident among Mormons in other parts of the world. In recent years the church has met with unexpected success in Latin America and the Third World. Many of these converts are repelled both by the economic theories and practices of the ruling classes as well as the various Marxist alternatives. Because Mormonism in these areas is still very much in flux, it is still too early to tell whether updated nineteenth-century Mormon economic principles can be implemented successfully on a large scale. More-over, as long as the hierarchy is dominated by North Americans, massive innovative experiments in this direc-tion are not very likely.

IV

The economic takeover of the kingdom of God was related to its decline in political power. As long as the kingdom had political clout, it had some means of defense
against the outside world. A brief history of the political
kingdom is thus essential to an understanding of the rise
and fall of the Mormon empire.

When Victoria was crowned Queen of Great Britain and
Ireland in Westminster Abbey on June 28, 1838, the
Mormons took little notice of an event whose pomp and
ceremony prompted the Turkish ambassador to mutter
repeatedly: "All this for a woman!" Confident that they
were instruments in the hand of God to create on earth
that kingdom which they believed Daniel had predicted
some 2300 years earlier, the Saints had little awe for
monarchs of either sex. In a letter addressed to the Queen
in 1841, Mormon apostle Parley P. Pratt wrote: "Know
assuredly, that the world in which we live is on the eve of a
REVOLUTION, more powerful in its beginnings—more
rapid in its progress—more lasting in its influence—more
important in its consequences—than any which man has
yet witnessed upon the earth." The present political and
religious establishments, the letter solemnly affirmed,
were destined to vanish, and God was about to set up "a
new and universal Kingdom, under the immediate administration of the Messiah and his Saints."[21]

It is doubtful that Pratt's letter caused the queen any
sleepless nights. Yet if the young monarch had read
another letter, written three years later, by Pratt's fellow
apostles Brigham Young and Willard Richards, to Reuben
Hedlock, leader of the British Mormons, informing him
that the kingdom of God was "organized and although as
yet no bigger than a grain of mustard seed, . . . in a
flourishing condition, and our prospects brighter than
ever," she might have been well advised to inform herself
of these "prospects."[22] For her subjects swelled the ranks
of the Mormon kingdom by the thousands. If these

converts—largely from classes of displaced and restless yeomen, artisans, and mechanics—had remained in Britain, their newly acquired aspirations, which were not only religious, but social, economic, and even political, might well have been an additional source for the kind of turmoil stirred up by Chartists and anti–corn-law leagues that so annoyed and perplexed the queen in the restless 1840s. Their migration to the New World, of course, helped relieve the pressure on the constituted authorities in Britain. Thus, ironically, Pratt's anticipated revolution of the kingdom of God may well have done its small part in helping to prevent revolution in Great Britain.

At the same time, the influx of these immigrants into the Mormon kingdom in Nauvoo, Illinois, further heightened tensions between Saints and Gentiles at a time when Joseph Smith was actively engaged in establishing a political government that was intended as the nucleus for a future world state. For by 1844 the Mormon prophet had come to the realization that the "new heaven and the new earth," especially its social and economic programs, could be accomplished only through political independence from the world. When, on May 12, 1844, he declared before an assembly of Saints, "I calculate to be one of the instruments of setting up the kingdom of Daniel by the word of the Lord, and I intend to lay a foundation that will revolutionize the whole world,"[23] it is unlikely that very many members of his audience understood the full meaning of his words. For few of them knew—most likely identifying the foundation of the kingdom of God with the organization of the Mormon church in 1830—that the prophet had secretly begun the establishment of a literal, temporal government for the "kingdom of Daniel" two months earlier.

If Smith waited until 1844 before he formally organized the government of the kingdom, the logic behind that move goes back to the very beginning of the new religion, because he never conceived of Mormonism as merely another sect. At the very least, it was a sect to end all sects,

though the prophet, in more positive terms, conceived of
it as a kingdom that—like the one in Daniel's vision—
would fill the earth. At a general church conference in
Nauvoo held in April, 1844, Sidney Rigdon told those
present that "we were maturing plans fourteen years ago
which we now can tell.... There we sat in secret and
beheld the glorious visions and powers of the kingdom of
heaven pass and repass.... We talked about the people
coming as doves to the windows, and that nations should
flock unto it; that they should come bending to the standard of Jesus, ... and of whole nations being born in one
day ... and we began to talk about the kingdom of God as
if we had the world at our command."[24]

Smith and Rigdon soon learned, however, that if whole
nations could be born in a day, then only according to the
reckoning of the Lord's time. The building of the Mormon
kingdom was a precarious adventure of sometimes slow
and sometimes spectacular advances alternating with dis-
heartening setbacks and defeats. That a new Jerusalem, a
new city of Zion, should be built on the North American
continent had been predicted in the Book of Mormon. A
revelation in September, 1830, vaguely identified the location of the new Zion "on the borders, by the Lamanites,"
to which the prophet promptly sent a group of missionaries to proselytize among the Indians. Another revelation instructed the prophet "to bring to pass the gathering of mine elect ... unto one place upon the face of this
land." In the summer of 1831, Smith declared that Independence, Missouri, was "the center place" of Zion. A
revelation instructed the Saints to purchase land, "that
they may obtain it for an everlasting inheritance." The first
to obey the call of the gathering to Missouri were the
members of the Colesville branch. On August 2, they laid
the foundation of the first house in the future capital of the
kingdom of God. As part of the dedicatory ceremony,
Sidney Rigdon charged the Saints "to keep the law of God
on this land which you never have kept in your own lands."
Later intimations by Rigdon suggest that in addition to the

spiritual laws of the church and the law of consecration and stewardship, the "law of God," even in these early days, already had political significance as well.[25]

In spite of these ambitious plans, Smith did not envision an immediate influx of large groups of Mormon settlers into Missouri. "Concerning the residue of the elders of my church, the time has not yet come, for many years, for them to receive their inheritance in this land."[26] A major reason for this delay was that as a result of a fortuitous detour on the part of those missionaries who had been sent to the "borders, by the Lamanites," Sidney Rigdon and his followers had been converted to Mormonism. Taking advantage of this opportunity the Mormon prophet, as we have seen, therefore chose Ohio as an initial gathering place for the Saints. This was in keeping with the emerging image of Zion as a gigantic tent supported by stakes. While the center stake was to be driven in Jackson County, Missouri, other stakes, radiating from this core, would be erected as needed to support the ever growing tent of the kingdom, until it would cover the entire North and South American continents, and finally the world.

In 1831, the center stake was a mere twig in comparison with the veritable pole that arose in Kirtland, Ohio. According to one observer, the town "presented the appearance of a modern religious Mecca. Like Eastern pilgrims [the Mormons] came full of zeal for their new religion. They came in crude vehicles, on horseback, on foot. They came almost any way, filling on their arrival every house, shop, and barn to the utmost capacity."[27] Many of these immigrants were poor, and the resulting economic crisis was in part responsible for the failure of the law of consecration and stewardship. As an answer to economic problems, as well as to a growing spirit of dissension, the prophet devised an ambitious public works project, the building of a temple.

Unlike later Mormon temples, such as the one in Nauvoo, and the ones in Utah (and at the present time in various parts of the world—whose primary function is the performance of marriages for time and eternity, and vicarious ordinances for the dead) the temple at Kirtland was intended as a meeting house and a school: "even a house of prayer, a house of fasting, a house of faith, a house of learning, a house of glory, a house of order, a house of God."[28] Still open to visitors, the well-preserved building, in its outward appearance, is virtually indistinguishable from a New England meetinghouse, though its interior is divided into two floors to accommodate its dual function. Richly carved interior woodwork attests to the craftsmanship and dedication of the pioneer artisans. Although the building of the temple required great sacrifices of the Saints, it fulfilled its purpose, contributing significantly to the revival of the lagging Kirtland economy, and, more importantly, reviving within the hearts of the Saints a spirit of unity and commitment to kingdom of God. Like all later temples, the one in Kirtland became a symbol for the Saints, a permanent reminder of the kingdom of God, both spirtually and temporally, to which they had committed their lives. The dedication of the temple, in 1836, was the occasion for spiritual manifestations very much like those that had occurred among the early Christians at the day of Pentecost. Jesus Christ, as well as several prophets of the Old Testamant, appeared personally to Joseph and Oliver Cowdery.[29]

In spite of these events, the stake in Kirtland was soon to be uprooted. Too many of the Mormons, including the prophet himself, became involved in the speculative fever of the 1830s. When, as a result of the panic of 1837, the Kirtland economic bubble burst, the Mormon community quickly disintegrated, largely as a result of internal conflict. Many of the Saints blamed their misfortunes on the prophet. Not surprisingly, the temporal kingdom became a major issue in the controversy, dividing those who accepted the prophet's leadership in all things spiritual and temporal from those who believed that Joseph should have stuck to religion and not gotten involved in the affairs of the world.[30]

Meanwhile, the Saints in Jackson County had experienced serious troubles of their own, though these were primarily a result of conflict with their Gentile neighbors, who became convinced that the Mormons were attempting to establish themselves not merely as another religious faith, but were intent on setting up "a temporal kingdom or government, and they would not be subject to the laws of the state, but should make their own laws, have their own civil officers to execute them, Joseph, the prophet, being dictator, aided by revelation and his cabinet or council."[31] Though the Missourians distorted Mormon ambitions, their perception of the kingdom of God as a cohesive social unit was correct. The individualistic, competitive values of the Missourians were clearly incompatible with those of the Saints. Outnumbered by their enemies, the Mormons had to flee their land and homes in 1834.

Smith, after an unsuccessful attempt to obtain satisfaction in the courts, decided to meet force with force. "Behold, I say unto you, the redemption of Zion must needs come by power," he declared in a revelation. He gathered an army of about two hundred men that was "to go up . . . unto the land of Zion . . . and organize my kingdom upon the consecrated land, and establish the children of Zion upon the laws and commandments which have been, and which shall be, given unto you."[32] On May 5, 1834, Zion's Camp, as the expedition was named, left Kirtland. Upon arrival in Missouri, however, the prophet realized that the Mormon cause in Jackson County was lost. Choosing discretion before valor, he realistically disbanded his army. For the time being, the dispossessed Saints resettled in the neighboring counties of Clay and Caldwell.

Judged from its immediate results, Zion's Camp was a quixotic adventure, and yet one of long-range significance for the future development of the political kingdom because it set the precedent for the establishment of the military arm of the kingdom. All future Mormon military organizations, including the Nauvoo Legion, as well as the militia of that same name organized by Brigham Young in

Utah, and the Army of Israel that directed the exodus to the Great Basin, were patterned after Zion's Camp. The expedition also provided valuable training and experience for future leaders of the kingdom. Few of the participants forgot that they had been charged to "organize my kingdom"; many of them participated in the organization of the political kingdom of God in Nauvoo in 1844.[33]

After the Kirtland debacle, Smith and those of his Ohio followers that remained loyal joined their Missouri brethren to establish a new Zion, with Far West in Caldwell County as the center. More than five thousand Mormons flocked to the new gathering place. All available men volunteered their labor for the excavation of a temple site. Again, the Saints entertained high hopes for the establishment of the kingdom of God. And again, they encountered difficulties with their Gentile neighbors, who repeated some of the same accusations that had been levelled against the Saints in Jackson County: "the general teachings of the presidency were, that the kingdom they were setting up was a *temporal* as well as a spiritual kingdom; that it was the little stone spoken of by Daniel."[34]

Even within the church, the Saints were still divided over the precise nature of their religion. None other than Oliver Cowdery had to answer charges "for virtually denying the faith by declaring that he would not be governed by any ecclesiastical authority or revelations whatever in his temporal affairs." Crowdery replied that

> the very principle of ... [ecclesiastical authority in temporal affairs] I conceive to be couched in an attempt to set up a kind of petty government, controlled and dictated by ecclesiastical influence, in the midst of this national and state government. You will, no doubt, say this is not correct; but the bare notice of these charges, over which you assume a right to decide is, in my opinion, a direct attempt to make the secular power subservient to church direction—the correctness of which I cannot in conscience subscribe—I believe that the principle never did fail to produce anarchy and confusion.[35]

Cowdery's prompt excommunication made very clear to all those who refused to conceive the kingdom of God as a total reality the direction in which Mormonism was moving.

That direction also was not to the liking of the Gentiles.
As a result, open warfare broke out in Caldwell County.
On October 25, about seventy-five Mormons and a mob of
Missourians engaged in a skirmish known as the battle of
Crooked River. Five days later, "a large company of armed
men, on horses," massacred seventeen Mormon men and
two boys, and wounded another dozen, at Haun's Mill,
where they had taken refuge with their families. Encouraged by Governor Lilburn Bogg's infamous extermination
order, the Missourians did not rest until they had driven
every Mormon from the state.[36]

During the winter of 1839/40, the ragged band of refugees found hospitality in the neighboring state of Illinois, at Commerce, a town located at a swampy bend of
the Mississippi River. Within a year, the industry and en-
ergy of the Mormons had transformed the sleepy river
hamlet into a bustling and growing town that the prophet
renamed "Nauvoo, which means in Hebrew a beautiful
plantation." Those few Saints who checked their Hebrew
dictionary in vain for the new word could well have reasoned that any man who had the daring to stamp the most
spectacular city in Illinois out of a fever-infested swamp
surely had the right to name the place, even if it meant
coining a new word. The act was fittingly symbolic of the
prophet's will and imagination.[37]

In Nauvoo, more than at any of the other Mormon
settlements, Smith gave full rein to these powerful twin
traits. It is as if he sensed that he did not have much time
left. Ironically, if he had restrained himself, perhaps he
would have avoided his violent death, which was at least in
part a result of his feverish experimentation in the realms
of society, economics, and politics. It was in Nauvoo that
the prophet secretly initiated some of his closet associates
into the theory and practice of plural marriage and that he
organized the secret Council of Fifty that would take
charge of the temporal affairs of the kingdom of God and
would in time become the actual government of the Kingdom.

Still, while it lasted, Nauvoo was one of the most spectacular cities on the western frontier. By 1844, it boasted a
population of about 12,000. Among the numerous visitors
attracted to the kingdom on the Mississippi two of the
most notable were Josiah Quincy, who became mayor of
Boston in 1845, and his cousin Charles Francis Adams, son
of John Quincy Adams. Neither stayed to worship, but
both were impressed. And to this day Mormons take pride
in quoting Quincy's remark, that "It is by no means improbable that some future text-book, for the use of generations yet unborn, will contain a question something like
this: What historical American of the nineteenth century
has exerted the most powerful influence upon the de-
stinies of his countrymen? And it is by no means impossible that the answer to that interrogatory may be thus
written: *Joseph Smith, the Mormon Prophet*."[38] The Mormon
prophet undoubtedly would have agreed with Quincy's
verdict. Rarely did he feel any uncertainty about his place
in history.

About the future of Nauvoo, however, he became increasingly less confident, as the activities of the Council of
Fifty in the spring of 1844 bear out. Smith soon came to
the realization that an overt political kingdom of God in
the State of Illinois would only intensify the conflict between Mormons and Gentiles and might well lead to the
destruction of all he had lived and worked to accomplish.
The grand visions of the kingdom of God, which had
quickened his imagination from the very beginning of his
career, simply could not be realized as long as he and his
followers had to mingle with hostile Gentiles. By 1844,
moreover, it had become all too obvious that Mormonism,
because of its fundamental antipluralist nature, would
come into conflict with a pluralistic American society no
matter how sincere the initial overtures of good behavior
might be on both sides. The non-Mormons, quite obviously, never would have tolerated a fully organized Mormon kingdom of God in their midst. And so Smith began
to look around at some uninhabited lands, such as Texas,

Oregon, and Vancouver Island, where he might implement his plans without Gentile interference.

At the same time, Smith embarked on these alternatives
with a considerable degree of ambivalence. The heady atmosphere of power and accomplishment which stirred the
Mormons in Nauvoo was much to the prophet's liking.
"Excitement has almost become the essence of my life," he
once exclaimed. "When that dies away, I feel almost lost.
When a man is reined up continually by excitement, he
becomes strong and gains power and knowledge."[39]
Therefore, when the difficulties with the Gentiles in Illinois began to increase, Joseph, while seriously con-
templating the possibility of emigration, also considered a
rather spectacular alternative, namely, to run for the presidency of the United States in the election of 1844. During their visit to Nauvoo, Quincy and Adams had been
told by the Mormon prophet "that he might one day so
hold the balance between the parties as to render his election [as president of the United States] . . . by no means
unlikely."[40]

Why did Smith decide to run for the presidency?
Among the enemies of Mormonism it has been axiomatic
that the prophet's power in Nauvoo had gone to his head.
In a fit of megalomania he deluded himself into thinking
that he was a kind of superman to whom nothing was
impossible. Perhaps so. There were, however, more realistic reasons for Smith's candidacy. One was political. In
Illinois the Mormons had made a practice of selling their
vote to the highest bidder, which was to their advantage in
the short run, but had ultimately antagonized both Whigs
and Democrats. Owing political debts to both, the prophet
could extricate himself best by running on a Mormon
ticket. At the same time, his candidacy seems to have been
more than a matter of political expediency. In any case, he
dispatched an army of missionaries across the country to
plead the Mormon cause. George Miller's hopeful opinion, that "if we succeeded in making a majority of the
voters converts to our faith, and elected Joseph president,

in such an event the dominion of the kingdom would be forever established in the United States," was, of course, a doubtful proposition at best. Yet apostle Willard Richards remarked with irrefutable logic that "if God goes with them, who can withstand their influence?"[41]

As it turned out, Richards's faith was never put to the test. On June 27, shortly before the nomination of James K. Polk as the Democratic candidate against Henry Clay, Joseph's presidential aspirations were ended by assassins' bullets fired by a mob that stormed the jail at Carthage, Illinois, where the prophet was held on charges on treason.

His death, like that of his brother Hyrum, was the direct result of his social and political innovations in Nauvoo. When a number of pluralistically oriented Mormons got wind of the secret Council of Fifty and the rumors of polygamy, they attempted to challenge the prophet's authority and power by publicizing these principles and practices in a dissenting newspaper called the *Expositor*. Smith promptly had the first (and only) issue of the paper confiscated and the press destroyed, without due process, charging libel. Outraged Gentiles, who had nervously watched the growth of a monolithic Mormon empire in Illinois for some time, seized upon this opportunity to have Smith arrested. The mob that lynched the Smith brothers comprised the leading members of the community, the same kind of people that Leonard Richards, in his superb study of antiabolitionist mobs, has called "gentlemen of property and standing"; they claimed their actions were sanctioned by a "higher law" because they had been unable to challenge the Mormons by political and legal means, going so far as to use the American Revolution as a precedent.[42]

Though the death of the prophet temporarily dampened anti-Mormon activities in Illinois, Smith's successor Brigham Young realized that if the Saints remained in Nauvoo they faced a precarious future at best. Following up on Joseph's earlier plans the new leader began removal of the Saints to the Great Basin of the American West in the spring of 1846. Under his personal guidance an advance party arrived in the Valley of the Great Salt Lake in July, 1847, followed by a steady stream of emigrants from the eastern United States and later Europe, especially Britain and Scandinavia.[43]

Young established a political kingdom of God, ruled by the Council of Fifty under the direction of the hierarchy, and announced polygamy to a startled and outraged world. The Saints drew up an ambitious map for a State of Deseret that covered what are now parts of California, Oregon, Arizona, New Mexico, Colorado, and Wyoming, and all of Nevada and Utah. This vast territory had come into the possession of the United States as a result of the Mexican War under the treaty of Guadalupe-Hidalgo of 1848. When Congress hammered out the political future of the Mexican cession in the Compromise of 1850, the boundaries of Deseret were drastically reduced, and Congress assumed the administration of a new territory, called Utah.[44]

Needless to say, these developments were not exactly to the liking of the Saints, who did not take kindly to the presence of federal "carpet-bag" officials in their midst. Young ignored them as best he could. The territorial government may have held de jure political authority, but Brigham and his council were still the de facto rulers of the kingdom. Inevitably, the federal officials learned the realities of political power in Utah. When their negative dispatches added news of polygamy, politicians in Washington professed moral outrage.

In 1856, the news from Utah entered national politics when the Republican candidate for the presidency, John C. Fremont, ran on a platform of abolishing the "twin relics of barbarism, slavery and polygamy." Not surprisingly, few southerners were taken in by this obvious political maneuver to give the Republicans intersectional legitimacy. Ironically, it was the victorious Democrat, James Buchanan, who felt called upon in 1857 to send an ill-starred expedition to Utah, as much to suppress po-

lygamy as an alleged Mormon rebellion. As Richard Poll
has pointed out, the Democrats were in dire need of steal-
ing some of the thunder from the Republicans to prove
to a reform-minded North that they too, were against at
least one relic of barbarism.[45]

The Utah War, as it turned out, was a rather half-hearted
attempt to bring the Mormons to terms. Congress might
deliver rhetorical cannonades against social and political
conditions in Utah, but "votes were cast in terms of national political considerations." Advocates of popular
sovereignty were painfully aware that too zealous a
crusade might backfire. If one relic of barbarism could be
rendered criminal, what about the one—slavery?

Such sentiments may in part account for the inglorious
end of "Buchanan's blunder." The nation simply had no
stomach for a war that might be a nasty one, since the
Mormons let it be known that they would not be pushed
around any more. Young had gone so far as to work out
plans for a scorched earth policy. Mormon militia attacked
wagon trains of military supplies, giving substance to the
Mormon rhetoric of defiance.

Ever ready to see the hand of God in historical events,
the Saints now speculated that perhaps the time had come
to achieve their political independence. In a private message to Thomas L. Kane, staunch Gentile friend of the
Mormons, Young was so indiscreet as to suggest that "the
time is not far distant when Utah shall be able to assume
her rights and place among the family of nations." Yet
hopes of independence for the kingdom of God had to be
deferred when as a result of the mediating efforts of none
other than Kane himself the Mormon kingdom remained
part of the United States.[46]

With the outbreak of the Civil War the Mormons
quickly faded from the center stage of American politics.
To a question of what he planned to do about the Mormons, Lincoln replied: "I propose to let them alone." He
compared the Mormon question to a knotty green hem-
lock log on a newly cleared field. The log being too heavy

to move, too knotty to split, and too wet to burn, he thought it best to "plow around it." Congress, more militant, did pass an antibigamy law in 1862, but the administration failed to enforce it.[47]

Having vanquished slavery in 1865, the government now focused its attention on "reconstructing" the South. Although several antipolygamy bills were introduced in the 1870s, none of them were passed, though federal officials in Utah made increasing efforts to assert their authority vis-à-vis the Mormon kingdom. After the termination of congressional reconstruction in 1877, the Republicans, not surprisingly, now made renewed efforts to eradicate the surviving twin of the relics of barbarism.

The judicial groundwork for the crusade was prepared in 1879, when the Supreme Court, in the test case of *Reynolds* vs. *United States,* upheld the constitutionality of the Anti-Bigamy Act of 1862.[48] Having the full force of the law behind it, the government now used its power and authority to renew the attack on the Mormon kingdom. President Rutherford B. Hayes recorded in his diary on January 13, 1880: "Laws must be enacted which will take from the Mormon Church its temporal power. Mormonism as a sectarian idea is nothing, but as a system of government it is our duty to deal with it as an enemy of our institutions, and its supporters and leaders as criminals."[49] Nevertheless, it was not until 1882 that Congress provided the legislative teeth in the Edmunds Act, which not only outlawed polygamy, but also denied all those convicted of "unlawful cohabitation" the right to vote or to hold office.

Under the watchful eye of a federal commission set up to enforce the law, the courts zealously prosecuted offenders. The Mormons defiantly resisted. Many of them proudly went to jail. Others, including church leader John Taylor, went into hiding rather than submit to the humiliating circumstances under which these trials were conducted. The Edmunds-Tucker Law of 1887 further in-

creased the pressures on the Saints. Under its provisions,
witnesses were compelled to testify, including wives
against their husbands; the right to vote, to hold office, and
to serve on juries was reserved only to those who, under a
test oath, pledged obedience to the antipolygamy laws.
Church property in excess of $50,000 was subject to
escheat proceedings, and the church itself disincorporated.
Because they considered even these extreme measures insufficient, the crusaders, in 1889, introduced the Cullom-
Struble bill in Congress, which proposed disfranchisement
of all Mormons by providing that mere belief in the doctrine of polygamy was sufficient to bar an individual from
the franchise and from holding office. Realizing the futility
of further resistance Mormon leaders finally decided to
give in to the demands of the government in order to save
the church from annihilation. On September 25, 1890,
President Wilford Woodruff issued a statement denying
that the church still solemnized polygamous marriages:
"And I now publicly declare that my advice to the Latter-
day Saints is to refrain from contracting any marriage forbidden by the law of the land." On October 6, 1890, this
"manifesto" was unanimously sustained at a general church
conference.[50]

Because polygamy and the political kingdom were
interdependent, defeat of the one was virtually synonymous with defeat of the other. Indeed, though a number of
crusaders appeared to have made polygamy their main
target, the political kingdom was the bigger game, as
Senator Frederick T. Dubois of Idaho made clear:

> Those of us who understand the situation were not nearly so much
> opposed to polygamy as we were to the political domination of the
> Church. We realized, however, that we could not make those who
> did not come actually in contact with it, understand what this politi-
> cal domination meant. We made use of polygamy in consequence as
> our great weapon of offense and to gain recruits to our standard.
> There was a universal detestation of polygamy, and inasmuch as the
> Mormons openly defended it we were given a very effective weapon
> with which to attack.[51]

In the wake of the manifesto, the influence of the Council of Fifty appears to have declined to the point of impotence. Whether or not the council is still in existence today, its political influence is clearly insignificant. The Mormons disbanded their own political organization, the People's Party, prior to the admission of Utah to the United States in 1896, and divided along national party lines as Democrats and Republicans. Indeed, it is ironic that in view of the social and economic aspirations of the Mormon kingdom the political orientation of the Mormon hierarchy in the twentieth century has been conservative, favoring the Republican Party, though individual Mormons are of course free to vote as they please. When the hierarchy, in the 1930s, made no secret of its opposition to Franklin Roosevelt's New Deal, the majority of Saints, ignoring the political advice of their leaders, voted Democratic.

The reality of political pluralism in contemporary Mormon culture is perhaps best exemplified by the fact that in 1979 the highest ecclesiastical body of the church, the Council of the Twelve, included among its members one man who had been campaign manager of a former congressman and who was coordinating Senator Edward Kennedy's campaign in six western states, as well as a conservative extremist who had for years been active in the John Birch Society.

5

Changing Perspectives on Sexuality and Marriage

Mormonism is destined to thoroughly revolutionize the world with regard to the intercourse of the sexes.

Orson Pratt

Mormonism, it is clear, has experienced a social and intellectual transformation of such magnitude that a resurrected Joseph Smith, returning to earth today, might well wonder if this was indeed the same church he had founded, given the disappearance of the political kingdom, of economic cooperation, and of plural marriage. These are the most obvious examples. Although the demise of all three institutions must be attributed to external as well as internal pressures, the interplay of these factors in the dynamics of change is particularly revealing in the case of sexuality and marriage, providing some glimpses into just how Mormonism was transformed from a nineteenth-century religious movement that encompassed all facets of human existence to its contemporary status as one of numerous denominations within the spectrum of American pluralism.

I

Early Mormon attitudes regarding sex and marriage were derived from their New England heritage. In colonial America sexual attitudes and behavior were firmly rooted in a biblically oriented Calvinism or Anglicanism and in a social order reflecting the values of these religions. Fornication and adultery, as well as other, less common sexual transgressions were regarded not only as heinous sins but

147

crimes and were punished severely. For later generations "puritanism" became a synonym for sexual repression. As Edmund Morgan's revisionist study pointed out long ago, however, the Puritans were far from being the sexual prudes that a hostile literature made them out to be. They regarded sex in marriage not only as a means of procreation but also as a natural expression of the love between husband and wife. Celibacy in healthy persons was regarded as unnatural and against the will of God, as, of course, was sexual transgression. In either case, man was wilfully rejecting the laws of God.[1]

However severely they condemned sin, the Puritans realized that living as they did in a fallen world, even they could not be absolutely certain about the state of their souls. Virtue could be achieved only at the cost of eternal vigilance. First and foremost it was the responsibility of the family to monitor the behavior of its members. The community, likewise, saw to the enforcement of morals, a task made easy by a relative lack of privacy. If these institutions should fail, the law held immorality in check. When sin, nevertheless, did strike, the Saints rarely panicked. Realizing that there, but for the grace of God, went they, the Puritans had a relatively relaxed attitude toward transgressors, no doubt encouraged by a stable social order in which rather infrequent premarital pregnancies and illegitimate births suggest a close correlation between prescription and behavior.

From about 1675 on, however, we can observe an increasing divergence between belief and conduct. By 1790, the premarital pregnancy record in America exceeded 25 percent of firstborn children, suggesting a dissolution of the social and intellectual underpinnings of traditional society. As the social controls of the community slackened, sexual mores slackened also. From this time on, however, the statistics begin a steady downward trend that reaches a low point of less than 10 percent by 1860.[2]

Interpreted without a context, such data might suggest that nineteenth-century Americans had reestablished the

stable social order of a traditional society. The social and
intellectual climate of the period, however, points to a
different conclusion. By the 1820s and 1830s, the decades
of the birth of Mormonism, American culture had moved a
long way down the road from the relatively stable social order of colonial America to the increasingly atomistic society of capitalistic individualism; from the tra-
ditonal Calvinism that saw God as the center of the
universe to an Arminianized evangelism that saw man as
the center; and from a society in which behavior was
largely controlled by the norms of the community to a
society in which moral standards were internalized.
Teetotalism and sexual restraint became two of the most
important means of expressing this modern attitude. Once
again, as in colonial society, prescription and behavior
coincided, but for very different reasons.[3]

As social control gave way to self-control, Americans
developed a perfectionism that would brook no compromise with sin. In colonial society, sex within marriage
was regarded as intrinsically wholesome. In the nineteenth
century, however, an army of sexual reformers began to
extol the virtues of sexual continence bordering on celibacy, even in marraige. If we can believe the rising chorus
of antisexual rhetoric, severe doubt was cast upon God's
wisdom or at least propriety for having made human propagation a function that at best was indelicate. Relatively
perfunctory in their attacks on public vice, these reformers
raised their crusade to a pitch of near-hysteria as they in-
veighed against the supposedly ubiquitous sexual excesses
practiced within the privacy of the marraige bed or, even
worse, by the individual alone.[4]

In the opinion of one historian, such attitudes "may have
had a therapeutic value when [they] took hold in the
1830s, giving men and women an explanation and a set of
cures for the frightening world they found themselves in."
Another explanation for this seemingly puzzling shift in
attitudes may be found in the individualistic, anti-
institutional ethos of the period, which placed the burden

of reform on the individual rather than on society. If the
world was less than perfect, it was the fault of the individual. As a result, private sins assumed an unprecedented,
monumental significance. Charles Rosenberg's assertion
that masturbation was widely regarded as the "master vice"
of the period finds a plausible explanation in the social and
intellectual climate of antebellum America.[5]

Sexual attitudes thus had undergone a profound transformation. To colonial Americans the idea that one particular form of sexual transgression was a "master vice"
would have been incomprehensible. As vigorously as they
disapproved of departures from the sexual norms, such
lapses were merely sins among many other sins. For many
nineteenth-century reformers, however, sin had virtually
become synonymous with sex.

II

These were the kinds of sexual attitudes emerging as
Mormonism made its debut in America. Such values, however, were not congenial to the early Saints, who scarcely
fit into the pluralistic cultural pattern emerging in the antebellum period. As we have seen, Joseph Smith's millennial kingdom was intended as an alternative to the presumed deficiencies of American society rather than as an
instrument for its reform. Mormonism, at least in its early
phase, attempted to restore a society that reflected traditional values. Eventually, Joseph Smith envisioned a radical reordering of the family and of relations between the
sexes, innovations scarcely foreshadowed in the Book of
Mormon, which in its sexual ethos shared many of the
values of colonial society. Though Puritans would have
regarded Smith's idea of modern revelation as heretical,
they would have been comfortable with the kind of Book
of Mormon theology that asserted that the Fall "was the
cause of all mankind becoming carnal, sensual, devillish."[6]

To the early Mormons this passage appears to have been
a fact of life rather than a source of anxiety. There is little

evidence suggesting that the Saints—at least prior to the death of Joseph Smith—shared the sexual concerns of their modern American contemporaries. As in traditional society, adultery, fornication, and other less common sexual transgressions were severely condemned, and unrepentant sinners excommunicated. But an examination of early church trials suggests that sexual offenses were but one cause among many for excommunication. Although demographic evidence for this early period is scant, it is quite likely that the sexual conduct of the Saints was on the whole exemplary by the standards of the period. Unfortunately, it is all but impossible to document such changes. A perusal of diaries, journals, and letters for this early period is most unrewarding. When it comes to sex, the Saints left little record.[7]

To modern, psychologically-oriented scholars, this silence may itself speak volumes. Perhaps the sexual repression was so severe that it remained totally submerged. Yet it should be remembered that it was the age in which the sexually obsessed reformers articulated their concerns ad nauseam. If sexuality had been one of the Mormons' chief concerns, it is unlikely that they would have remained silent on that issue, especially since the new religion, like Puritanism, was very much a religion of the word. That, in fact, was one of its great attractions. Ideally, aspiring Saints would be baptized only after the Truth had been revealed to them by the Spirit, but the preparation for that manifestation, as we have seen, involved a rational process of study.

Mormonism was an ideology preparing the way for a new social and religious order and was not particularly evangelical or revivalistic in its appeal. The converted Saints, to be sure, would manifest through their conduct that they had been "born again," but what set the Mormons apart from the world more than anything was their ideological identification with the kingdom of God that resulted in a close correlation between belief and behavior. It is true that many of the Gentiles, likewise, lived lives of moral rectitude. But what they lacked, in the opinion of the Saints, was the true and everlasting gospel. Most of those who accepted Mormonism followed its moral regulations gladly. Yet it is unlikely that these, rather than the message of the restoration, of priesthood authority, and of the gifts of the Spirit, became the central concern of their lives.

In addition to these intellectual or theological motivations, there were social reasons that may help explain why the early Saints did not share the sexual concerns of their contemporaries. It appears that during the antebellum period, conceptions of sexuality were tied to changing perceptions and conditions of class. Some historians have suggested that at this time in England and on the continent middle-class sexual morality became a necessary adjunct and expression expected of those who became the producers and managers of the nation. In an upwardly mobile society, this ethos was imitated by all those who had middle class aspirations. This kind of "victorianism" also served to provide a sense of identity, to set the middle class off from both the lower classes and the aristocracy, who were either unable or unwilling to live by bourgeois moral precepts.[8] In spite of increasing stratification, class boundaries in America were clearly less defined than in Europe. Charles Rosenberg has argued persuasively that "a good many Americans must . . . have been all the more anxious in their internalization of those aspects of life-style which seemed to embody and assure class status."[9]

Sociologist Joseph Gusfield's study of the "bourgeoisification" (I love that word!) of antebellum American cultural values provides striking support for this argument. For the overwhelming majority of those involved in the temperance movement, for example, abstinence became a symbol for the internalization of moral values and behavior. Because "there would be no compromise with Evil in any of its forms," sexual conduct would be of equal concern to upwardly mobile Americans.[10] The Saints, however, felt that they had escaped the psychological, social, and economic pressures of class. Although in their new world temperance and sexual restraint were part of the social order, neither served as a means for social transformation.

The prophet's dietary rules as revealed in the Word of Wisdom illustrate this clearly. Viewed superficially, these directives appear to be a typical expression of the temper of the times. Yet the very wording of the revelation is alien to the emerging spirit of "necessary moral action"; "To be sent greeting; not by commandment or contraint, but by revelation and the word of Wisdom." It is, of course, too much to say that among the Mormons the use of alcohol was governed by the same legal and moral sanctions that made moderate drinking in colonial America socially and morally acceptable. Nevertheless, Joseph Smith remained a moderate drinker all his life, and it is perhaps safe to suggest that until his death the Word of Wisdom was honored almost as much in the breach as in the observance—a further indication that Mormon social norms, in many ways, resembled those of the seventeenth century more than those of the nineteenth.[11]

There is, of course, a point at which the analogy between drinking and sex breaks down. Neither Mormons nor Puritans would have agreed with Benjamin Franklin's moderate use of "venery" if it occurred outside of marriage. When applied to fornication or adultery, the concept of moderation, in the opinion of the Mormons, ceased to have meaning. Rather, it can be said, the Mormons, like the Puritans, had a positive attitude toward sex in marriage and did not share the hysterical attitude of the reformers regarding masturbation. Lest I be misunderstood, I am not suggesting that the Saints condoned the "secret vice." All I am saying is that, having removed themselves from the presumed corruptions of the Gentiles, they had no reason to invent a "master vice" in order to cope with the pressures of modernization. Mormons, for example, exhibited little if any anxiety over gender roles. Yet as Charles Rosenberg has shown, concern with masturbation was strongly connected to such anxieties, and was, by some, regarded as an "ultimate confession of male inadequacy." Masturbation was also regarded as socially isolating, thus conflicting with the male role demands for social and economic achievement. The social and economic communitarianism of Mormonism may well have minimized such pressures.[12]

Because the early Saints failed to articulate their attitudes regarding this delicate topic, it is only by way of circumstantial evidence that it may be possible to document this supposition. An autobiographical statement by Joseph Smith suggests an implicit lack of concern over issues that agitated moral reformers of the day. We cannot, of course, know what transgressions the prophet conjured in his readers' minds as he confessed, "I was left to all kinds of temptations; and, mingling with all kinds of society, I frequently fell into many foolish errors, and displayed the weakness of youth and the corruption of human nature, which I am sorry to say led me into diverse temptations, to the gratification of many appetites offensive in the sight of God." But given the preconceptions of the day, it is hard to believe that his detractors would have gone out of their way to read trivial foibles into the passage. The sentence, surely, has a potential for offending the squeamish. Certainly, those editors who much later changed "corruption" to "foibles," and struck out the phrase, "to the gratification of many appetites," must have been sensitive to the uses that could be made of this passage. By that time (1902), as we shall see, Mormons had adopted the "modern," nineteenth-century attitudes of their erstwhile antagonists. Quite possibly, the young Joseph was not only more ingenous but also more "traditional" in his response to his imperfections.[13]

Having thus far stressed the traditional aspects of Mormon culture and Mormon sexuality, I hasten to add that, even in its early phase, Mormonism contained many of the germs of its later evolution into a "modern" religion. Emerson's statement that Mormonism was "an after-clap of Puritanism," while containing a great deal of insight, was clearly an oversimplification. Even the Book of Mormon contains too many Arminian heresies to make the comparison stick, and the prophet's later pronouncement that "men will be punished for their own sins, and not for Adam's transgression" was fully compatible with the beliefs of one form of liberal Protestanism. Still, having extricated themselves from the pressures of modernization, the Mormons, unlike their Gentile contemporaries, were not compelled to push for a frantic internalization of mores—sexual or otherwise.

With the benefit of hindsight, it is clear that many of Joseph Smith's unorthodox ideas were already contained in the Book of Mormon. By 1833, with the publication of the prophet's early revelations in the Book of Commandments, the novel side of Mormonism became more apparent. Continual altercations with the Gentiles, for the time being, prevented the full realization of many of these ideas. It was not until the early 1840s, when the Mormon prophet believed he had placed the kingdom of God on a firmer footing in Nauvoo, that he was able to press for the further realization of his innovative religious, political, and social ideas.

III

Plural marriage was the most dramatic of these. Because of the extreme complexity of the origins of Mormon polygamy, all I can do in a brief study such as this is to summarize the most important points. On July 12, 1843, Joseph Smith secretly dictated a revelation pertaining to the doctrine of celestial marriage—the new and everlasting covenant, that sanctioned the principle of plural marriage. Part of the justification, in the revelation, was restorationist. In times past the Lord had given concubines and wives to Abraham, Isaac, and Jacob, as well as to David, Solomon, and Moses. In the latter days God was revealing the principles upon which these ancient patriarchs were justified, together with a stern injunction that "all those who have this law revealed unto them must obey the same . . . and if ye abide not that covennant, then ye are damned; for no one can reject this covenant and be permitted to enter into my glory." The major purpose of plural marriage was "to multiply and replenish the earth, according to my commandment, and to fulfil the promise which was given by my Father before the foundation of the world, and for their exaltation in the eternal worlds, that they may bear the souls of men; for herein is the work of my Father continued, that he may be glorified."[14]

Although it was only in the 1840s that Smith began to teach polygamy to his most trusted followers, and to practice it himself, there is strong evidence suggesting that some of the ideas behind it may have originated in the prophet's mind as early as 1831, when he was engaged in retranslating the Old Testament. An unpublished revelation to a group of missionaries who had been sent to the Indians in Missouri in 1831 indicated that at a future date they would be permitted to take Indian women as plural wives, though none of them did.[15] In 1835, the church made the first of a number of pronouncements denying charges of polygamy at a time when rumors were spreading that Smith had taken up with Fannie Alger, a seventeen-year-old orphan. One dissident faction, the Reorganized Church of Jesus Christ of Latter Day Saints, ironically, uses these denials as evidence that Smith never taught or practiced plural marriage, claiming it was instituted by Brigham Young, who needed the authority of a dead prophet who could not defend himself to launch the odious practice in Utah. This denial, however, is untenable in the face of overwhelming evidence to the contrary. Recent scholarship has shown conclusively that it was Smith who inaugurated plural marriage in theory and practice.[16]

In Nauvoo, Smith initiated some of his close and trusted associates into the new and everlasting covenant. Brigham Young later claimed that "it was the first time in my life that I desired the grave, and I could hardly get over it for a long time." Smith himself claimed that he took the fateful step only after God had repeatedly commanded him to do so. According to Eliza R. Snow, one of the most renowned of his plural wives, the prophet hesitated to carry out the fateful commandment "until an angel of God stood by him with a drawn sword, and told him that, unless he moved forward and established plural marriage, his priesthood would be taken from him and he should be destroyed."[17] Realizing the explosive potential of polygamy, Smith publicly denied and condemned the practice until his death. As a matter of fact, the Book of Mormon contained a passage denouncing polygamy, though with the significant escape clause that "if I will . . . raise seed unto me, I will command my people."[18]

Privately, Smith made it clear that plural marriage was an important part of the social order of the kingdom of God. But the prophet did not believe it safe to publicize polygamy until the kingdom of God had established a political and legal framework capable of sanctioning the practice. It may be more than coincidental that the revelation concerning the new and everlasting covenant was given more than a year after an important revelation that had launched the political organization of the kingdom. Because most states had bigamy laws, plural marriage could be practiced legally only within a separate political kingdom of God. It is for this reason that Brigham Young prudently deferred the public announcement of polygamy until he had established a quasi-independent kingdom of God in the Rocky Mountains.

Polygamy, perhaps more than most other principles of Mormonism, could identify the Saints as a peculiar people who had removed themselves from the mainstream of American culture. It could serve as a rallying point and a symbol of identification for a people who in spite of many idiosyncratic qualities of their faith shared many of the basic cultural characteristics of their fellow Americans. Perhaps even more important, polygamy irrevocably tied its practitioners to Mormonism. For polygamists it was virtually impossible to defect from the kingdom. As we have seen, many opponents of Mormonism realized this only too well and conducted the antipolygamy crusade of the 1880s not only on moral grounds but more importantly as a means of destroying the kingdom.

To all but devout Mormons and antipolygamy crusaders the origin of polygamy presents a perplexing and intriguing historical problem. The Saints, of course, simply accepted it as a commandment of God, given for the reasons stated in Smith's revelations. The anti-Mormons had an equally simple explanation: A lecherous Joseph Smith and some of his lecherous associates had to devise a system that would allow them to exercise their sexual appetites freely without arousing the outraged protest of their wives and more straightlaced followers. A more sophisticated version of this "lecher school" is Fawn Brodie's, who argues that although Joseph loved his wife Emma dearly, "monogamy seemed to him an intolerably circumscribed way of life." At the same time, "there was too much of the Puritan in him" to allow him to be content with clandestine affairs. Therefore, in order to calm his own conscience, "he could not rest until he had redefined the nature of sin and erected a stupendous theological edifice to support his new theories on marriage,"[19]

The plausibility of Brodie's theory is supported by some additional evidence. If it is true that for Joseph monogamy had always been an intolerably circumscribed way of life, this was even more the case in those last few turbulent years in Nauvoo prior to his assassination. Like many public figures, in his day as well as our own, he had a charismatic personality attractive to both men and women. This resulted in some very strong male friendships—and in the case of John C. Bennett in the exploitation of the prophet by someone who projected a great deal of personal magnetism of his own. Yet it is quite clear that Joseph exhibited no overt homosexual tendencies. But like John F. Kennedy and Martin Luther King in our own day, he had a magnetic attraction for women. At the same time, his own

marriage appeared to be less than fulfilling. Though Joseph
gave Emma some reason for jealousy, she apparently
needed very little provocation in any case. In view of the
fact that she was in the shadow of Joseph this is perhaps
not too difficult to understand. As the leader of the
church, he was the one who absorbed all the attention and
adulation of his followers. A woman's role, in the
nineteenth century especially, was very much that of
helpmate, and in the case of Emma under conditons more
trying than those experienced by most women of the time.
The history of Mormonism had been a turbulent one, and
the itinerant years of persecution had taken their toll on
Emma. In those years she had borne Joseph nine children,
of whom only four lived to maturity. It is not surprising,
then, that a traveler to Nauvoo in 1843 described Emma as
"very plain in her personal appearance." But, if we can
trust contemporary descriptions, these same years, if anything, had enhanced the physical attractiveness of the
prophet, who was a year younger than his wife.

   In the culture of Victorian America, even more so than
in our own times, there prevailed a sexual double standard
regarding age. Joseph, at thirty-eight, was a man in the
prime of life; Emma, at thirty-nine, was on the threshold of
becoming an old woman. Lest we be too harsh on antebellum Americans, this prejudice was more than skin
deep but rested on some very fundamental biological and
cultural assumptions that, contrary to our own "enlightened" ideology, subtly prevail to this very day. Nancy
Friday, for example, has shown that many women who
go out of their way to be sexually attractive before
marriage, accept the role models of their own mothers
after marriage, and (often unconsciously) suppress their
sexuality—all the brave exhortations of the women's magazines to the contrary notwithstanding.[20] How much more
would this be the case if today's women's magazines, like
those of the nineteenth century, disseminated opinions
such as Sarah Grimke's, who insisted that woman was in-
nately superior to man because "the sexual passion in man

is ten times stronger than in woman."[21] Indeed, according
to polite middle class opinion, a "lady" had no sexual passion whatsoever. As we shall later see, Mormons did not
necessarily accept such middle class notions. But it is also
true that culturally Emma never fit comfortably into Mormonism and aspired very much to middle class respectability. It is ironic (and for Emma tragic) that when
she remarried after Joseph's death, her second husband
had several extramarital liaisons without the benefit of
religious sanction.[22]

One of the first non-Mormons to take issue with the
crusaders against polygamy was George Bernard Shaw,
who argued that Smith's puritanical followers would have
quickly deserted him if they had suspected him of lecherous
proclivites. Unfamiliar with the demographic realities of
western America, Shaw thought that the major purpose of
polygamy was to provide husbands for a surplus of women
and ensure the rapid population of the Mormon frontier.
Grateful for support from such an unexpected quarter,
some Mormons convinced themselves that Shaw was right.
The theory provided a kind of sociological respectability
for plural marriage after its demise and found some cur-
rency in textbooks at a time when the frontier thesis was in
vogue. The fact, of course, is that even in Mormon Utah
women were in short supply. As a matter of fact, in some
communities there was considerable competition between
younger and older men for nubile women. Furthermore,
as Stanley Ivins had demonstrated, plural marriage had an
adverse effect on the birth rate. Fertility of women in
polygamous marriages was lower than that of women in
monogamous marriages—possibly because polygamous
husbands tended to be older and hence less virile or possibly because (and Shaw was most likely right) many
polygamists were not motivated by sexual desires.[23]

This is one point on which a number of recent historians
agree who are otherwise dissatisfied with previous interpretations of the origins of polygamy and who argue that it
can be understood only in the broader context of antebel-

lum American culture. The most prominent—and the most brilliant—of these is Lawrence Foster, who has presented the most ambitious and the most plausible explanation for the origins of plural marriage thus far.[24] Foster argues that Mormon polygamy was but one of numerous attempts in antebellum America to establish alternative family systems by millennial religious groups who had rejected existing marriage and family patterns, such as the Shakers and the Oneida Perfectionists of John Humphrey Noyes. Foster regards the Mormon introduction of polygamy "as part of a larger effort to reestablish social cohesion and kinship ties in a socially and intellectually disordered environment," or at least one that Mormons perceived as such. (After all, a large group of Americans were quite satisfied with the absence of institutional restraints.) Moreover, as we can now see in retrospect, this did not mean the absence of all restraints. That America was moving rapidly toward the privatization of the economy, of the family, of religion, even politics, is true. A momentus shift had occurred in the locus of authority. External restraints on the individual by the state, the church, the community, and even the family, had been greatly diminished. At the same time, Americans were internalizing the individualistic, competitive values of a capitalistic society that placed a premium on restraint and self-control. To those who were in tune with the temper of the times, this was in fact an exciting development.

When Joseph Smith had his vision, this transformation was by no means complete. To him, the competing churches were presenting a Babel of confusing voices, although, as we now know, evangelical religion became one of the major suppliers of gyroscopes that kept all those individualistic Americans on their steady course toward progress and success—though it is doubtful that Smith would have approved in any case. But the point here is that in the 1830s and 1840s many Americans still lacked this internal gyroscope, so that the perception of social disorder on the part of dissenters was quite accurate. As I

have already indicated, the breakdown of external authority in the wake of the revolution led to a dramatic rise in
premarital pregnancies and drunkenness. The paternalistic
reform movements of the early nineteenth century were
virtually powerless to deal with these problems and reveal
rather the anxieties of patricians who have lost their status
and influence. Their crusades for temperance and attempts
to solve the problem of slavery through African colonization are two cases in point. The lower orders no longer
listened to their exhortations to sobriety, while colonization required the massive support of the federal government at a time when such support was regarded as inimical
to the encouragement of private initiative. Both temperance and abolitionism became successful only after they
appealed to the individual directly, as evangelical religion
did, without any institutional intermediaries, in keeping
with Emerson's pronouncement that "an institution is the
lengthened shadow of one man."[25]

The kind of people who became Mormons or Shakers or
Oneida Perfectionists found themselves thoroughly at sea
in this kind of world. As they saw it, the old rules no
longer applied, the new rules of the dominant culture had
not yet been clearly defined, and in any case were not to
the liking of the dissenters. In such an age of fluidity and
transition it is therefore not surprising to find significant
social and cultural minorities choosing to believe that social reality was arbitrary and that they could persuade
others to follow their alternative visions. In the words of
Foster, "Smith was attempting to demolish an old way of
life and to build a new social order from the ground up."[26]
The conditions of the new and everlasting covenant illustrate this point forcefully: "All covenants, contracts,
bonds, obligations, oaths, vows, performances, connections, associations, or expectations, that are not made
and entered into and sealed by the Holy Spirit of promise . . . are of no efficacy, virtue, or force in and after the
resurrection from the dead; for all contracts that are not
made unto this end have an end when men are dead."

Although this revelation has direct applicability only to life after death, these covenants have to be entered into in this life under the authority of someone "on whom this power and the keys of this priesthood are conferred." Contracts conducted under the auspices of eternity were clearly superior to those concluded only for time—like those of the Gentile world.[27]

We have already seen that Mormons regarded baptisms of other churches as invalid. In the early days of millennial enthusiasm in Ohio and Missouri, some of the Saints, erroneously, to be sure, believed that traditional property arrangements, likewise, were superseded and began to help themselves to the belongings of their Gentile neighbors. We have also seen that the concept of a political kingdom of God evolved to the point where it was regarded as the only legitimate governmental authority under heaven. It is as if the Mormons had reinvented Locke, who had remarked that "in the beginning, all the world was America." But the Mormons also learned that America was no longer a tabula rasa—that the slate would have to be wiped clean before a new beginning could be made. In the meantime, they had to struggle as best they could against a hostile world and nullify its laws as far as realistically possible within their emerging kingdom while creating their own laws that would usher in the new heaven and the new earth.

Perhaps no institution could serve this dual purpose more effectively than marriage and the family. In antebellum America the nuclear, monogamous family was fast becoming the cornerstone of the social order as the importance of other, traditional institutions declined. This modern family had a seemingly paradoxical function. On the one hand, it served as a haven and retreat from the pressures of a heartless and competitive world. On the other hand, it created and nourished—aided by evangelical religion—the identities of self-motivated individuals who had achieved the direction and discipline to compete successfully in the modern world of trade, commerce, and manufacture. Thus, by striking at the American family, Mormonism was attacking not only the social but also the economic and even psychological foundations of antebellum America.[28]

Joseph Smith was extremely sensitive to the shift in the locus of authority that had led to the decline of the status of the father to the benefit of his inner-directed children. He insisted that the patriarchal order in the home must be restored "if social chaos is to be avoided." "Multitudes of families are now in confusion and wretchedly governed. This is a great evil."[29] A major cause was lack of affection between husband and wife. A contemporary observer of these conditions and an intimate of Joseph Smith, John D. Lee, reported on the prophet's response to these problems at Nauvoo in 1842:

> At about the same time the doctrine of sealing for an eternal state was introduced, and the Saints were given to understand that their marriage relations with each other were not valid. That those who had solemnized the rites of matrimony had no authority of God to do so. That the true priesthood was taken from the earth with the death of the Apostles and inspired men of God. That they were married to each other only by their own covenants, and if their marriage relations had not been productive of blessings and peace, and they felt it oppressive to remain together, they were at liberty to make their own choice, as much as if they had not been married. That it was a sin for people to live together, and raise or beget children, in alienation from each other. That there should exist an affinity between each other, not a lustful one, as that can never cement that love and affection that should exist between a man and his wife.[30]

With the restoration of the true priesthood, of course, this alienation could be reversed, and men and women could find eternal happiness in the new and everlasting covenant.

The Mormons were not the only ones who perceived a sense of isolation and alienation in antebellum America. Tocqueville, who, like Joseph Smith, had an uncannily accurate perception of the temper of the times, remarked: "The woof of time is every instant broken, and the track of generations effaced. Those who went before are soon forgotten; of those who will come after, no one has any idea ... Thus not only does democracy make every man forget his ancestors, but it hides his descendants and separates his contemporaries from him; it throws him back forever upon himself alone and threatens in the end to confine him entirely within the solitude of his own heart."[31] the Mormon prophet, as we have seen, taught "that the earth will be smitten with a curse unless there is a welding link of some kind or other between the fathers and the children."[32] This link was marriage under the new and everlasting covenant. To be binding "for time and eternity," such marriages had to be "sealed" by proper priesthood authorities in temples especially dedicated for this purpose. Monogamous marriages performed in this manner were just as eternally binding as polygamous unions. Polygamous marriages, of course, have officially been discontinued since the so-called manifesto of 1890. Nevertheless, Joseph Smith made it unmistakably clear that the highest degree of glory in the celestial kingdom, the attainment of Godhood, was reserved for those who had entered into polygamous relationships. It was polygamy that presented the most direct and visible challenge to the American social order. It was polygamy that more than any other Mormon institution came to symbolize the new heaven and new earth.

It is not surprising, then, that the promulgation of such ideas would lead to tension and conflict, not only between the Mormons and the world, but also among the Saints themselves. By the time of Joseph's martyrdom, theological and social innovations had accelerated at such a pace that they threatened to spin out of control. Social cohesion, in Nauvoo, was clearly loosening. The prophet's experimentation with "celestial marriage," if continued in the ad hoc fashion of those secretive liaisons of that last year prior to his death, had a potential for sexual anarchy. Certainly, the impact even on his most trusted followers was nothing less than traumatic. In fact, the prophet himself seems to have had second thoughts as he launched social and sexual practices in direct conflict with the Judaeo-Christian ethic and the established mores of American society. According to one of his followers, Smith had to be assured by revelation that he had not committed adultery. To his detractors, particularly those within the church who were beginning to look askance at his vigorous round of experimentation and innovation, such a revelation could be viewed as a justification for sexual transgressions.[33]

IV

After the death of Joseph Smith Mormonism continued to totter in precarious balance and began to split into numerous sects. Although Brigham Young professed to continue in the tradition of his predecessor, more conservative policies imply a recognition of the centrifugal forces that were pulling Mormonism apart during the Nauvoo years. If polygamy in Utah, publicly announced in 1852, was a major aberration from the social mores of Protestant America, its public, institutionalized, carefully regulated practice implied social controls going far beyond those recorded in the days of Joseph Smith. At the same time, its external controls contrasted sharply with the internal controls and self-repression that were the essential features of "modern," antebellum American morality.[34]

There is some evidence to suggest that in Utah Mormons developed a greater degree of self-consciousness about matters sexual. An increasing defensiveness in Mormon publications seems directly related to the announcement of polygamy in 1852. Anticipating or responding to charges of sexual profligacy, the Saints began to compare their supposedly superior sexual morality to a sexually corrupt Babylon. Because the Gentiles, not suprisingly, stressed the idea that polygamy provided a convenient means of sexual gratification for the man, the Saints now emphasized more strongly than before the idea that the primary if not the only purpose of marriage, monogamous or polygamous, was to have offspring. Sexual relations,

said Heber C. Kimball, were not "to gratify the lusts of the
flesh, but to raise up children." One of sociologist James
Hulett's informants reported that "his father was sexually
interested in his wives only for the purposes of procreation, and the Principle could not be lived in any other
way."[35]

When M. R. Werner, a biographer of Brigham Young,
coined the phrase "puritan polygamy," he probably was
not far off the mark. At any rate, it was an impression
consistent with the observations of Richard Burton, the
famous English traveller and linguist, who visited the city
of the Saints in 1861. Burton reported that "All sensuality
in the married state is strictly forbidden beyond the requi-
site for ensuring progeny,—the practice, in fact, of Adam
and Abraham." He quoted one of his informants, Belinda
Pratt, as saying that according to the Old Testament, during prescribed periods of gestation and lactation, sexual
relations were prohibited: "should her husband come to
her bed under such circumstances, he would commit a
gross sin both against the laws of nature and the wise provisions of God's law, as revealed in His word; in short, he
would commit an abomination."[36]

In the opinion of Heber C. Kimball, any man violating
the divine laws of sexual conduct had no right to procreation: "if I am not a good man, I have not just right in this
Church to a wife or wives, or to the power to propagate my
species. What, then should be done with me? Make a
eunuch of me, and stop my propagation." His hyperbolic
solution, however, appears to have been intended for the
life after death, in keeping with Parley P. Pratt's statement
that "If they choose in this world to follow the wicked lusts
and pleasures of the moment, . . . then . . . death closes the
scene, and eternity finds them poor wanderers and outcasts from the commonwealth of the celestial family, and
strangers to the covenant of promise."[37]

Thus, the principle of deferred compensation found its
way into the sexual economics of the kingdom of God,
"this being the world of preparation and that the world of

enjoyment," as Pratt put it. Under the "law of forfeiture," in the next life the women of all those innumerable men who had proved themselves "wholly unfit to sustain the sacred relationship of a husband . . . will most assuredly be given to the comparatively few men who keep themselves pure, and fulfil the laws made known to them from heaven." Implicit in this logic was a theoretical argument in favor of polygamy—at least in the next life. Eternal marriage was an essential requirement for entry into the highest degree of glory in the celestial kingdom. Therefore, if there was an excess of righteous women over men eligible for the highest degree, simple justice dictated that a righteous man take more than one wife in order to assure that all eligible women attained the exaltation they deserved. The polygamous husband, in turn, was thus given the opportunity all the more to increase his kingdom.[38]

For those who were able to control their sexual impulses, the rewards were truly awesome. According to an article in the *Millennial Star,* "the fountains of life are the source of His glory, dominion, and power. They are the germ of an infinitude of good if used only for pure and righteous purposes, and of unlimited evil if perverted and corrupted. Either way the consequences resulting are incalculable, and can only be measured by the mind that can grasp eternities of existence." Those who had the vision to live their lives in conformity with such insights and entered into the eternal covenant of plural marriage, said Brigham Young, would "hold control over the elements, and have power by their word to command the creation and redemption of worlds or to extinguish such by their breath, and disorganize worlds, hurling them back into their chaotic state. This is what you and I are created for." What, by comparison, were the sinful pleasures of this world?[39]

This awesome conception of the power of sex was supported by a positive philosophy of sex that the Gentiles found nothing less than blasphemous. In the opinion of Mormons, the traditional Christian world view was

essentially hostile to human sexuality, supported as it was
by a metaphysical dualism that elevated the soul above the
body, mind above matter, the spirit above the flesh. Seen
from this perspective, sex was at best a necessary evil to
ensure the continuation of the human race. But because in
Mormon theology the dichotomy between mind and matter has been eliminated, because, as Joseph Smith said, "all
spirit is matter," and "nothing exists which is not material,"
sex, in theory, does not represent the corruption of the
flesh against the sublimity of the spirit.

This spirit-matter continuum is complemented by a rejection of the traditional Christian view of man as a con-
tingent being—that is dependent on the existence of God.
In the view of Joseph Smith, man is coeternal with God—a
"necessary being"—and like God without beginning and
end. In a certain sense, sexuality is a part of man's eternal
nature, even if its manifestation in mortality differs from
that in other forms of existence. Orson Pratt asked
rhetorically: "Will that principle of love which exists now,
and which was has existed from the beginning, exist after the
resurrection?" His answer was in the affirmative.[40]

One of the most important consequences of this prem-
ise, and one that distinguished Mormonism radically from
many other Christian religions, is that sexuality is not a
result of sin. This could hardly have been otherwise, since
at least some Mormon leaders believe that the human
spirits, in the preexistence, were begotten "upon the same
principle that we reproduce one another." Consistent with
such beliefs, Mormons rejected the notion of original
sin.[41]

Pushing this literal-mindedness to its extreme, Mormons argue that divine sexuality is but an elevated form of
human sexuality. Mary's conception of Christ was interpreted as meaning that though she had not been touched
by mortal man, God had literally begotten His Son as we
are by our fathers. For some Mormon authorities, it followed further that Christ, too, was required to fulfil the
law "to multiply and replenish the earth." In the opinion of

Apostle Orson Hyde, Jesus begat children, and in so doing "only did that which he had seen his Father do." It followed that both God and Christ were married.[42]

It remained for a woman, Eliza R. Snow, plural wife of Joseph Smith and later Brigham Young, to puruse this idea to its logical conclusion in perhaps the most popular and certainly the most Mormon of all hymns, "O, My Father":[43]

> In the Heav'ns, are parents single?
> No! The thought makes reason stare!
> Truth is reason, truth eternal
> Tells me I've a mother there.

The next step might well have been the worship of this heavenly mother along with God the Father. For a number of compelling reasons, however, this did not happen. Most Mormons were Protestants before conversion. However much they saw Mormonism as a repudiation of the sectarianism of the Protestant tradition, they were emotionally unprepared for a practice that might have reminded them too much of "popery." For most Protestants, Maryolatry was one of the most distasteful excesses of Catholicism, and worship of a Mormon heavenly mother might have been too reminiscent of that practice.

A second, and perhaps more important reason was the Mormon belief that leadership was a male prerogative. The Mormon priesthood was for males only. They were under greater obligation than women to do right, and under greater condemnation if they sinned. "Whatever may be the character, conduct, or wishes of woman, the Lord expects man to do right, independent of her influence." According to Mormon theology, it was Eve who had been led astray by the serpent. Adam, on the other hand, had not been deceived, but had accepted the forbidden fruit from Eve in the full knowledge of what he was doing and had made a rational choice between two conflicting divine commandments. In emulation of Adam, man was to be "a great centralizing power which will draw

congenial spirits under his control." Therefore, "the man
should stand at the head of and be the controlling power in
his family, and they should yield the most implicit obedience to his counsels." It was the man who held the responsibility for the salvation of his family, "and if he leads
them astray, he will have to answer for it in their stead."[44]

Woman's role was clearly more circumscribed. Since her
sexuality was regarded as passive, she lacked the broad
sphere enjoyed by man for the exercise of her free agency.
Although she was "one of the choicest gifts of God to
man," the Lord intended that she "should be obedient to
the man. He made her the weakest of the two, and im-
planted in her nature a disposition to cleave to man, and a
desire to please him and be obedient to his wishes." It is
"under the guidance of a noble lord striving to magnify his
manhood, [that] she becomes all that God and nature designed her to be." Such ideas, still current among contemporary Mormons, are a major reason for their strong opposition to the Equal Rights Amendment.[45]

In the opinion of at least one nineteenth-century observer, however, Mormons in those days did not generally
place their women on a pedestal. According to Richard
Burton, the Mormon woman was "not petted and spoiled
as in the Eastern States; the inevitable revolution, indeed,
has rather placed her below par, where, however, I believe
her to be happier than when set upon an uncomfortable
and unnatural eminence."[46] This situation, however, may
have been more a result of necessity than of ideology. In
the Mormon frontier environment, social realities, simply,
worked against the male ideal envisioned by many a Mormon patriarch. For if the Mormon women had meekly
submitted to the male bias of their presumed superiors, it
is doubtful that the group led by Brigham Young would
have become the largest and most successful of the
numerous movements claiming to be the heirs of Joseph
Smith. As Leonard Arrington has observed, the survival of
Mormon society in the Great Basin hinged largely upon
the courageous and self-reliant family leadership of all

those innumerable pioneer women whose husbands were forever abroad, on foreign missions, or who could devote only a limited amount of time to each family because of their polygamous obligations.[47] Inevitably, this would result in a high respect for women, even in polygamy. Significantly, it is only after Mormonism succumbed to the forces of modernization that we begin to encounter among the Saints what Christopher Lasch has called "that pious cant about the sanctity of motherhood, the sanctity of home and hearth, which was the real mark of women's degradation" in the nineteenth century. Women in territorial Utah, in many ways, had more in common with their sisters in colonial America than with their nineteenth-century American contemporaries.[48] Male roles, likewise, were determined at least as much by the social and economic realities of subsistence agriculture as by the ideology of priesthood supremacy. It was not until the twentieth century that the Mormon woman was raised onto that same pedestal from which her nineteenth-century antagonist had barely escaped.

V

This transformation in sex roles was part of a larger process of the "embourgeoisement" of Mormon culture after the Civil War—a period during which the Saints began to adapt to the forces of modernization by internalizing their sexual mores. By its very nature this process cannot be imposed by ecclesiastical fiat, but is by and large a spontaneous response to cultural change to which the institution must adapt itself if it wishes to survive. The plausibility of this theory is supported by the work of anthropologist Mark Leone, in whose opinion modern Mormonism developed a high degree of "adaptability" in its value system, which derived, to a large extent, from the sensitivity of its members to the cultural environment, as well as the ability of the Saints to influence the world around them: "Under the guise of strict literalism exists a diffuseness, individual inventiveness, and variability through time that contradicts usual views of the Mormon belief system." What Leone has done, essentially, is to apply sociologist Robert Bellah's concept of "modern religion" to Mormonism; both have an ability to absorb and generate change.[49] Certainly, without this adaptability it is doubtful that Mormonism would have been able to survive the elimination of those social, economic, and political institutions that were virtually synonymous with its cultural identity in the nineteenth century. These institutions rested on a theology that made Mormonism a "religion of the word," one that had a strong ideological orientation, stressing belief as much as behavior. As late as 1867, this emphasis is illustrated in the Godbeite heresy, which represented a more "modern" view by refusing to acknowledge the prophet's right to dictate to them "in all things temporal and spiritual." In its excommunication trial, "the High Council affirmed that this was contrary to church doctrine," and that the defendants "might as well ask whether [they] could honestly differ from the Almighty."[50]

The social and intellectual transformation that occurred is perhaps best illustrated by the statement of church president Joseph F. Smith in 1903, during the controversy over the seating of Mormon apostle Reed Smoot in the United States Senate: "Our people are given the largest possible latitude for their convictions and if a man rejects a message that I may give him *but is still moral* and believes in the main principles of the gospel and desires to continue his membership in the church, he is permitted to remain and he is not unchurched" (my italics). By this time, Mormonism was well on its way to adopting the kind of self-revising value system that Bellah describes in *Beyond Belief,* and that Leone sees as the key to modern Mormonism.[51]

Among American Protestant churches, this transformation had largely occurred in the antebellum period. Under the impact of a pluralistic denominationalism, the churches emphasized conduct more than belief, thus serving as effective tools of modernization. Tocqueville acutely observed: "Go into the churches, you will hear morality preached, of dogma not a word."[52] Mormonism now went the route of its erstwhile antagonists. Between 1880 and 1920, Mormonism experienced a profound cultural transformation reminiscent of the shift from Puritan to Yankee, of the shift from belief to behavior, of the shift from the total system in which religion encompassed all facets of life and the social order to one in which religion became "self-revising" to adapt itself to social, economic, and political change.

Internalized moral norms became an essential compass in this restless new world. As among the modernizing Protestants of antebellum America, abstinence from alcohol and sexual restraint became important means of acquiring those basic characteristics that would help them survive effectively in an individualistic, capitalistic, competitive environment. It is therefore no accident that in this period we perceive an intensified campaign for observance of the Word of Wisdom and an increase in excommunications due to sexual transgression (even though excommunications in general declined in this period). As among antebellum Protestants, sin was increasingly equated with sex, if not according to official doctrine, certainly according to the manner in which church authorities enforced compliance with sexual norms, thus shaping a quasi-official attitude. An early indicator of this changing climate of opinion was the expurgation of Joseph Smith's autobiography.[53]

These changes reflected a profound change in social reality. As long as the Saints controlled not only the religious, but also the social, economic and political institutions of the kingdom of God, numerous community sanctions could be applied to enforce sexual morality. As in Puritan society, sexual transgressions were not only sins but crimes, punishable by the legal code. And as in colonial society, the community informally enforced its moral values. This was facilitated by a relative lack of privacy reinforced by settlement patterns. Like the New England village, the Mormon village consisted of houses that clustered in close proximity. Few families could afford separate rooms for each of their members.[54]

At the same time, in a society that was primarily agrarian sexual pressures were somewhat minimized because most young people were able to marry early. Brigham Young encouraged young men to marry at the age of eighteen. Richard Burton reports that "girls rarely remain single past sixteen."[55] Thus the need for strict sexual control of adolescents was diminished. But as society became more urbanized and industrialized, early marriage became socially less desirable, or even possible. As marriages were postponed to a later age, sexual pressures understandably increased, thus necessitating greater sexual control. The need for greater control, however, coincided with the dissolution of traditional institutions. Given the premium Mormons continued to place on sexual purity, internalization of sexual mores was a necessary and inevitable response to social change. At the same time, it was precisely because of profound cultural changes that sexual morality became all the more important to the Saints. Leonard Arrington suggested that in this period the Word of Wisdom became a symbol of identification.[56] Sexual morality may well have become an even more profound symbol of identity. Again, we are reminded that sex served an analogous function among upwardly mobile, antebellum, middle-class Americans.

This social transformation had its early beginnings at about the same time that Mormonism experienced an internal backlash against polygamy. Having been branded as sexual outcasts, the Saints may well have felt that they had to "out-Victorian" the Victorians in order to become respectable members of American society. Quite possibly, Mormons went through a response analogous to the one Charles Rosenberg has observed among aspiring members of the lower orders of Victorian England and America, who achieved a modicum of autonomy and respectability through "repression of sexuality."[57] Nevertheless, if the polygamy backlash contributed to the embourgeoisement of Mormon culture, a more profound and important reason, I believe, was the internalization of modern behavior patterns. In fact, the development of the modern Mormon personality may have contributed as much to the ultimate demise of polygamy as did the crusade of the Gentiles.

By the 1870s polygamy was passively resisted by many traditionally oriented Saints who fully supported the kingdom but nevertheless continued to practice monogamy. At the same time, the "twin relic" was more actively opposed by a growing number of Mormons who were beginning to embrace the social, economic, and political values of modern America. I believe it is possible to argue that when the Saints, by the turn of the century, gave up the political kingdom of God, communitarianism, and plural marriage, they did so as much from an internal response to modernization as from external pressure. It is not improbable that had it not been for the antipolygamy crusade, this relic of barbarism, unlike its twin slavery, might have died with a whimper rather than a bang.

In any case, the demise of polygamy signified the beginning of the end for Mormonism as a total institution. By the 1880s, the modern market economy was invading Utah with a rush. Because its leaders had kept the government of the political kingdom secret, they were able to hang on to it a bit longer. But with the death of plural marriage the political kingdom seems to have died on the vine. The signs of the times were clearly irreversible. By the end of World War I, most Saints had become as modern as their erstwhile antagonists.

VI

In recent years, the American sexual drama has opened to another scene. Some commentators have called its ethos

postmodern, characterized by norms that are becoming
increasingly tolerant of pre- and extramarital sex, abortion,
and nonjudgmental attitudes toward masturbation and
homosexuality. Twentieth-century American society has
clearly moved away from sexual self-control and self-
repression—those inner-directed norms of nineteenth-
century individualism—toward "sexual liberation." Mormons understandably see such norms as a threat to their
own values and are discovering that internalization of morals leading to self-control is increasingly difficult to
achieve. Considerable evidence points to an emerging
tendency of Mormons to return to traditional, externally
sanctioned mechanisms of social control. In recent times
these have resulted not only in stricter surveillance of sexual morality and observance of the Word of Wisdom, especially among adolescents, but also in stricter standards of
grooming and dress, for example, at Brigham Young University. For better or for worse, it is these symbols of
behavior that are increasingly determining who and what a
Mormon is. Modern Mormons have clearly joined what
Martin Marty has called "a nation of behavers."[58]

Yet it may come as a shock to modern Americans that
these same Mormons still profess to believe in the principle of plural marriage. As a matter of fact the entire Mormon belief system is still very much intact. Supporting
Marty's thesis, Jan Shipps has demonstrated that anti-
Mormon crusaders were offended not so much by Mormon beliefs but by their sociopolitical behavior. After the
Saints wholeheartedly embraced political pluralism, economic individualism, and the monogamous nuclear family
they were permitted to believe as they chose. A telling
illustration of this attitude is the remark of a prominent
participant in the Smoot hearings to the effect that he
preferred "a polygamist that didn't polyg [Smoot] to a
monogamist that didn't monog."[59]

This raises an interesting question about the possible
reintroduction of polygamy among Mormons. It is not
inconceivable that a postmodern American society may

extend its liberalized attitude toward sexual behavior to the principle of plural marriage, and that at some future date the United States Supreme Court may overturn *Reynolds* vs. *United States,* just as the Warren Court overturned *Plessy* vs. *Ferguson.* Should that happen, what would the response of Mormons be? My crystal ball, admittedly, is cloudy. Nevertheless, I can hardly believe that the Saints would be overjoyed at such a decision. No doubt they will be able to avoid the unpleasant prospect of reintroducing polygamy should they be faced with such a choice. That, however, does not make such a situation any less ironic.

6

The Transformation of Racial Thought and Practice

Any man having one drop of the seed of Cain ... in him cannot hold the priesthood.

Brigham Young

In the previous chapters I have emphasized those aspects of Mormonism that reveal its distinctiveness within the larger matrix of American culture. At the same time I hope I have also made it clear that Mormons shared many of the values and beliefs of their antagonists, for better or for worse. One of the less endearing features of both societies was the growth of a deep-seated racial prejudice against nonwhites that coincided in each case with the search for a national identity. At the same time, Mormon racial attitudes differed subtly from those of the dominant culture.

I

Racial prejudice, of course, was no invention of the nineteenth century. The story of the relations between white colonists and Indians and blacks is not a pretty one, to say the least. Nevertheless, colonial Americans were less overtly racist than their nineteenth-century descendants. The Puritan concept of the elect, for example, was paradoxical. The Saints, who were always looking for reassurance that they had been saved, could all too easily be led to believe that God's special favor was upon "His Englishmen," as John Milton had put it. Yet they also knew that there was no surer sign of falling from grace than spiritual pride. After all, God could save whom he chose. This included Indians and blacks. The social order,

179

likewise, tended to blunt the sharp edge of racial prejudice. In the social stratum of colonial America, both servants and slaves were on the bottom. Thus, the low status
of the slave was as much a matter of class as of race. In the
hierarchical, ascriptive social order of the time all individuals were regarded as members of the community, were all
equally children of God. Under the aspect of eternity,
distinctions of class and race were temporal and temporary
ephemera.[1]

According to the book of Genesis, moreover, the
human race had a common origin. All mankind was descended from Adam and Eve. Although in the eighteenth
century students of the origin of man began to doubt the
version in Genesis, they persisted in the belief that mankind descended from one common ancestor. Racial differences were explained as having environmental origins,
especially geography and climate. In America, these ideas
were disseminated by Samuel Stanhope Smith, who published a treatise on the subject in 1787.[2] He regarded the
various colored races as degenerations from the white
norm, but also believed in the possibility of regeneration,
interestingly enough, through racial intermixture. In spite
of its obvious ethnocentric bias, this theory did acknowledge the common humanity of all races. In the words of
historian Winthrop Jordan, "even the most barbarous of
men must be presumed to retain the capacity for civilization, for no people have lost entirely a capacity originally
endowed upon them by their creator." In America such
theories were applied especially to the Indians, who were
widely regarded as having descended from the House of
Israel, specifically through the Lost Ten Tribes.[3]

II

When Joseph Smith published the Book of Mormon in
1830, it is doubtful that he was familiar with the specific
details of this racial theory. Yet the very same general
notions were implicit in the popular versions of the red

sons of Israel accounts, which are clearly mirrored in the
story of the Book of Mormon, billed, among other things,
as a history of the Indians. The Book of Mormon,
however, modified the traditional opinion of most
nineteenth-century Americans that the Indians were descendants of the Lost Ten Tribes by claiming, rather, that
they belonged to the Tribe of Joseph (the one sold into
Egypt by his brothers) through his son Manasseh. The
Saints believed that they themselves were primarily of the
tribe of Ephraim, Joseph's other son, and were therefore
related to the Indians or "Lamanites," as they were called
in the Book of Mormon. These Lamanites were descended
from the prophet Lehi, who had been commanded by God
to escape the impending Babylonian captivity of the Jews
and had been led with his family to the New World where
he became the progenitor of a thriving civilization. His son
Nephi, who obeyed the counsel of his father and walked in
the ways of the Lord, became the founder of a civilization
of farmers and builders of cities, while his son Laman, who
rejected the religious and moral teachings of his father,
became the leader of a band of outcasts who adopted a
nomadic way of life and continually harassed the more
civilized Nephites, as they came to be called. In punishment for their wickedness, God cursed these Lamanites,
and "they became a dark, and loathsome, and a filthy
people, full of idleness and all manner of abominations."[4]

If to the modern mind this account of the racial origins
of the Indians appears naive and simplistic, it is quite in
keeping with the intellectual assumptions of the period in
which the Book of Mormon was published, as we have
seen. Although the Book of Mormon does not say so directly, later exegeses suggest that the curse upon the
Lamanites may have been a natural result of their savage
way of life. It was because they wore fewer clothes than
their Nephite brethren and were more frequently exposed
to the sun and weather that they turned into a "dark, and
loathsome" people. This explanation was supplemented by
a widespread belief in a correlation between the physical

and moral worlds. An immoral way of life would reveal itself in a person's face. You could tell a liar, thief, murderer, or adulterer by looking at him or her. Moral degeneration led to physical degeneration. Some Mormons, for example, also believed that apostates would turn darker and in time become like the Indians.[5] Like contemporary "ethnologists," Mormons also believed that the process could be reversed. The Book of Mormon held out the hope to the Lamanites that if they turned from their wicked ways they would once again become a "white and delightsome people." In the early days of Mormonism, some Saints appear to have expected that Indians, stepping from the waters of baptism, would become white.[6]

Like Samuel Stanhope Smith, Joseph also suggested a more effective process. In an unpublished revelation on July 17, 1831, during a missionary journey to the Indians of western Missouri, he announced that it was the Lord's will "that in time, ye should take unto you wives of the Lamanites and Nephites, that their posterity may become white, delightsome and just." This metamorphosis, however, was more than a biological process, for the revelation continued with the comment that "even now their females are more virtuous than the gentiles." Although the idea of racial regeneration through miscegenation ran counter to the moral sensibilities of most antebellum Americans, it was an idea in full harmony with the current state of biological opinion.[7]

If we can recognize in this romantic Mormon attempt to "raise" the Indians to their own cultural level a not so subtle form of condescension, it is nevertheless appropriate to point out that within the cultural context of the 1830s—at a time when in the eyes of most Americans the only good Indian was a dead Indian—such an attempt at racial elevation was rather daring. Indeed, the sympathetic attitude of the Mormons toward Indians was a major cause for conflict with the Gentiles. The most obvious reason was political, because many Americans believed that the Mormons were attempting to ally themselves with the In-

dians against their common enemies. At the same time,
racial attitudes of Saints and Gentiles were beginning to
diverge in some basic assumptions. Even as the Mormons
continued in their environmentalism, American racial attitudes took a turn for the worse.

That this should be so is not at all surprising when we
realize that racialism came to play a major role in the creation of an American national identity. As I have suggested
earlier, for all their racial prejudices, colonial Americans
lived in a relatively stable, hierarchical social order, supported by their national identity as Englishmen. In the
wake of the revolution they had to build a new identity at
the very time when the traditional social order had all but
dissolved. In the rhetoric of Jacksonian ideology, the old
world of *artificial* privilege had made way for the new
world of *natural* equality. In the opinion of some theorists,
there was no distinction more artificial than class and more
natural than race. Thus, all those antebellum Americans
who had been left behind in the race for the main chance
could at least console themselves that they shared a natural
equality with their betters—a white skin.[8]

This logic dictated that nonwhite races would no longer
be regarded merely as inferior, as they had been in colonial
society, but as totally distinct and separate. Under the auspices of the American school of ethnology the old en-
vironmentalist, monogenist theory of racial origins was replaced by a new, polygenist theory which maintained that
the races of man were separate species rather than varieties
of the same species. Not suprisingly, the white race ranked
the highest, the black race the lowest. Any intermixture
would lead to the deterioration and final destruction of the
higher race. In its most extreme form the theory maintained that whites and blacks were as distinct as horses and
donkeys, and that the offspring, like mules, could not reproduce, though the effect was not quite as sudden, and
would take several generations.[9]

Although the Mormons developed racist theories of
their own, they stopped short of this kind of blatant racist

ideology, which infected the North as much as the South. As biblical literalists, Mormons could not reconcile polygenism with Genesis. They found the doctrine equally difficult to reconcile with the regenerationist teachings of the Book of Mormon. Another reason was cultural. The social order of the Saints, clearly, was more compatible with that of colonial America than that of the ninteenth century.

Of course, the victims of such prejudice might have found the distinction to be an academic one. Though nineteenth-century Mormons, on the whole, followed a racial policy vis-à-vis Indians more enlightened than that of the Gentiles, their ethnocentrism was as ingrained as that of other Americans. Whether the Mormons would have been able to cope with mass conversions of Indians is doubtful. But as the history of Mormon missionary efforts among the Indians proved, such prospects were not forthcoming. If its true that Joseph Smith was highly sensitive to the cultural environment of his times, it is possible that he may have regarded the assimilation theory of the Indians as quite safe for a people who had already proved singularly unassimilable into American culture. Equally significant is the fact that the Mormon prophet developed no such doctrine for another racial group that had shown a great deal more ability to assimilate—the American Negro.

III

Just exactly when, how, and why Mormon prejudice against Negroes developed into discriminatory policy is a matter of considerable controversy, though its existence is an incontrovertible fact. For more than a century and a quarter the Mormon church denied the priesthood to blacks, a policy publicized by Brigham Young in 1852 after the arrival of the pioneers in Utah. Because there is no evidence that Joseph Smith made an unequivocal, authoritative statement regarding black ineligibility for the

priesthood, some scholars believe that the policy was in
fact initiated by Brigham Young, while others insist that,
because Young based virtually all of his teachings on the
authority of Joseph, this would be particularly true of a
doctrine as controversial and far-reaching as priesthood
denial to blacks.[10]

Who is right? Unfortunately, the question has been
clouded by ideology. As long as the hierarchy excluded
Negroes from the priesthood, the prophetic authority of
Joseph provided the most effective linchpin for the doctrine. For that same reason liberal historians who wanted to
undermine a practice they regarded as reprehensible felt
they could do so most effectively by pulling the pin.

The most ambitious and brilliant attempt to divorce
Joseph's authority from the "Negro doctrine" is a seminal
essay by Lester Bush for *Dialogue* (Spring, 1973), an unofficial journal published by a group of Mormon intellectuals.[11] Bush argues that the Negro doctrine lacks
official sanction by revelation, and merely grew as an historical accident in response to persecution. Once having
been established, it was reaffirmed by a succession of
Mormon leaders, each of whom erroneously had been led
to believe that the policy had been officially originated by
Joseph Smith. The Mormon Negro policy, according to
Bush, therefore represents a kind of "unthinking decision"
analogous to Winthrop Jordan's account of the origins of
American Negro slavery and racism. In Bush's opinion,
Smith was quite open-minded about race, as evidenced by
the fact that he allowed the ordination of Elijah Abel, a
Negro, to the office of elder in the church, later permitting
his advancement to the position of a seventy, a missionary
calling of considerable trust and responsibility.

Defenders of the theory that Smith was indeed responsible for originating priesthood denial to blacks argue
that Abel was ordained to the priesthood before the
prophet had received any revelations to the contrary. The
latter, so the argument goes, were not received until
sometime after 1835, when Joseph translated the Book of

Abraham, to be published in 1842. According to the Book
of Abraham, the Egyptian pharaoh "was a descendant from
the loins of Ham, and was a partaker of the blood of the
Canaanites by birth. . . . and thus, from Ham, sprang that
race which preserved the curse in the land." The first
pharaoh was a grandson of Noah, "who blessed him with
the blessings of the earth, and with the blessings of wisdom, but cursed him as pertaining to the Priesthood."[12]

In the minds of nineteenth-century Americans, Negroes
were unquestioningly wedded to the Hamite genealogy of
the Canaanites. By linking the Book of Abraham to the
unexamined assumptions of the Hamite genealogy the
Mormons clinched the scriptural basis for priesthood denial. Bush shrewdly recognized that with the demise of this
genealogy under the onslaught on modern scholarship the
scriptural rug had been pulled out from under the Negro
doctrine. Not that Bush questioned the scriptural authenticity of the Book of Abraham. Rather, it had become a
non sequitur. There was simply no way to link Noah's
curse on pharaoh to the modern Negro through these
scriptures. If Bush is right, the Negro doctrine has been
disconnected from the prophetic authority of Joseph,
and Mormon racial discrimination has lost its historical
rationale.

Paradoxically, Bush was able to pull the pin of revelation
only on the assumption that the Book of Abraham was
indeed an authentic record of the writings of Abraham and
not a product of the imagination of Joseph Smith. As I
have mentioned in chapter 1, however, the authenticity of
the Book of Abraham has been seriously challenged by
scholars after the discovery of the original papyrus from
which Smith claimed he had made his translation. If Smith
rather than Abraham was the author of these scriptures,
Bush's case loses much of its force since Joseph shared the
general belief of his day in the authenticity of the Hamite
genealogy. In that case modern scholarship is irrelevant, for
the crucial question becomes not whether there is, in fact,
a link between Ham and the modern Negro, but whether

Smith *believed* there was. In that case, the Book of Abraham is indeed the linchpin in the Negro doctrine. The fact that neither Joseph nor Brigham Young apparently felt it necessary to use the Book of Abraham as proof text does not negate my point. I am reminded of Jacob Burckhardt's comment that "everywhere in the past we encounter things which remain unexplained only because they were completely self-understood in their time."[13]

IV

If Joseph was the author of the Negro doctrine, there are plausible historical reasons why he should have been. As Lester Bush himself acknowledges, the Saints shared many of the cultural assumptions and prejudices of their times. These were sometimes reinforced by historical circumstances. For example, one reason given by the Missourians why the Mormons were driven out of Jackson County in 1833 is that they harbored abolitionist sentiments, certainly a dangerous opinion to hold in a border state such as Missouri. It is perhaps true that the Missourians merely used the slavery issue as an excuse to rid themselves of the unwelcome Mormons. Yet it should be remembered that in the same year the Reverend John D. Pinney of Columbia, South Carolina, became the incomprehending victim of a mob scene as a result of some innocent remarks concerning African colonization. Because this incident occurred in August, Elder W. W. Phelps, editor of *The Evening and the Morning Star,* lacked its cautionary example when he made some favorable comments about colonization in its July issue. That same number also admonished the Saints to take "great care" to adhere to the Missouri laws pertaining to "free people of color." The old settlers of Missouri, nevertheless, were outraged, charged the Mormons with an attempt to tamper with the institution of slavery, and refused to accept a Mormon clarification on the question of slavery in an "extra" edition of the *Star,* which went so far as to assert that "we feel in duty bound to state, in this *Extra,* that our intention was not only to stop free people of color from emigrating to this state, but to prevent them from being admitted as members of the Church." Even this extreme position proved insufficient to save the Mormons from the wrath of the Missourians, who, by November, had driven most of the Saints from their homes in Jackson County at gunpoint.[14]

The Saints seem to have learned their lesson and from then on discouraged missionary activities among blacks. The Mormons, however, hardened their racial position not only as a result of persecution. Between 1830 and 1844, Mormonism (under the leadership of Smith) also evolved and changed theologically and institutionally. Elijah Abel (Mormons seem to have been oblivious to the irony of the name) was ordained to the priesthood at a time when Mormonism was dominated intellectually by the ambivalent theological and racial attitudes expressed in the Book of Mormon. As Smith developed his complex and grandiose vision of the kingdom of God, racial tolerance fit less consistently into this social edifice. Mormon nationalism, like American nationalism, was supported by the search for racial identity. By the Nauvoo period, therefore, I believe, Mormon "racism" had become a logical if temporary expression of kingdom building. Far from representing an unthinking decision, the Negro doctrine fits consistently into the evolution of the kingdom.

This intepretation is supported by the history of the Mormon experience following the death of the Mormon prophet. Those who rejected the Nauvoo experiment, and most of what it stood for, and who preferred the earlier, less complex form of Mormonism as expressed primarily in the Book of Mormon, such as the Reorganized Church, freely admit blacks to the priesthood, whereas the Utah Mormons, continuing in the Nauvoo tradition, until recently resisted any attempts at liberalization.

Mormon racial attitudes were also related to their response to the crisis of the family. In a general way, this response was analogous to that of their Gentile perse-

cutors. American Protestants were racists for some of the
same reasons that they pursued antipolygamy crusades. In
both instances, sex became a major issue of concern. That
polygamy, in the eyes of the Gentiles, represented a threat
to the family has already been established. There is also
considerable evidence that northern fears of miscegenation can be ascribed, in part, to apprehensions regarding
the safety of hearth and home. The cult of womanhood
and domesticity, to some extent, appears to have been a
response to racial fears. This argument is admittedly cir-
cular. For it is also true that apprehensions regarding the
changing status of women and the family helped trigger an
increasingly virulent racism.[15]

Because the Mormons shared many of the sexual and
racial attitudes of their Gentile adversaries, many Mormon
references to interracial sex between blacks and whites are
indistinguishable in tenor from those of their fellow
Americans. On one level, miscegenation was frowned
upon because in most instances it represented illicit sexual
relations. From the perspective of Christian morality, it
was merely one form of fornication or adultery, usually
between a white man and a black woman. John Taylor
seems to have responded to these values when he called
prostitution a "grand institution" in the North, and then
continued by lamenting that "this niggerism in the South is
about the same kind of thing, only a change of colour."[16]
William Appleby, however, complained about what was
clearly regarded as a larger problem, though it did not
involve a direct violation of the Christian sex code, when
he recorded in his "History of the Signs of the Times" that
"It is no uncommon thing (we have witnessed it) in the
cities of the Eastern and Northern States to see a large
black negro, married to a white girl,—a great many persons calling themselves rich, and wished to be thought
respectable, believes in, and upholds amalgamation in
those states. In some places Coloured Pastors preside over
White Congregations. Colored school Teachers, Attor-
neys at Law &c." Appleby entered this passage under a

rubric he called "confusions," thus providing us with a clue to the reasons for his apprehensions.[17]

Miscegenation between blacks and whites, in the Mormon mind, introduced "confusions" on several levels. First of all, any kind of premarital and extramarital sex, according to the Mormon code, was a sin "next to murder." Second, interracial marriages simply faced too many obstacles—largely a result of racial prejudice, to be sure—to be successful. Whether such prejudice was right or wrong, its reality threatened such unions, potentially endangering the institution of marriage if too many people followed such a pattern. Third, even if such marriages were successful, they would create "confusion" because the resulting children were neither black nor white, thus threatening the kinship patterns of Mormon family trees at a time when the idea of membership in the House of Israel was taken literally.

It is true that Smith had taught that through the "Spirit of Elijah" the entire human race would ultimately be welded together into one family. But this welding was to be a highly structured affair, proceeding along lines of kinship and of race. God had singled out the seed of Abraham for special blessings, because of his faithfulness. These blessings continued especially through the lineage of Jacob, who had wrestled with the Lord, and was called Israel. His twelve sons became the progenitors of the Twelve Tribes of Israel, who were scattered abroad, and through whose seed the blessings of Abraham were to be carried to the far corners of the earth. Among the most favored of the tribes of Israel were Judah, through whose lineage Christ was born, and Joseph, whose two sons, Ephraim and Manasseh, were the progenitors of peoples that would especially affect the history of the New World.

The story of the Book of Mormon purports to be the history of a group of descendants of Manasseh, who migrated to America and became the ancestors to the American Indians. The descendants of Ephraim, presumably, had been dispersed through Western Europe and were the an-

cestors of the Anglo-Saxon and Germanic peoples. It was
through them that the North American continent was settled, and through them that the Gospel of Jesus Christ was
restored. Joseph Smith believed that he was a literal descendant of Ephraim. The great work of "restoration"
which he initiated was intended not only as a return to
fundamentalist Christian foundations but also as a "re-
discovery" of the tribal identities of the human race, beginning with Ephraim and Manasseh. Ephraim, especially,
had been scattered like a leaven through the "Gentile"
nations. It was the purpose of the restoration to sift out the
scattered "remnants," to "gather" them to Zion, and to
establish, through them, the kingdom of God. Ephraim
had a special talent for government. Those who had
founded the American republic were largely of the blood
of Ephraim. The United States itself, believed Smith, was
preparatory to the establishment of the kingdom of God.

Therefore, as Mormon missionaries went abroad to
preach the Gospel, they were proselytizing not in a narrow
religious sense, but were literally gathering in those belonging to the House of Israel. This concept of the
"gathering" became one of the fundamental, essential principles of the kingdom. Mormon missionaries instructed
their converts that gathering to Zion was one of the basic
tests of orthodoxy. "None of the Saints," admonished
Orson Pratt, "can be dilatory upon this subject, and still
retain the spirit of God. To neglect or be indifferent about
gathering, is just as displeasing in the sight of God as to
neglect or be indifferent about baptism for the remission
of sins."[18]

Although in theory the voice of the Lord was "unto all
people," many, perhaps the majority, would "harden their
hearts" like the Nephites of old and thus become candidates for the impending destruction God had decreed for
the wicked. Reminiscent of their Puritan ancestors, who
believed they were the grain sifted out of a whole nation,
the Mormons regarded themselves as a saving remnant
that had been gathered from the nations of the earth, like

wheat from tares. And like their New England forebears, they saw themselves not only as a people of God, a community of saints, in the spiritual sense, but as families, friends, and neighbors engaged in building a Godly commonwealth that included houses and barns, flocks and herds, schools and workshops. Like their ancestors, they were building a nation.

In the nineteenth century, such an enterprise would, of course, be fraught with even more difficulty than in the seventeenth. To be successful, it would have to be even more deliberate, require even more planning and discipline than the "city upon a hill." The Puritans had been a relatively homogeneous group, the Mormons much less so, even though New Englanders and "Yorkers" made up the bulk of early converts, soon to be joined by migrants from Upper Canada. Immediately upon its opening in 1837, the British mission became a spectacular success. Soon, missionaries fanned out over the Continent and Scandinavia, gathering the poor of Europe "homeward" to a moveable Zion that had to flee periodically before the wrath of its Gentile neighbors.[19]

To weld such an increasingly heterogeneous group into citizens of the kingdom of God required both symbols and institutions of unity and identity. Important among these were the personality and stature of the prophet, the authority of his evolving hierarchy, the entire organizational structure of the church, the mobilization of the Saints for public projects, especially the building of temples, such as in Kirtland, Nauvoo, and later on in Utah, and the peculiar practices and beliefs of Mormonism. Racial concepts were among the most important of these symbols.

If to a genealogist the identification of the chosen Israelites might have presented virtually insurmountable difficulties, the missionaries let faith be their guide. The spirit, they believed, would lead them to those in whose veins the blood of Israel coursed with vigor. These were the sheep that would hear the master's voice. After baptism, presumptive membership in the House of Israel generally

received confirmation and precision through a patriarchal blessing. In keeping with the idea of the patriarchal
order, the first patriarch of the church was Smith's father,
Joseph, Sen. It was the function of the patriarch to
pronounce blessings upon the faithful, which frequently
took the form of a brief, prophetic guide to the recipient's
life. But the chief purpose of the blessing was to identify
the tribe of Israel to which the Saint belonged. In time,
this practice caused some confusion as occasionally some
members of a family were identified by a particular patriarch as belonging to one tribe, while another patriarch
might identify other members as belonging to another tribe.
As a result, the church in later years redefined the
significance of such blessings as *assigning* recipients of a
blessing to a tribe rather than as *identifying* their membership. This modern clarification also helped counter the
racist implications of such blessings and complemented, in
its logic, the currently prominent idea that all those who
join the Mormon church become members of the House
of Israel by adoption.

    In the nineteenth century, however, the idea of adop-
tion seems to have been used to accommodate the excep-
tional, non-"Anglo-Saxon" convert and to explain
anomalies rather than as an opening to include large numbers of non-Israelites in the Mormon kingdom.[20] Such
all-inclusiveness would have threatened the very reason
why Smith promulgated the idea of the House of Israel in
the first place. If early Mormonism represents a pre-
industrial frame of mind, then it appears that this kind of
instant tribalism may well be interpreted as an attempt to
return to kinship patterns that were threatened, indeed
breaking up, in a society that was becoming increasingly
atomized as a result of social dislocations triggered by accelerating changes in urban-rural patterns and in geographic mobility. Many early Mormon converts were "displaced" persons, looking for the security of family and
kinship.

    These expectations, at least in the first two decades of

Mormonism, remained for the most part a faint hope. As
we have seen, Gentile persecutions and internal dis-
sensions caused dislocations perhaps even more intense
than those many Saints had experienced before their conversion. Although these experiences were conducive to
the formation of an unusally strong group solidarity, they
also continued to break up many ties of family and kinship.
Because Mormons, in the nineteenth century, were social
outcasts, virtually all who joined them either lacked strong
ties of this kind, or were forced into wrenching separations
from families and friends. But this process continued even
after conversion, as many Mormons apostatized from their
new faith, often further fragmenting family ties. Sectarian
divisions, which in the nineteenth century created several
Mormon sects, continued the atomizing process. After the
death of Joseph Smith, for example, only one branch of his
family, the descendants of his murdered brother Hyrum,
followed Young to Utah.

These experiences suggest why nineteenth-century
Mormonism developed a cosmic world view of rationality
and order reminiscent of the western mind of the
eighteenth century. In the face of an unstable reality they
created a stable and orderly world of the mind. In a real
world in which racial, sexual, and family identities were
forever threatened, these identities could be anchored se-
curely in an ideal world beyond time and history.[21]

This ideal world of the "ought," in the Mormon mind,
was transformed into an ultimate reality through the
mechanism of a quasi-Newtonian world view. The laws of
cause and effect were both mechanical and spiritual. Relations between the sexes, between families, between
tribes, among the entire human race, were established according to laws laid down in eternity. They could not be
violated with impunity. The Lord had set boundaries between nations, kindred, tongues, and people. These
boundaries existed for a purpose. When the Children of
Israel moved into the Promised Land they were commanded to drive out and destory the Canaanites. Because

they disobeyed and intermingled with the earlier inhabitants, the Lord's wrath was kindled against the Israelites. They had violated not only temporal laws prohibiting
social intercourse, but eternal laws designed to preserve
their racial identity.

V

It is perhaps not suprising, then, that when the Saints, like
a modern Israel, sojourned to their own promised land
they were mindful of the racial injunctions their God had
issued to their predecessors. Though there were no
Canaanites to rout, Brigham Young wanted to make sure
that the time would not come when he might have to. This
may explain the hardening of racial attitudes after the
Saints had removed themselves from the world of the
Gentiles, with only a handful of blacks (servants) in their
midst. Certainly, Brigham Young's opinion regarding miscegenation appears extreme: "Shall I tell you the law of
God in regard to the African race? If the white man who
belongs to the chosen seed mixes his blood with the seed
of Cain, the penalty, under the law of God, is death on the
spot. This will always be so."[22]
    There is no record that Young ever applied this "law."
In any case, it is doubtful that he had much reason to do so,
since Mormon missionaries were instructed not to proselytize among blacks. Slaveholders who converted to
Mormonism were encouraged to sell or manumit their
slaves before gathering with the Saints in Utah. Though
Young was not averse to slavery on principle, he did not
think it practical as an institution in the Great Basin kingdom. Young, of course, also knew that the majoirity of
mulattos were the offspring of white Southern men and
their female slaves.
    One of the most effective ways of discouraging blacks
from becoming Mormons was to deny them the priesthood. This, of course, was a male prerogative, whose
"blessings" were extended to women through marriage.

Only those who held the priesthood could enter into the "new and everlasting covenant," to be sealed in the temple for "time and eternity." Thus, when Brigham Young declared in 1852 that "any man having one drop of the seed of [Cain] . . . in him cannot hold the priesthood," he brought into the open a doctrine that made it very unlikely that he would ever be called upon to administer "death on the spot."[23]

The reference to the "seed of Cain," while not inconsistent with the traditional justification for slavery, represents a shift in emphasis from the stock biblical genealogy through the "curse of Ham" as passed on to Canaan. When asked what "chance of redemption there was for the Africans," Young answered that "the curse remained upon them because Cain cut off the lives of Abel. . . . the Lord had cursed Cain's seed with blackness and prohibited them the Priesthood." Noah's curse on Ham's posterity, in fact, may have been a kind of added insult to an injury incurred because of Ham's marriage to a "Canaanite" through whom his descendants would have inherited Cain's curse in any case.[24]

While the Cain-Ham genealogy seemed sufficient justification for the Negro doctrine to most Mormons, a few of them began to perceive an inconsistency with the Second Article of Faith, in which Joseph Smith had asserted that "men will be punished for their own sins, and not for Adam's transgression." That Cain should be punished for killing Abel seemed reasonable; but what about his posterity? Orson Hyde and Orson Pratt were the first to address themselves to this problem and concluded that the explanation lay in the Mormon doctrine of the preexistence. As summarized and extended by Mormon historian and "general authority" B. H. Roberts in 1885, the linkage between the two doctrines is as follows: In the great war in heaven some spirits "were not valiant" in defense of the principles of righteousness against Lucifer. These spirits, though worthy of attaining their second estate, a human body, had "rendered themselves unworthy of the Priesthood and its powers." Black skin was a mark that would identify these shirkers, ensuring that they could not usurp blessings to which they were not entitled.[25]

This rationalization became the cornerstone of the Negro doctrine well into the twentieth century. At the same time, under the onslaught of modern, secular scholarship, the connection between the Cain-Ham genealogy and modern blacks could no longer be maintained. By the 1960s even conservative Mormon authorities were compelled, however reluctantly, to admit that upon careful reading the scriptural authority of the Book of Abraham was insufficient to sustain the Negro doctrine. The linkage between the doctrine of the preexistence and the Negro doctrine, likewise, was relegated to the realm of unsubstantiated speculation. Having thus been deprived of any scriptural basis for denying the priesthood to blacks, the Mormon hierarchy, nevertheless, persisted in a practice that was being increasingly attacked by civil rights activists from without the church, and by intellectuals within. In 1968, Mormon philosopher Sterling McMurrin publicized a private statement made to him by church president David O. MacKay in 1954, to the effect that the church had "no doctrine of any kind pertaining to the Negro," and that the priesthood restriction was "a practice, not a doctrine, and the practice will some day be changed." As a sequel to this private statement, the First Presidency, in 1969, officially announced that Negroes are "not yet to receive the priesthood, for reasons which we believe are known to God, but which He has not made fully known to man."[26]

It was shortly thereafter, in 1973, that Lester Bush rehearsed the long and depressing history of Mormon racial prejudice and concluded with the following pessimistic note:

> As relieved as the educated Mormon may be at not having to stand squarely behind the curse on Cain or a non sequitur from the Pearl of Great Price, nor ultimately to defend a specific role for blacks in the pre-existence ..., there is little comfort to be taken in the

realization that the entire history of this subject has been effectively declared irrelevant. For if the priesthood restriction now stands independently of the rationales that justified its original existence, the demonstration that these rationales may have been in error becomes an academic exercise.[27]

VI

Hindsight has confirmed Bush's assessment, though in a manner that he undoubtedly did not anticipate. For when on June 8, 1978, the First Presidency of the Mormon Church, in an historic letter, made the unexpected and dramatic announcement that "all worthy male members of the Church may be ordained to the priesthood without regard for race or color," this change, however momentous, might well have been effected by a mere policy directive. Instead, the letter emphatically made it known that the change had come by way of revelation.[28]

Why? The researches of Bush and others, after all, seemed to have made it very clear in the first place that God had never given a specific revelation regarding priesthood denial. Why, then, should God, by revelation, rescind an order he had never given? That argument, of course, had been advanced by Mormon intellectuals for a number of years, without visible effect. Indeed, on reflection, it becomes clear that revelation was the only way out for the Mormon leadership (something Bush himself conceded).[29] However correct the historical reconstruction of the problem may have been, its implications were so devastating that the leadership could not possibly accept it. After all, if Mormon prophets were guided by revelation, why had the Lord made it so hard to discover his will on a matter of such monumental significance? Quite obviously, then, the Lord had indeed made known his will—though to his prophets only, and not to historians.

What Bush had done, as we have seen, was to absolve Joseph Smith from complicity in the whole depressing racist plot, banking on the assumption that the prophetic

authority of the founder of Mormonism would carry the
day. What Bush and the intellectuals did not fully understand was that by implication they were undermining the
prophetic authority of Smith's successors. After all, if
these leaders had been wrong on the "Negro question,"
what might historians discover next! The Mormon leadership shrewdly understood that it was a great deal easier for
God to change his mind than for a prophet. That approach
also allowed the hierarchy to evade such inevitable and
hard questions as why God had not spoken sooner, or
why, if he was no respecter of persons, he had withheld his
highest blessings from a substantial portion of the human
race at all.

Another reason for making the change unambiguously
revelatory was the precedent of the manifesto regarding the
cessation of plural marriage of 1890. Wilford Woodruff
seemed to have caved in so obviously to pressures of the
United States government that his insistence that he had
indeed acted under revelation has always seemed somewhat suspect to all but the most credulous among the
faithful. Indeed, Mormon apologists ever since have
seemed to be protesting far too much in their emphatic
assertion that Woodruff never would have issued the
manifesto unless expressly demanded to do so by God.
Though included in the Doctrine and Covenants, the prosaic statement stands in glaring contrast to Smith's language of revelation.[30] By unambiguously stating that the
change of priesthood denial was arrived at by revelation,
the church leadership clearly has not been unmindful of
Woodruff's unfortunate manifesto.

Another intriguing question is, why did Kimball act
when he did? Ironically, the change might have come some
years earlier had it not been for the militancy of civil rights
activists both without and within the church. The long-
range impact of changing racial attitudes in America on
church policy is of course beyond question. Indeed, without the civil rights movement the traditional racial policy

might still be in effect today. At the same time, the immediate impact of the movement caused a resistance to change among some influential Mormon leaders of a liberal bent, if only for tactical reasons. Even those sympathetic to change could not very well make it appear that the church was giving in to outside pressure. The leaders were thus caught in a double bind. If they rescinded the Negro doctrine, they would stand condemned as pragmatists who had succumbed to social pressures, just as their predecessor Woodruff had. If they resisted, they would stand condemned as racists. Fortunately for the leadership, racial tensions in America have calmed considerably in recent years. Clearly, when the First Presidency issued its statement in 1978, they were not responding to overt pressures from civil rights leaders or intellectuals.

That is not to say that the leadership was not responding to some very profound pressures indeed, but from very different quarters. First of all, the change is the result of a cultural transformation that has been at work for some time. If my hypothesis is correct that nineteenth-century Mormon racial attitudes were intimately connected to the establishment of the kingdom of God and to the search for a national identity, then one might well have expected the early demise of Mormon racism after the metamorphosis of the kingdom. In fact, those dissident Mormons who had rejected "corporate" Mormonism as it manifested itself in plural marriage and the political kingdom, who had refused to follow Young to the Rocky Mountains, and who had started the Reorganized Church with headquarters in Independence, Missouri, never felt it necessary to invent a Negro doctrine. Unlike the Utah Mormons, they refused to canonize the Book of Abraham, regarding it as one of Smith's more adventurous and unreliable excursions into "revelation." The Reorganized Church has always admitted Negroes to full membership, including the privileges of the priesthood.[31] Having given up polygamy and the political kingdom by the early twentieth century, Utah Mormons were now closer to their Missouri dissidents than to

their own historical Nauvoo tradition of the kingdom. If
they had given up their policy of excluding the Negro from
the priesthood, their similarity to the Reorganized Church
would have been even more complete.

The fact that this did not happen, however, does not
necessarily invalidate my hypothesis. Indeed, racism may
well have become all the more important as a means of
reasserting a difference that could now be little more than
symbolic. In their search for symbols of identification, as
we have seen, the Utah Saints now began to emphasize
strict observance of the Word of Wisdom and to stress a
Victorian, middle class sexual morality. Having been
forced through too many traumatic changes in too short a
time, the Saints may well have clung to their racial concepts as a source of stability, as a symbol of ideological
permanence that seemed to have some substance behind
it. After all, the only way they could insist on the permanence of other aspects of the social reality of Mormonism
was to pretend that some of its most fundamental institutions had never existed, or had been of peripheral
importance at best. Seen from this perspective, then, racism may well have symbolized a kingdom of God that was
now irretrievably lost. It is ironic, of course, that racism
was also one of the symbols of an American middle class
society that Mormonism had resisted for more than half a
century.

Having gained a sense of security in their new bourgeois
identity by the 1970s, Mormons were now prepared to
shed that symbol which also stood as a paradoxical reminder of an almost forgotten past. Clearly, not many
Saints were anxious for a restoration of the kingdom in the
modern world. Furthermore, Mormon racial teachings
were becoming as unfashionable among contemporary
Americans as polygamy had been a century earlier. To
professionally and academically successful Mormons, and
to those who had political aspirations, especially, the
Negro policy was becoming an acute embarrassment.[32]
Thus, when Kimball issued his historic revelation, there

was a palpable sigh of relief throughout Mormonism, a feeling of gratitude that what one Mormon intellectual, in a fit of romantic irrationality, called "the Mormon cross," had been lifted at last.[33] Of course many Mormons, at the turn of the century, had responded in the same fashion to the demise of polygamy. The revelation granting the priesthood to blacks, then, was a delayed reaction to one aspect of cultural change.

It was also a direct response to a more palpable and more important manifestation of social change. When Mormon missionaries, in the nineteenth century, first fanned out into the four corners of the world, their success in Asia and Africa and Latin America was very limited indeed. Even the Catholic countries of Europe "hardened their hearts" to the message of the new gospel. In the Protestant countries of Europe, on the other hand—in Britain, in the Germanies, in Scandinavia, they reaped a spectacular harvest of converts who were gathered to Zion. These were those who were regarded as belonging to the House of Israel. It was only after World War II that missionaries began to have measurable success in the Catholic countries such as Ireland, Italy, and Spain. Finally, beginning in the 1960s, thousands in the countries of the Third World, particularly in Latin America, and even in Africa, turned to the new gospel from America. At the same time, missionaries now found Protestant Western Europe a hard soil for their message, claiming that Britain, West Germany, and Scandinavia had been virtually "tracted out."

What is the explanation behind this pattern of conversion? It appears that Mormonism has been most successful in countries undergoing rapid change, such as the United States, Upper Canada, and Western Europe in the nineteenth century, Southern Europe after World War II, and the Third World at the present time. As I have suggested earlier, Mormonism seems to appeal to individuals who have been dislocated in a rapidly changing world, who are searching for stability and order, but who are at the same

time looking for a better future. Mormonism helps these
people back into the future.

Ironically, the conservative Mormon leadership in Utah
has been caught up in the process. It was largely as a result
of recent, spectacular conversions in the Third World that
the hierarchy finally had no choice but to adapt to the new
reality. What, for example, were Mormon leaders to do
after World War II when thousands of Ibo in Nigeria were
converting to Mormonism without benefit of missionaries.
By 1963, the church was finally persuaded to send elders
from the United States to administer various Mormon ordinances, only to be stopped by the Nigerian government
who refused resident visas to the Mormons after discovering the Negro doctrine. The growing success of the church
in Latin America, especially Brazil, also made the racial
question acute. In Brazil, after all, racial mixture is quite
common, and not always easily detected. Should Brazilian
converts, in emulation of Hitler's policy regarding Jews,
furnish genealogical proof of white ancestry before being
ordained to the priesthood? As a matter of fact, that had
been a long-standing policy the church had followed in
South Africa. But Brazil was another country and another
age. Although those male members who were obviously
black were refused ordination to the priesthood until
1978, the burden of proof was upon the church and not
the members. It was quite obvious that some time before
the official revelation of 1978, some Brazilians were ordained to the priesthood who had Negro ancestry. When
the church announced in 1975 that a temple would be
built in Sao Paulo, the die was in effect cast. For under the
old policy neither males nor females with "Negro blood"
could have been allowed into the temple. To have a large
population of second class Saints in Brazil in the 1970s was
clearly unthinkable.

Seen from this perspective, then, Kimball, in a way, was
bowing to the inevitable reality of social change in much
the same way that Woodruff was bowing to the pressures
of the federal government in 1890. It has been predicted

that within a decade Mormons in the Third World will outnumber their North American coreligionists. What effect this will have on the future of Mormonism remains to be seen. Sao Paulo, of course, is more than 5,000 miles from Salt Lake City. For North American Mormons this means that the racial question is still largely theoretical. One important test of Mormon racial tolerance will come when and if large numbers of American blacks are converted to Mormonism, and when members in local congregations are asked to admit these black converts to fellowship.

Sociologist Thomas F. O'Dea has suggested that the manner in which modern Mormons handle the question of race is a "diagnostic test" of their ability to adapt to the modern world. When he wrote his essay, that question was still very much in the open. Quoting Mormon President David O. McKay's reply to one interviewer to the effect that blacks would not gain the priesthood "while you and I are here," O'Dea was not entirely optimistic about the outcome.[34] In the meantime, Kimball's revelation has been a sobering turn for the better. And if O'Dea is right that "race" is indeed a diagnostic test, then there is hope that modern Mormonism will also adapt to the social and political realities of a world that includes not only the Mormon "haves" of North America, but also the rapidly growing number of Mormon "have-nots" of the Third World. If the current trend continues, it is quite likely that should a generation from now a series such as this one include a volume on the Mormons, its title might appropriately be "Mormonism in a World Perspective."

Epilogue:
Mormonism and
the Shifting
Sands of Culture

History . . . spins against the way
it drives.

Herman Melville

In the preceding chapters I have attempted to delineate the changing contours of Mormonism against the shifting backdrop of American culture. For about three quarters of a century the two cultures, though sharing many beliefs and symbols, were operating on different assumptions and moving toward different and often conflicting goals. Yet when the Mormon kingdom, around the turn of the century, disintegrated as suddenly and completely as the Puritan oligarchy in Oliver Wendell Holmes's celebrated poem of the wonderful "One-Hoss-Shay," conflict eased virtually overnight. In view of the seeming bitterness of the struggle the rapid metamorphosis of the kingdom of God into an eminently respectable middle class religion holding up all the virtues of the Protestant ethic is nothing less than a modern miracle.[1] How is it possible that within a generation a people that had been the very epitome of an antibourgeois mentality became one of the mainstays of American middle class culture?

I

One not very original interpretation that I have already hinted at is that the Mormons were backing into the future—that one fine day, rather to their own surprise, they were marching in lockstep with America. Those

familiar with the Weber thesis will recognize my indebt-
edness. Max Weber's Protestants, of course, were
tradition-minded people who had little inkling that their
famous "ethic" was catapulting them headlong into the
modern world.[2] The same was true of the Mormons who,
while building their antimodern kingdom of God, developed those modern habits of initiative and self-discipline
that helped dig the grave of the kingdom and ushered in a
new breed of Mormon thoroughly at home in the corporate economy of American and its corollaries, political
pluralism and the bourgeois family.

This is not to suggest that the Saints were an oppor-
tunitistic and feckless lot. Like their Puritan forebears, the
Mormons were not consciously and deliberately pushing
toward these ends. In fact, the *perception* of the new realities came somewhat later than the substantive transformation of Mormon culture. The cumulative and irreversible change in the character of Mormon life proceeded
quite gradually and imperceptibly for nearly three generations while the Saints clung to an ideology that was increasingly out of step with social reality. Between 1890
and 1910 "the always-tenuous equilibrium between
ideology and action" was restored—to the degree that it is
possible to establish an equilibrium between what people
think and what they do. In the preceding generation Mormons had begun to act more and more like Americans
while continuing to think in the paradigm of the kingdom.
To borrow the language of Thomas S. Kuhn, Mormon
thought now underwent a paradigm shift: the Saints began
to *think* like Americans.[3] I find this model particularly
appealing because it helps explain how the change was
both evolutionary (social) and revolutionary (intellectual).

Given the power of ideology of the kingdom as articulated by Joseph and as implemented by Young, the relative
speed of the shift nevertheless needs explanation. A
number of historical analogies suggest that "outmoded"
ideologies are capable of hanging on for incredibly long
times in the face of social change so powerful and perva-

sive as to put into question the validity of the "equilibrium" theory. The Mormons, it has been suggested,
yielded only before superior force—were compelled to
change by an intolerant America at the threat of extinc-
tion.

Now it is true that the Saints put up a good show against
the antikingdom crusade. Many leaders and followers went
to jail. Others defied the law and went into hiding. Mormon folklore abounds with stories of the "raid." Yet to me
there is something unreal about the whole episode. Every
history of the conflict reproduces a picture of thirteen
Mormon bishops surrounding George Q. Cannon (a coun-
selor in the First Presidency), at the Utah Territorial Pen-
itentiary, all dressed in zebra-striped prison garb. They
look at us, somewhat smug, self-satisfied, well-fed. In
those days conflict was obviously conducted by civilized
rules. But then, perhaps, both sides were merely acting out
a play. Life in Utah, as they say, went on.[4]

Some hard-liners, it is true, were holding out to the bitter end. President John Taylor, who went into hiding and
died in exile, certainly was playing no charade. Yet, that
also was part of the script. The fact is, the Mormons could
not very well have given up the kingdom without some
outside pressure. From a psychological perspective the
raid may well have been a face-saving operation for the
Saints.

This leads us to the next question: why had the Saints
lost their will to fight? Why were they so anxious for the
establishment of social and intellectual equilibrium? If it
was not the antipolygamy crusade that precipitated the
most pivotal transformation in Mormon history, what was it
that prepared the way for change? In order to answer that
question, I wish to proceed by way of an analogy.

In his justly famous essay "Errand into the wilderness"
Perry Miller attempts to explain the changing meaning of
America for the Puritans of Massachusetts Bay. He begins
by contrasting their venture with that of the Pilgrims of
Plymouth, who "were reluctant voyagers; they had never

wanted to leave England, but had been obliged to depart because the authorities made life impossible for Separatists." Having escaped from a wicked world, they were anticipating its destruction from their hiding place. Miller sees in the Pilgrims "the prototype of the vast majority of subsequent immigrants—those Oscar Handlin calls 'The Uprooted': they came for better advantage and for less danger, and to give their posterity the opportunity for success."[5]

Not that the Puritans of Massachusetts Bay were impervious to such motives. But the driving force behind their journey was "a positive sense of mission." They had been sent by their God on an errand into the wilderness to establish a city on a hill, one that would eventually lead to the regeneration of old England. We all know, of course, what happened. Old England did indeed regenerate, quite beyond the fondest dreams of John Winthrop and his fellow Saints. At the beginning of the English Civil War the Puritans in America were waiting with bated breath for the word from home that their day had come, that their errand would be duly recognized. Instead, the English Puritans were almost like a new generation of Egyptians "who knew not Joseph." To them, the errand of New England had become irrelevant. The Saints of America had lost their audience, and with it the reason for their original errand, and thus their identity. Plunged into a profound spiritual crisis as reflected in their jeremiads, the Saints now were forced to focus inward upon themselves and discovered that they were left with a second errand, an errand into the wilderness on their own terms, an errand that led them to the establishment of an American identity.

Recognizing the limitations of analogies, I nevertheless find this one instructive for my purposes. Many of the early Mormons were New Englanders, and many of them the kind for whom that second Puritan errand into the wilderness had not borne much fruit. They were the kind of people whom the rising American empire was passing by, those who did not make it in the first wave to western

New York and the Ohio country, who were finally driven
out by economic hardship to find only meager opportunities when they arrived in western New York. Many of
them, perhaps even most of them fit Miller's Pilgrim
prototype. The Smith family certainly did.

Yet Joseph was one migrant who in time found himself
embarked on a different course. Imbued with a powerful
sense of mission, he embraced the kind of gospel in which
his God would send him precisely on the kind of errand on
which John Winthrop believed he had been sent. The
metaphor of the errand into the wilderness fits Mormonism extremely well. For Joseph Smith, separation
from the world was analogous not to the experience of
William Bradford but of Winthrop. Like Winthrop, the
Mormons were forever agonizing over the meaning of
their apparent separation from the world. Like Winthrop,
they continually insisted that they had not really left it.
Like Winthrop, Smith dreamed of building a city on a hill,
though it was up to Brigham Young to fulfill that dream.
On May 29, 1847, while camped at the banks of the Platte
River, and still facing nearly two months' journey to their
promised land, Young spoke of "the 'standard' or 'ensign'
that would be reared in Zion to govern the kingdom of
God, and the nations of the earth, for every nation would
bow the knee and every tongue confess that Jesus was the
Christ; and this will be the standard—*The Kingdom of God
and His Law.*' . . . there would be an invitation to all nations under heaven to come unto Zion."[6] Immediately
upon their arrival in the Great Salt Lake Valley, the
pioneers named a mountain northeast of the settlement
"Ensign Peak" as a symbol of their endeavor. From this
perspective, then, the proper metaphor for the Mormon
migration is not a quest for refuge, or manifest destiny, or a
quest for empire, but an errand into the wilderness—in
fact very much like Winthrop's errand.

Like their Puritan ancestors, the Latter-day Saints were
plunged into an identity crisis at the end of the first generation, and like that of their ancestors, it was triggered by a

civil war. With the opening of hostilities between the Union and the Confederacy in 1861, the Saints confidently expected that the two sides would exhaust each other until a desperate United States would call upon the Mormon kingdom to save the nation from the brink of destruction.[7] The American republic would be reorganized in more perfect form under the auspices of the kingdom of God, in preparation for the triumphant return of the Savior at his Second Coming. Under the direction of the Council of Fifty, a shadow government was organized initially to take over the state government of Utah. Its more ambitious purpose was to become the government of the United States, and ultimately the government of the "Empire of Christ." In an address to this body in 1863, Brigham Young remarked: "We should get all things ready, and when the time comes, we should let the water on the wheel and start the machine in motion."[8]

But the time never came. Under the leadership of the American republic the Lord's Truth was marching on to a victory in which the Saints had no part. They kept the secret meetings of their shadow government going for a number of years, but to no avail. To make things worse, unlike their Puritan ancestors, the Mormons were not free to resolve their identity crisis by redefining their errand into the wilderness on their own terms. A victorious United States, having vanquished the anti-Christ of the "slavocracy," now embarked on a crusade against the surviving twin relic of barbarism, polygamy. The desperate attempt of the Saints to hold on to the original meaning of their errand is underscored by the fact that in some of them this crusade helped revive their flagging sense of identity. Some of the more desperate among them, in fact, seem to have persuaded themselves that they had misread the signs of the times when they had identified the Civil War as the signal heralding the consummation of their errand into the wilderness. Now they fastened upon the antipolygamy crusade as the fulfilment of prophecy. Any day the Lord would come out of His hiding place to slay the wicked.[9] Such expectations, of course, were a gross distortion of the original meaning of the errand. In any case, the Lord did not see fit to go along with such a drastic change in the meaning of His will. Instead, the Saints were left to ponder the meaning of the victory of the United States over polygamy and the kingdom of God.

II

The reconstruction of their past, as it turned out, was one of the most effective ways of creating a new identity. In the first decade of the twentieth century ambitious young Mormons were beginning to enter graduate schools in California and the East. These students, while professing pride in their Mormon heritage, regarded polygamy and "kingdom" building as acute embarrassments and were anxious to be thought of as patriotic and loyal Americans. Several of them were historians, and a few of these attempted to show through a study of Mormon history that the congruences between Mormonism and American culture far outweighed the differences. One of the most successful was Andrew L. Neff, who as a young man in 1903 conceived of writing a "Mormon epic" that was strongly influenced by the ideas of Frederick Jackson Turner. In a letter to one of his former teachers at Brigham Young University, Neff wrote: "To my mind the greatest fact in American history is the spread of settlement from the Atlantic seaboard to the Pacific Ocean. And I hope to ascertain the relative part of Mormons in blazing the trail and opening up the continent to settlement."[10]

Neff was not the only Mormon historian who saw in the Turner thesis a ready-made vehicle for the Americanization of the Mormon past. In fact, several of these scholars probably would have invented Turner had he not existed, so readily did they apply the frontier hypothesis to Mormon history. If Joseph Smith harbored some ideas that were not in complete harmony with American democratic values, he was in good company. Such alien "germs," however, had never successfully sprouted in American soil. What did take root on the Mormon frontier was a hardy plant that was very much in the true tradition of American democracy. Whatever departures may have occurred from the main currents of American thought and behavior were mere "back eddies," explainable as temporary if necessary responses to a hostile environment. The State of Deseret, for example, had as its model the State of Franklin. In these histories the political kingdom of God was conspicuously absent. When polygamy made a quick and embarrassed appearance, it was for demographic reasons; once the population had become viable the practice quickly disappeared; in any case, only 2 or 3 percent adhered to the "principle," and then with great reluctance.[11]

These historians, by Americanizing the Mormon past, were thus creating an Orwellian version of their history, in keeping with the idea that sometimes change is best accomplished under pretense that it is not going on. The paradigm shift would be at its most effective if the Saints could somehow be persuaded that the new paradigm, in fact, was not new at all because the entire Mormon past could be explained from this Americanized perspective. Thus, by changing the perception of themselves, these Mormons were not only altering the past but were also attempting to control the future.

The history of Mormonism in the twentieth century reveals the extent of their success. As Ernst Troeltsch pointed out, the dream of a visible, earthly kingdom of God has been one of the chief criteria of many of the sects of Christianity.[12] He also observed that the history of most sects is characterized by a subtle but continuous process of transformation, resulting in their metamorphosis into a church. The metamorphosis of the Mormon kingdom provides a striking example of this thesis. From a cultural perspective modern Mormonism differs fundamentally from the Mormonism of the nineteenth century—though

little official change in theology has occurred. Yet the sectarian aspects of Mormonism have vanished into a forgotten past. Thus, while providing "cognitive distance"
through its theology, Mormonism has in fact become a
mainline religion (at least in Utah) that is socially acceptable nearly everywhere in the western world. Mainline
religions, as Martin Marty has observed, often produce as
well as embrace "very worldly looking cultures,"[13] perhaps
symbolized in Mormonism by the popularity of Donny and
Marie Osmond among the middle-brow Saints and Gentiles alike.

It is this alleged compromise with Babylon that has
aroused the ire of "sectarian" reformers, who want to return the church to its true historic self—to the days of
plural marriage, communitarianism, and the political kingdom, and to an identity that is separate from modern
American culture. Perhaps no phenomenon establishes a
former sect more firmly among mainline faiths than the
fact that it spawns sects dedicated to its reform. Needless
to say, Mormon leaders vigorously attempt to disassociate
themselves from such movements.[14]

Mormon history, then, is ironic. When Brigham Young
assumed the leadership of the main body of the church in
Nauvoo after the death of Joseph Smith, many Saints refused to follow him because they could not accept
polygamy and the political kingdom. Ultimately, in protest, they found themselves united in the Reorganized
Church with headquarters in Independence, Missouri,
whose leaders, officially, have categorically denied that
Joseph originated a temporal kingdom and its unorthodox
marriage practices. These Latter Day Saints (without a
hyphen and with a capital D) never shared the alienation
from American culture of their western cobelievers in the
prophetic mission of Joseph Smith and the divinity of the
Book of Mormon, and have always fit comfortably into the
religious pattern of American pluralism, resembling very
much one of the smaller, fundamentalist-oriented Protestant denominations. Today, having declared war on

polygamists and kingdom builders, Utah Mormons fit as readily into the American cultural mainstream as their schismatics from Independence.

III

This cultural mainstream, as I have already suggested, was not something static. To be more precise, the stream did not forever flow in one direction, but continued to change its course. In the first part of chapter 2 I suggested that antebellum American culture might be compared to millenarian movements in the Third World as described by Kenelm Burridge, who had identified three stages of development: of "old rules," "no rules," and "new rules." By way of analogy, I suggested that the age of federalist hegemony might be called the period of old rules, the age of "freedom's ferment" the period of no rules, and the age of the consolidation of corporate capitalism the period of new rules.

Paradoxically, it was the age of freedom's ferment, of no rules, that made Mormonism possible. At the same time, I believe I have made it clear that the Mormons were repelled by this age of "boundlessness," and were anxiously attempting to restore order in the world. Religious pluralism, the negative state, and laissez-faire capitalism, in the opinion of the Saints, were clearly inimical to such order. A society governed by individual promptings of the revivalist spirit and the invisible hand of the marketplace held out little assurance for the kind of social stability for which the Saints yearned. In response, the Mormons established their corporate kingdom of God, which clashed with the values of the age of boundlessness. Yet these values, at least as represented by the laissez-faire capitalism of the period, especially as exemplified in its marriage with evangelical religion (the kind of economic order arising in Rochester and Rockdale) lasted for only two generations. If historians such as John Higham, Robert Wiebe, and Arthur Chandler are correct, then the age of new rules was the age of consolidation (Higham), representing a search for order (Wiebe), which substituted for Adam Smith's invisible hand Alfred Chandler's visible hand of the managerial revolution.[15] This revolution ushered in the age of corporate capitalism, a world radically different from and in virtual opposition to the Jacksonian world of William Leggett and Theodore Sedgwick, which drew so much of its inspiration from Adam Smith.

The Mormons, as we have seen, found this new economic order quite congenial and participated with enthusiasm in the managerial revolution, many of them ending up as senior executives in the corporate world.[16] From the perspective that I have largely adopted in this book, this Mormon enthusiasm for corporate capitalism represented a dramatic transformation in Mormon values. Yet it should be recognized that there was an equally significant if less dramatic shift in American cultural values.

From a different perspective, the Mormon transformation represented a radical change in content, not in structure—a shift from one corporate endeavor to another. In his prosopographical study of the Mormon hierarchy, Michael Quinn has untangled a complex, interlocking corporate web of senior church officials whose pyramidal structure is supported by a strong network of family and kin.[17] In spite of a facade of amateurism, these men in fact represent a dedicated and hardworking group of professionals who are devoting their entire lives to the corporate well-being of the organization they are serving. Conservatism and loyalty are among the characteristics most valued by this group. According to Quinn, the main end the Mormon hierarchy has served from its inception has been control. In some of the preceding chapters I have illustrated the extraordinary success of the brethren in exerting control over politics, the economy, and social relations. While it is true that church leaders were forced to relinquish much of their influence in these areas, they were able to expand their power in other areas of corporate endeavor. Lawrence Foster has effectively summarized Quinn's main points: "Whenever one avenue of control became blocked or partially blocked, concerns for control became redirected into other areas of life. In effect, the more things changed, the more they stayed the same at the deepest level. Few would be likely to take strong exception to the conclusion that 'the extent of the Mormon hierarchy's control over its adhering society seems without parallel in U.S. history.' Even Puritan New England, perhaps, was not such an effectively closed system."[18]

Understandably, then, any challenge to this control was met with the most profound resistance. As I have indicated earlier, for example, the hierarchy resisted any change on the Negro doctrine as long as it was being pressured from outside. The same is true of such issues as feminism. When in 1979 Mormon feminist Sonia Johnson challenged the hierarchy's opposition to the Equal Rights Amendment, she was excommunicated. In the trial, church authorities would admit no evidence relating to Johnson's stand on ERA, insisting that she was on trial not for her social or political *opinions*—which she was entitled to hold—but for her active opposition to the leadership of the church and her implicit rejection of the principle of divine revelation.[19]

So far, Dr. Johnson is very much the exception among Mormons. Most of her former fellow Saints are the willing heirs of a tradition that has reconciled individual enterprise with corporate obedience, a tradition that modern corporations no doubt envy, plagued as they are with a continuing struggle of harmonizing individual goals with corporate goals.

IV

In this final chapter I have painted with bold strokes, outlining a number of hypotheses that would require the writing of another book for thorough testing. Thus a cynic might well ponder whether history is not merely a shifting

and variable set of circumstances in search of an author.
Wishing to conclude on a less cynical—though not necessarily more optimistic—note I recall Herman Melville's
homely but poetic observation that history "spins against
the way it drives," leading me to the sobering reflection
that not even the Saints are exempt from its ironies.

Notes

Preface

1. Moses Rischin, "The New Mormon History," *American West* 6 (March 1969): 49.

1   *The Birth of Mormonism*

1. Henry Stommel and Elizabeth Stommel, "The Year without a Summer," *Scientific American* 240 (June 1979): 176–86.
2. On the early history of the Smiths, see Lucy Mack Smith, *Biographical Sketches of Joseph Smith the Prophet and His Progenitors for Many Generations* (Liverpool, 1853), and Richard Anderson, *Joseph Smith's New England Heritage: Influences of Grandfathers Solomon Mack and Asael Smith* (Salt Lake City, 1979).
3. As reproduced in Fawn M. Brodie, *No Man Knows My History: The Life of Joseph Smith the Mormon Prophet* 2d ed. (New York, 1971), p. 427. For a recent discussion of the trial, see Marvin S. Hill, "Joseph Smith and the 1825 Trial: New Evidence and New Difficulties," *Brigham Young University Studies* 12 (Winter 1972): 223–33.
4. "Writings of Joseph Smith," in the Pearl of Great Price (Salt Lake City, 1967), 2:30–59.
5. Most scholars see this incident as a turning point in Smith's career—in fact the beginning of his prophetic role. Jan Shipps has called attention to the need for distinguishing between Joseph's numerous visions, which in his subjective experience

originated with God, and his continuing revelations, such as this
one, in which God responds to man's specific questions and
needs ("The Prophet Puzzle: Suggestions Leading toward a
More Comprehensive Interpretation of Joseph Smith," *Journal
of Mormon History* 1 [1974]: 3–20, esp. p. 18).

6. William J. Whalen, *The Latter-day Saints in the Modern
World* (Notre Dame, Indiana, 1964), p. 30.

7. Mormon apologists insist that Smith merely used these
terms to satisfy copyright requirements. Current editions carry
the line "Translated by Joseph Smith, Jun."

8. *An Address to All Believers in Christ* (Richmond, Mo., 1887),
p. 12.

9. John A. Clark, *Gleanings by the Way* (Philadelphia, 1842),
pp. 256–57; Joseph Smith 2:60.

10. Howard A. Davis, Donald R. Scales, and Wayne L. Cow-
drey, with Gretchen Passantino, *Who Really Wrote the Book of
Mormon?* (Santa Ana, Calif., 1977). For a refutation, see Lester
E. Bush, Jr., "The Spalding Theory Then and Now," *Dialogue* 10
(Autumn 1976): 3–20. For Brodie's refutation see *No Man
Knows My History,* pp. 442–56.

11. For an excellent discussion, see ibid., pp. 34–49.

12. Michael Coe, "Mormons and Archaeology: An Outside
View," *Dialogue* 8, no. 2 (1973): 40–48.

13. Dee F. Green and John L. Sorenson, "The Prospects for a
New World Archaeology," *Dialogue* 4 (Summer 1969): 71–94;
Hugh Nibley, *Lehi in the Desert* and *The World of the Jaredites*
(Salt Lake City, 1952); Richard L. Bushman, "The Book of
Mormon and the American Revolution," *Brigham Young Uni-
versity Studies* 17 (Autumn 1976): 3–20.

14. "The Centennial of Mormonism," *American Mercury* 19
(1930): 5.

15. Phyllis Greenacre, "The Impostor," *Psychoanalytic Quarterly* 27 (1958): 359–82; quoted in Brodie, *No Man Knows My
History,* pp. 418–19.

16. *Millennial Harbinger* 2 (February 1831): 85.

17. Brodie, *No Man Knows My History,* p. 69.

18. *Biographical Sketches,* p. 87.

19. *The Mormons* (Chicago, 1957), p. 24.

20. Thus William Lawrence Foster, "Between Two Worlds:
The Origins of Shaker Celibacy, Oneida Community Complex
Marriage, and Mormon Polygamy" (Ph.D. diss., University of
Chicago, 1976), p. 198. Conversation with Jan Shipps.

21. I. Woodbridge Riley, *The Founder of Mormonism: A Psychological Study of Joseph Smith, Jr.* (New York, 1902).

22. Doctrine and Covenants, sec. 9.

23. *The Origin of Consciousness in the Breakdown of the Bicameral Mind* (Toronto, 1978), pp. 361–78, and quotations on p. 44. See also Albert Rothenberg, *The Emerging Goddess: The Creative Process in Art, Science, and Other Fields* (Chicago, 1979).

24. In a stimulating essay, anthropologist Luther P. Gerlach asked, "What, we can wonder, would happen if our scholarly paradigm was based on or at least admitted the existence of God, spirit forces, or the like?" ("Pentecostalism: Revolution or Counter-Revolution?" in Irving I. Zaretsky and Mark P. Leone, eds., *Religious Movements in Contemporary America* [Princeton, N.J., 1974], p. 671).

25. Jaynes, *The Origin of Consciousness,* pp. 318–19.

26. Mario S. De Pillis, "The Quest for Religious Authority and the Rise of Mormonism," *Dialogue* 1 (Fall 1966): 68–88; Jaynes, *The Origin of Consciousness,* p. 320.

27. Oliver Cowdery, *Defense in a Rehearsal of My Grounds for Separating Myself from the Latter Day Saints* (Norton, Ohio, 1839); Brodie, *No Man Knows My History,* p. 74.

28. Joseph Smith 2:5–20.

29. *The Varieties of Religious Experience* (New York, 1925), p. 445; also: "the evidence for God lies primarily in inner, personal experiences."

30. For various accounts of the First Vision, see Dean C. Jesse, "The Early Accounts of Joseph Smith's First Vision," *Brigham Young University Studies* 9 (Spring 1969): 275–96; James B. Allen, "Eight Contemporary Accounts of Joseph Smith's First Vision—What Do We Learn from Them," *Improvement Era* 83 (April 1970): 4–13. See also Richard Lloyd Anderson, "Circumstantial Confirmation of the First Vision through Reminiscences," *Brigham Young University Studies* 9 (Spring 1969): 373–404. Fawn Brodie rejects this evidence in the second edition of *No Man Knows My History,* pp. 405–25. Wesley P. Walters challenges the authenticity of the "Palmyra Revival" in "New Light on Mormon Origins from the Palmyra Revival," *Dialogue* 4 (Spring 1969): 60–81; his interpretation is challenged by Richard L. Bushman, "The First Vision Story Revived," ibid., pp. 82–93. The Mormon position is summarized in Milton V. Backman, Jr., *Joseph Smith's First Vision* (Salt Lake City, 1979).

31. Joseph Smith 2:22.

32. Ibid., 2:24; Jaynes, *The Origin of Consciousness,* p. 371.

33. "Joseph Smith: the Verdict of Depth Psychology," *Journal of Mormon History* 3 (1976): 73–83.

34. Erik H. Erikson, *Childhood and Society* (New York, 1950); *Identity and the Life Cycle* (New York, 1959); I am quoting Brink, "Joseph Smith," p. 83.

35. Joseph F. Kett, "Growing Up in Rural New England, 1800–1840," in Tamara K. Hareven, ed., *Anonymous Americans: Explorations in Nineteenth-Century Social History* (Englewood Cliffs, N.J., 1971), pp. 1–16; quotations from pp. 5, 12.

36. For a stimulating interpretation suggesting that in order to understand Smith we must understand *how* he performed his prophetic role, see Shipps, "The Prophet Puzzle."

37. The best study of this relationship is Marvin S. Hill, "The Role of Christian Primitivism in the Origin and Development of the Mormon Kingdom, 1830–1844" (Ph.D. diss., University of Chicago, 1968); see also idem, "The Shaping of the Mormon Mind in New England and New York," *Brigham Young University Studies* 9 (Spring 1969): 351–72.

38. Joseph Smith, *History of the Church of Jesus Christ of Latter-day Saints,* ed. B. H. Roberts (6 vols.; Salt Lake City, 1948), 4:461.

39. Jay M. Todd, *The Saga of the Book of Abraham* (Salt Lake City, 1969); idem, "The Joseph Smith Egyptian Papyri: Translations and Interpretations," *Dialogue* 3 (Summer 1968): 67–105; Hugh Nibley, *The Message of the Joseph Smith Papyri* (Salt Lake City, 1975).

40. Shipps, "The Prophet Puzzle," p. 18.

41. Doctrine and Covenants, secs. 8; 9; 28:2, 11–12. For an excellent discussion of the "containment of charisma," see O'Dea, *The Mormons,* pp. 156–160.

42. Cowdery, *Defense in a Rehearsal of My Grounds for Separating Myself from the Latter-day Saints;* Whitmer, *Address to All Believers in Christ,* p. 31; reported in Brodie, p. 81.

43. Smith, *History of the Church,* 2:79.

44. Reported in Brodie, *No Man Knows My History,* pp. 98–99.

45. *Journal of Discourses* (26 vols.; Liverpool, 1854–86), 3:91; 8:38.

46. Mormon scientific beliefs derive from the cultural matrix discussed by Keith Thomas, *Religion and the Decline of Magic:*

Studies in Popular Beliefs in Sixteenth- and Seventeenth-Century England (New York, 1971). For the eighteenth-century American background see Herbert Leventhal, *In the Shadow of the Englightenment* (New York, 1976). R. Laurence Moore has established some significant parallels between Spiritualism and Mormonism. Both "appealed not to the inward illumination of mystic experience but to the observable and verifiable objects of empirical science." Both shared "a religious imagination that was graphic and literal. The plain people of Western New York responded to visual, exactly measured detail; and whether the subject was Hell, the Second Coming, the New Jerusalem, or the spirit world, really did not matter all that much to them; Mormons and spiritualists alike had a passion for collecting witnesses to certify the facts of their faith. Both in their own way strove after a religion whose evidences, however strange they seemed at first telling, fell entirely within the domain of advancing science" (*In Search of White Crows: Spiritualism, Parapsychology, and American Culture* [New York, 1977], pp. 7, 50).

47. Moroni 10:4.

48. Jaynes expresses the restorationist theme thus: the religious motivation of the Hebrews "was the nostalgic anguish for the lost bicamerality of *a subjectively conscious people.* This is what religion is" (*Origin of Consciousness,* p. 297 [my italics]).

2   *Mormonism and American Culture*

1. Unfortunately, we lack for nineteenth-century America the kind of magisterial interpretive synthesis that James A. Henretta provided for the eighteenth century in *The Evolution of American Society, 1700–1815* (Lexington, Mass., 1973). A useful introduction is Douglas T. Miller, *The Birth of Modern America, 1820–1850* (Indianapolis, 1970). On economic developments, see Douglass C. North, *The Economic Growth of the United States, 1790–1860* (New York, 1966). George Rogers Taylor, *The Transportation Revolution, 1815–1860* (New York, 1951) has become a classic. For the shift in the locus of authority in colonial society, see especially Richard Bushman, *From Puritan to Yankee: Character and the Social Order in Connecticut, 1690–1765* (Cambridge, Mass., 1967). See also Richard D. Brown, "Modernization and the Modern Personality in Early America,

1600–1865: A Sketch of a Synthesis," *Journal of Interdisciplinary History* 2 (Winter 1972): 201–28. The bipolar model of "modern-traditional" is, of course, highly controversial. As will become obvious from my discussion, I am not ascribing substantive or progressive meanings to the terms and merely wish to use them as a kind of shorthand for describing social and intellectual change.

2. William G. McLoughlin, "Revivalism," in Edwin Scott Gaustad, ed., *The Rise of Adventism* (New York, 1974), pp. 129–30, 134.

3. New York, 1969.

4. Alice Felt Tyler, *Freedom's Ferment: Phases of American Social History from the Colonial Period to the Outbreak of the Civil War* (Minneapolis, 1944); John Higham, *From Boundlessness to Consolidation* (Ann Arbor, 1969).

5. Foster, "Between Two Worlds," p. 265.

6. McLoughlin has expanded his essay in *The Rise of Adventism* into a book in this series: *Revivals, Awakenings and Reform: An Essay on Religion and Social Change in America, 1607–1977* (Chicago, 1978); Perry Miller, "The Evangelical Basis," in *The Life of the Mind in America from the Revolution to the Civil War* (New York, 1965), pp. 3–95.

7. *A Shopkeeper's Millennium: Society and Revivals in Rochester, New York, 1815–1837* (New York, 1978).

8. *Rockdale: The Growth of an American Village in the Early Industrial Revolution* (New York, 1978), especially parts 3 and 4, pp. 243–474.

9. Alexis de Tocqueville, *Democracy in America,* trans. Henry Reeve, ed. Phillips Bradley (2 vols.; New York, 1945), 1:314.

10. Sidney E. Mead, "Denominationalism: The Shape of Protestantism in America," in *The Lively Experiment: The Shaping of Christianity in America* (New York, 1963), pp. 103–33.

11. Ibid., p. 112.

12. William G. McLoughlin, "Introduction," to Charles Grandison Finney, *Lectures on Revivals of Religion* (Cambridge, Mass., 1960), pp. vii–lii; McLoughlin, *Modern Revivalism: Charles Grandison Finney to Billy Graham* (New York, 1959), p. 11.

13. Mead, in *The Lively Experiment,* p. 125.

14. Martin E. Marty, *A Nation of Behavers* (Chicago, 1976).

15. *The American Adam: Innocence, Tragedy, and Tradition in the Nineteenth Century* (Chicago, 1955); also David W. Noble, *The Eternal Adam and the New World Garden* (New York, 1968).

16. McLoughlin, *Modern Revivalism,* p. 103.

17. Ibid., p. 13.

18. *Righteous Empire: The Protestant Experience in America* (New York, 1970), pp. 68–69.

19. *Democracy in America,* 2:24.

20. *The Works of John Adams,* ed. Charles Francis Adams (Boston, 1856), 1:66; *The Writings of Thomas Jefferson,* ed. H. A. Washington (New York, 1859), 4:440–41.

21. Ether 2:21.

22. Marshall Davidson, "Whither the Course of Empire?" *American Heritage* 8 (October 1957): 52–61 contains the best available illustrations. My quotations are from the pictorial essay "nature" in Edwin C. Rozwenc and Thoms Bender, *The Making of American Society,* 2d ed. (2 vols.; New York, 1978), insert between pp. 292–93. On cataclysmic thought in antebellum America see Curtis Dahl, "The American School of Catastrophe," *American Quarterly* 11 (Fall 1959): 380–90; and Miller, *The Birth of Modern America,* pp. 42–66.

23. Quoted in Ernest Lee Tuveson, *Redeemer Nation: The Idea of America's Millennial Role* (Chicago, 1968), pp. 126–27.

24. 2 Nephi 10:11; 3 Nephi 21:4; Doctrine and Covenants, 101:80.

25. *Key to the Science of Theology* (Liverpool, 1855) pp. 79–81.

26. Peter Meinhold, "Die Anfaenge des amerikanischen Geschichtsbewusstseins," *Saeculum* 5 (1954): 65–86; Doctrine and Covenants, sec. 116.

27. Ithaca, N.Y., 1959.

28. Henry David Thoreau, *Maine Woods, The Writings of Henry David Thoreau,* Riverside edition (11 vols.; Boston, 1893), 3:85–86, 94–95. Thoreau saw this experience also as socially disruptive and after his return to society avoided nature in the raw. See especially Leo Stoller, *After Walden: Thoreau and Economic Man* (Palo Alto, Calif., 1959); excellent is Charles L. Sanford, "National Self-Consciousness and the Concept of the Sublime," in *The Quest for Paradise* (Urbana, Ill., 1961), pp. 135–54.

29. Doctrine and Covenants, 61:3–6, 14–24; canals, however were regarded as safe; on the levelling of mountains, ibid., 49:23.

30. Smith, *History of the Church,* 1:189, 357; Doctrine and Covenants, 57:2–3.

31. Doctrine and Covenants, 131:7–8.

32. *The Latter-day Saints' Millennial Star* 6 (1854): 19.

33. Smith articulated these ideas in the famous funeral sermon for King Follett, April 7, 1844 (*History of the Church,* 6:302–17).

34. Ibid. For exegeses see James E. Talmage, *Jesus the Christ* (Salt Lake City, 1922); Sterling M. McMurrin, *The Theological Foundations of the Mormon Religion* (Salt Lake City, 1965).

35. *The Patterns of Our Religions Faiths* (Salt Lake City, 1954).

36. 2 Nephi 2:11–27.

37. Abraham 3:26.

38. Fourth Article of Faith.

39. Doctrine and Covenants, sec. 137.

40. Ibid., 130:20.

41. Ibid., sec. 76.

42. Ibid., secs. 31–38.

43. Ibid., secs. 111–12.

44. Edward T. Jones, "The Theology of Thomas Dick and Its Possible Relationship to That of Joseph Smith" (M.A. thesis, Brigham Young University, 1969).

45. Abraham 3:1–23.

46. Doctrine and Covenants, 132:49, 63.

47. Ibid., 132:16–20.

48. "Religions on the Christian Perimeter," in *The Shaping of American Religion,* ed. James Ward Smith and A. Leland Jamison (4 vols.; Princeton, 1961), 1:214. Sterling McMurrin summed up Mormon theology as follows: "Mormon theology is a modern Pelagianism in a Puritan religion. Mormonism is a Judaic-like community religion grounded in the Puritan moral doctrine that the vocation of man is to create the kingdom of God. Its fundamentalism is rooted in the biblical literalism native to American religion. Its heresy is the denial of the dogma of original sin, a heresy that exhibits both the disintegration of modern Protestantism and the impact of nineteenth-century liberalism on the character of American sectarianism" ("Foreword," *The Theological Foundations of the Mormon Religion*).

3   *The Mormon Rationalization*
                                of Death

1. 1 Cor. 15:22.

2. David E. Stannard, "Death and Dying in Puritan New England," *American Historical Review* 78 (December 1973): 1305–30.

3. For this transformation, see Bushman, *From Puritan to Yankee;* and Rowland Berthoff, *An Unsettled People: Social Order and Disorder in American History* (New York, 1971), pp. 3–124. On nineteenth-century attitudes, see especially Lewis O. Saum, "Death in the Popular Mind of Pre–Civil War America," *American Quarterly* 26 (December 1974): 489.

4. Richard H. Shryock, *Medicine and Society in America, 1660–1860* (New York, 1960); Charles E. Rosenberg, *The Cholera Years: The United States in 1832, 1849, and 1866* (Chicago, 1962); Saum, "Death in the Popular Mind," p. 484.

5. David E. Stannard, "Death and the Puritan Child," *American Quarterly* 26 (December 1974): 456–76; Ann Douglas, "Heaven Our Home: Consolation Literature in the Northern United States, 1830–1880," ibid., pp. 496–515.

6. George H. Daniels, *Science in Jacksonian America* (New York, 1971); Shryock, *Medicine and Society in America,* p. 149: "Thus did Jacksonian Democrats proclaim their inalienable rights to life, liberty, and quackery."

7. John William Ward, "Jacksonian Democratic Thought: 'A Natural Charter of Privilege,'" in *The Development of an American Culture,* ed. Stanley Coben and Lorman Ratner (Englewood Cliffs, N.J., 1970), pp. 44–63.

8. *Unquiet Eagle: Memory and Desire in the Idea of American Freedom, 1815–1860* (Ithaca, N.Y., 1967), pp. 40–41.

9. Foster's "Between Two Worlds" is a comparative study of Shaker, Oneida, and Mormon attitudes toward sexuality and the family. Ernest R. Sandeen, "John Humphrey Noyes as the New Adam," *Church History* 40 (1971): 82–90.

10. 3 Nephi 28:8; patriarchal blessings, courtesy of the Historical Department of the Church of Jesus Christ of Latter-day Saints, Salt Lake City, Utah. Because of the sacred nature of these blessings, they are not accessible to the general public and are not for publication.

11. Diary of Millen Atwood, p. 1, and letter from Elizabeth Haven to Elizabeth H. Bullard, September 27, 1839 (typescripts of originals, Historical Department of the Church of Jesus Christ of Latter-day Saints).

12. In a revelation of February 9, 1831, the prophet provided one explanation for the mystery of death: "those that die in me shall not taste of death, for it shall be sweet unto them; And they that die not in me, wo unto them, for their death is bitter" (Doctrine and Covenants, 42:46–47). On Zion's Camp see

Doctrine and Covenants, sec. 105; Smith, *History of the Church,* 2:120.

13. Biography and Journal, p. 46 (typescript of original, Historical Department of the Church of Jesus Christ of Latter-day Saints).

14. Ibid., May 10, 1849, p. 269.

15. Sigmund Freud, "Thoughts for the Times on War and Death," in *Standard Edition of the Complete Psychological Works of Sigmund Freud,* ed. James Strachey (London, 1957), 14:289.

16. Appleby, Biography and Journal, May 10, 1849, p. 269; Psalm 91:7.

17. Doctrine and Covenants, 89:21; *Millennial Star* 11:373.

18. Quoted in Smith, *History of the Church,* 1:282.

19. Ibid., pp. 118–19.

20. *Manuscript History of Brigham Young, 1801–1844,* ed. Elden Jay Watson (Salt Lake City, 1968), p. 57.

21. Smith, *History of the Church,* 4:11.

22. Haven to Bullard, September 27, 1839.

23. Kenneth W. Godfrey, "Some Thoughts Regarding an Unwritten History of Nauvoo," *Brigham Young University Studies* 15 (Summer 1975): 417–24; William J. Reals and Sidney Merlis, "Mormon Winter Quarters: A Medical Note," *Bulletin of the Creighton University of School of Medicine* 4 (November 1947): 46–49. Reals and Merlis estimate the number of deaths along the trail at about six thousand.

24. Haven to Bullard, September 27, 1839.

25. *Manuscript History of Brigham Young,* p. 3.

26. Haven to Bullard, September 27, 1839.

27. Atwood Diary, p. 1; Appleby, "Biography and Journal," pp. 7–8.

28. Doctrine and Covenants 19:4–12.

29. Second Article of Faith.

30. "The Pornography of Death," *Encounter* 5 (October 1955): 50–51.

31. *The Complete Works of Ralph Waldo Emerson* (Boston, 1883), 1:87; 6:43, 100, 306; 10:130, 149.

32. 2Nephi 2:11.

33. Doctrine and Covenants, sec. 132.

34. *Millenial Star* 5:189.

35. N. B. Lundwall, ed., *The Vision, or, The Degrees of Glory* (Independence, Mo., 1945).

36. On the "crisis of the family" in antebellum American society, see Kirk Jeffrey, "The Family as Utopian Retreat from the City: The Nineteenth-Century Contribution," *Soundings: An Interdisciplinary Journal* 55 (Spring 1972): 21–41; Ronald G. Walters, "The Family and Antebellum Reform: An Intepretation," *Societas* 3 (1973): 221–32; Foster, "Between Two Worlds." Moroni 8:9.

37. Saum, "Death in the Popular Mind," p. 486.

38. "Death and the Puritan Child, pp. 470–71; Michael Paul Rogin (*Fathers and Children: Andrew Jackson and the Subjugation of the American Indian* [New York, 1975]) makes references to such anxieties (see pp. 8–11, 44–46, 114–17, 285–86).

39. On nineteenth-century American fertility and mortality, see J. Potter, "The Growth of Population in America, 1700–1860," *Population History; Essays in Historical Demography,* ed. D. V. Glass and D. E. C. Eversley (London, 1965), pp. 633–88; Wilson Grabill, Clyde V. Kiser, and Pascal K. Whelpton, "Long View," *The American Family in Social Historical Perspective,* ed. Michael Gordon (New York, 1973), pp. 374–96; Colin Forster and G. S. L. Tucker, *Economic Opportunity and White American Fertility Ratios, 1880–1860* (New Haven and London, 1972).

40. Doctrine and Covenants, 128:17–18.

41. *Sacred Hymns and Spiritual Songs for the Church of Jesus Christ of Latter-day Saints* (Salt Lake City, 1890).

42. *Writings from the Western Standard,* ed. George Q. Cannon (Liverpool, 1864), June 27, 1844.

43. B. H. Roberts, *A Comprehensive History of the Church of Jesus Christ of Latter-day Saints* (6 vols.; Salt Lake City, 1930), 2:418. I am indebted to Dr. David Musto for pointing out to me that from a psychological perspective, this is a classical case of response to death, consistent with observations recorded in psychological literature. About six weeks after the death of an admired or beloved person, survivors will sometimes unconsciously and temporarily mimic prominent characteristics of the deceased. Sometimes survivors will unexpectedly encounter the deceased, perhaps on a bus, or walking down the street, or in a crowd. See Sigmund Freud, "Mourning and Melancholia," *Complete Psychological Works,* 14:239–58.

44. 1 Peter 3:18–20; Joseph F. Smith, "Vision of the Redemption of the Dead," Pearl of Great Price.

45. Biography and Journal, p. 21; Alma 40:12.

46. Quoted in Mary Ann Myers, "Gates Ajar," in David E. Stannard, ed., *Death in America* (Philadelphia, 1975), p. 120.

47. Abraham 3:4, 9. On the basis of this and other Mormon scriptures, some Mormon scientists, among them a prominent metallurgist at the University of Utah, have questioned aspects of Einstein's theories of relativity. Allen E. Bergin, a psychologist at Brigham Young University, remarked: "There is just enough physics in the scriptures to show me that there is something basically wrong with his [Einstein's] notion of the velocity of light as a limiting factor in the universe. If the gospel is true, I think Einstein is wrong about that" ("Bringing the Restoration to the Academic World: Clinical Psychology as a Test Case," *Brigham Young University Studies* 19 [Summer 1979]: 471).

48. *On the Ragged Edge: The Life and Times of Dudley Leavitt* (Salt Lake City, 1973), p. 104.

4   *The Kingdom of God: Its*
                                     Economy and Politics

1. For an excellent survey of the literature, see David E. Smith, "Millenarian Scholarship in America," *American Quarterly* 17 (1965): 535–49. This should be supplemented especially by Tuveson, *Redeemer Nation.*

2. For an excellent summary of the Millerites, see David T. Arthur, "Millerism," in Gaustad, *The Rise of Adventism,* pp. 154–72.

3. *Revivalism in America: Its Origin, Growth and Decline* (New York, 1944), p. 41.

4. Douglas T. Miller, *Jacksonian Aristocracy: Class and Democracy in New York, 1830–1860* (New York, 1967); Edward Pessen, *Jacksonian America: Society, Personality, and Politics* (Homewood, Ill. 1969).

5. Stuart Bruchey, *The Roots of American Economic Growth, 1670–1861* (New York, 1968); Douglass C. North, *The Economic Growth of the United States, 1790–1860* (Englewood Cliffs, N.J., 1961).

6. The Ten Tribes were not the Indians, but would appear out of the "north"; Doctrine and Covenants, 110:11.

7. Doctrine and Covenants, 63:53; 130: 14–17; Smith, *History of the Church,* 5:336–37; 6:254; Richard Lloyd Anderson,

"Joseph Smith and the Millenarian Timetable," *Brigham Young University Studies* 3 (1961): 61.

8. T. B. H. Stenhouse, *The Rocky Mountain Saints* (New York, 1874), p. 489.

9. "To Transform History: Early Mormon Culture and the Concept of Space and Time," *Church History* 40 (1971): 108–17.

10. On the social origins of Mormonism, see especially Mario S. De Pillis, "The Social Sources of Mormonism," *Church History* 37 (March 1968): 50–79; and Laurence M. Yorgason, "Some Demographic Aspects of One Hundred Early Mormon Converts, 1830–1837" (M.A. thesis, Brigham Young University, 1974). Doctrine and Covenants, 1:2–4.

11. Michael Walzer, *The Revolution of the Saints* (New York, 1965), p. 319.

12. *Andrew Jackson: Symbol for an Age* (New York 1955), p. 10.

13. Doctrine and Covenants, 1:38.

14. Berthoff, *An Unsettled People*, pp. 270–74.

15. Doctrine and Covenants, 38:32.

16. James B. Allen and Glen M. Leonard, *The Story of the Latter-Day Saints* (Salt Lake City, 1976), p. 75; Leonard J. Arrington, "Early Mormon Communitarianism: The Law of Consecration and Stewardship," *Western Humanities Review* 7 (Autumn 1953): 341–69.

17. Review of *Building the City of God, Brigham Young University Studies* 17 (Winter 1977): 246.

18. Leonard J. Arrington, Feramorz Y. Fox, and Dean L. May, *Building the City of God: Community and Cooperation among the Mormons* (Salt Lake City, 1976) is the best interpretive survey of Mormon economic thought and practice. For the nineteenth century, however, it must be supplemented by Leonard J. Arrington's magisterial *Great Basin Kingdom: An Economic History of the Latter-day Saints 1830–1900* (Cambridge, Mass., 1958); see also Lowry Nelson, *The Mormon Village: A Pattern and Technique of Land Settlement* (Salt Lake City, 1952). On the breakdown of the traditional economic and social order I am quoting from Henretta, *The Evolution of American Society,* pp. 21–23.

19. Allen and Leonard, *The Story of the Latter-day Saints,* p. 362.

20. See especially Gordon Eric Wagner's stimulating "Consecration and Stewardship: A Socially Efficient System of Justice" (Ph.D. thesis, Cornell University, 1977); and Keith D.

Wilde, "An Interpretation of the Nature and Significance of Mormon Political-Economic Thought" (paper, Conference on Economics and the Mormon Culture, Brigham Young University, 1975).

21. *To Her Gracious Majesty, Queen Victoria* (Manchester, England, 1841), p. 5.

22. *Millennial Star* 23 (1862): 422.

23. Smith, *History of the Church,* 6:364.

24. Ibid., pp. 288–89.

25. Doctrine and Covenants, 28:9, 29:7–8, 57:3–5; B. H. Roberts, *A Comprehensive History of the Church of Jesus Christ of Latter-day Saints* (6 vols.; Salt Lake City, 1930), 1:250–56.

26. Doctrine and Covenants, 58:44.

27. Quoted in Ray B. West, *Kingdom of the Saints: The Story of Brigham Young and the Mormons* (New York, 1957), p. 39.

28. Doctrine and Covenants, 88:119.

29. Ibid., sec. 110.

30. R. Kent Fielding, "The Mormon Economy in Kirtland, Ohio," *Utah Historical Quarterly* 27 (October 1959): 831–56; Marvin S. Hill, C. Keith Rooker, and Larry T. Wimmer, "The Kirtland Economy Revisited: A Market Critique of Sectarian Economics," *Brigham Young University Studies* 17 (Summer 1977): 387–475; for the American and international economic conditions at the time, see Peter Temin, *The Jacksonian Economy* (New York, 1969).

31. Roberts, *Comprehensive History,* 1:314–36.

32. Doctrine and Covenants, 103:15–17.

33. Klaus J. Hansen, *Quest for Empire: The Political Kingdom of God and the Council of Fifty in Mormon History* (East Lansing, Mich., 1967), pp. 48–49.

34. U.S., Congress, Senate, *Testimony in Trial of Joseph Smith, Jr., for High Treason,* 26th Cong., 2d Sess., 1841, Senate Doc. 189, p. 23.

35. Roberts, *Comprehensive History,* 1:432–34.

36. Hansen, *Quest for Empire,* pp. 147–48.

37. The best study of Nauvoo is Robert Bruce Flanders, *Nauvoo: Kingdom on the Mississippi* (Urbana, Ill, 1965).

38. Quoted in William A. Mulder and A. Russell Mortensen, *Among the Mormons* (New York, 1958), p. 131.

39. Smith, *History of the Church,* 5:389.

40. Mulder and Mortensen, *Among the Mormons,* p. 142.

41. *Correspondence of Bishop George Miller with the Northern*

American Civilization, Columbia University, September 19, 1974).

9. "Sexuality, Class and Role," p. 143.

10. Gusfield, *Symbolic Crusade,* pp. 46–57.

11. Doctrine and Covenants, sec. 89; Leonard J. Arrington, "An Economic Interpretation of the 'Word of Wisdom,'" *Brigham Young University Studies* 1 (Winter 1959): 40–41. Significantly, references to violations of the Word of Wisdom were eliminated from the edition of the *History of the Church* published in 1902.

12. "Sexuality, Class and Role," p. 145; H. Tristram Engelhardt, Jr., "The Disease of Masturbation: Values and the Concept of Disease," *Bulletin of the History of Medicine* 48 (Summer 1974): 234–48.

13. Quoted in Davis Bitton, "B. H. Roberts as Historian," *Dialogue* 3 (Winter 1968): 31–32.

14. *Deseret News Extra* (September 14, 1852). Added to the Doctrine and Covenants as sec. 132 in 1876.

15. Ezra Booth, in letter to *Ohio Star,* 8 December 1831; quoted in Jerald Tanner and Sandra Tanner, *Mormonism Like Watergate?* (Salt Lake City, 1974), p. 9.

16. See especially Foster, "Between Two Worlds"; also Daniel W. Bachman, "A Study of the Mormon Practice of Plural Marriage before the Death of Joseph Smith" (M.A. thesis, Indiana-Purdue University, 1975); a useful survey of the scholarly literature is Davis Bitton, "Mormon Polygamy: A Review Article," *Journal of Mormon History* 4 (1977): 101–8.

17. Quoted in William Alexander Linn, *The Story of the Mormons* (New York, 1902), p. 280; *Biography of Lorenzo Snow* (Salt Lake City, 1884), p. 70.

18. Jacob 2:30.

19. *No Man Knows My History,* p. 297.

20. *My Mother/My Self* (New York, 1977), pp. 436–42.

21. Quoted in Ronald G. Walters, "The Erotic South," *American Quarterly* 25 (May 1973): 196.

22. Valeen Tippetts Avery and Linda King Newell, "Lewis C. Bidamon, Stepchild of Mormondom," *Brigham Young University Studies* 19 (Spring 1979): 375–88.

23. "The Future of Political Science in America," quoted in "George Bernard Shaw Speaks," *Improvement Era* 40 (July 1937): 413.

24. "Between Two Worlds," pp. 189–403.

25. "Self Reliance," in *Essays, First Series, The Works of Ralph Waldo Emerson*, 14 vols. (Boston, 1883), 2:61.

26. "Between Two Worlds," p. 226.

27. Doctrine and Covenants, 132:7.

28. For example William E. Bridges, "Family Patterns and Social Values in America, 1825–1875," *American Quarterly* 17 (Spring 1965): 3–11; Kirk Jeffrey, Jr., "The Family as Utopian Retreat from the City: The Nineteenth-Century Contribution," *Soundings* 55 (1972): 21–41; Ronald G. Walters, "The Family and Ante-bellum Reform: An Interpretation," *Societas* 3 (1973): 221–32.

29. Quoted in Lawrence Foster, "A Little-known Defense of Polygamy from the Mormon Press in 1842," *Dialogue* 9 (Winter 1974): 26; I am assuming here that a pamphlet, titled *The Peace Maker*, from which Foster quotes, represents the ideas of Joseph Smith.

30. Quoted in Foster, "Between Two Worlds," p. 258.

31. *Democracy in America*, 2:105–6.

32. Doctrine and Covenants, 128:18.

33. Joseph Lee Robinson, Journal, p. 22 (Historical Department of the Church of Jesus Christ of Latter-day Saints).

34. Leonard Arrington has suggested that "the conditions under which Brigham Young and the Twelve Apostles assumed leadership assured a hierarchical structure designed along authoritarian lines. The theophanous works of Joseph Smith were canonized into doctrine, and the doctrine and organizational structure of the church became more dogmatic and inflexible" ("The Intellectual Tradition of the Latter-day Saints," *Dialogue* 4 [Spring 1969]: 18). See also Ephraim E. Eriksen, *Psychological and Ethical Aspects of Mormon Group Life* (Chicago, 1922), pp. 35–36.

35. *Journal of Discourses* 5 (1858): 91; James Edward Hulett, "The Sociological and Social Psychological Aspects of the Mormon Polygamous Family" (Ph.D. diss., University of Wisconson, 1939), p. 37.

36. *City of the Saints* (London, 1861), p. 520.

37. *Journal of Discourses* 5:29; *Millennial Star* 5:193.

38. *Millennial Star* 17:726; see also *Journal of Discourses* 2:83. Hundreds of wives were "sealed" to Smith posthumously, among them the Empress Josephine. See Thomas Milton Tin-

ney, "The Royal Family of the Prophet Joseph Smith, Jr."
(typescript; Utah State Historical Society, Salt Lake City, 1973).

39. *Journal of Discourses* 3:356.

40. *Journal of Discourses* 12:186; see also McMurrin, *Theological Foundations,* pp. 3–5, 49–57; Doctrine and Covenants, 93:29;
Smith, *History of the Church,* 6:310–12. For a dissenting Mormon view see Lowell Bennion, "This-Worldly and Other-Worldly Sex: A Response," *Dialogue* 2:106–8: "We do not know
that it [sex] is eternal. As we know sex it is physical and biological as well as social and spiritual. Who can speak of the resurrected state in physiological terms with any knowledge or
meaning?"

41. *Journal of Discourses* 5:254; 6:101; Talmage, *Jesus the Christ,* p. 30.

42. *Journal of Discourses* 2:210; 8:115, 211; 13:207. For a
modern Protestant argument that Christ was married, see William Phipps, *Was Jesus Married?* (New York, 1971).

43. No. 138 in *Hymns; The Church of Jesus Christ of Latter-day
Saints* (Salt Lake City, 1948), Mormon apologists will no doubt
find remarkable parallels if not confirmation of the Mormon
position in the recently translated Gnostic gospels discovered in
1945 in the caves of Nag Hammadi in upper Egypt. See Elaine
Pagels, "The Suppressed Gnostic Feminism," *New York Review
of Books* 26 (Nov. 22, 1979): 42–49; *The Gnostic Gospels* (New
York, 1979).

44. *Millennial Star* 17:722–23; 19:717; 20:817; Ileen Ann Le
Cheminant, "The Status of Woman in the Philosophy of Mormonism from 1830–1845" (M.A. thesis, Brigham Young University, 1942).

45. Recently the case of Sonia Johnson, who was excommunicated from the Mormon church because of her opposition to the
anti-ERA stand of the hierarchy, received wide coverage in the
news media.

46. *City of the Saints,* p. 529.

47. "Blessed Damozels: Women in Mormon History," *Dialogue* 6 (Summer 1971): 22–31.

48. "The Mormon Utopia," *The World of Nations* (New York,
1973), p. 57. The most influential interpretation is Barbara
Welter, "The Cult of True Womanhood: 1820–1860," *American
Quarterly* 18 (1966): 151–74.

49. Mark P. Leone, "The Economic Basis for the Evolution of

the Mormon Religion," in Zaretsky and Leone, *Religious Movements in Contemporary America,* pp. 751–52; Bellah, *Beyond Belief* (New York, 1970).

50. Edward W. Tullidge, "The Godbeite Movement," *Tullidge's Quarterly Magazine* 1 (1880): 32.

51. U.S., Congress, Senate, *Proceedings before the Committee on Privileges and Elections of the United States Senate in the Matter of the Protest against the Right Hon. Reed Smoot, A Senator from the State of Utah, to Hold His Seat* (4 vols.; Washington, D.C., 1904–7), 1:97–99.

52. Quoted in Marty, *A Nation of Behavers,* p. 201.

53. See for example the minutes of the St. George Stake High Council, 1862–, as reported in Nels Anderson, *Desert Saints: The Mormon Frontier in Utah* (Chicago, 1942), pp. 346–48.

54. This is borne out by an examination of both the laws of the State of Deseret and those of the territorial legislature. According to the laws of the kingdom of God, adultery was punishable by death, though enforcement of the law cannot be documented. Gustive O. Larson suggests the possibility of enforcement in "The Mormon Reformation," *Utah Historical Quarterly* 26 (1958): 60–63. The community, however, condoned and perhaps encouraged extralegal action. See, for example, the celebrated case of *The United States* vs. *Howard Egan,* in October, 1851. Egan had tracked down and killed the seducer of his wife, James Monroe. In his plea for the defense Mormon apostle George A. Smith argued that by the standards of the community Egan had no choice but to kill Monroe. Egan was acquitted. See *Journal of Discourses* 1 (1854): 95–103. Nelson, *The Mormon Village.*

55. *Journal of Discourses* 12 (1869): 194; *City of the Saints,* p. 518.

56. "An Economic Interpretation of the 'Word of Wisdom,'" p. 47.

57. "Sexuality, Class and Role," p. 149.

58. Harold T. Christensen, "Mormon Sexuality in Cross-Cultural Perspective," *Dialogue* 10 (Autumn 1976): 62–75; Harold T. Christensen and Kenneth L. Cannon, "The Fundamentalist Emphasis in Contemporary Mormonism: A 1935–1973 Trend Analysis of Brigham Young University Student Responses" (manuscript).

59. "From Satyr to Saint: American Attitudes toward the

Mormons, 1860–1960" (paper presented at Annual Meeting, Organization of American Historians, Chicago, 1973), pp. 23–25.

6   *The Transformation of Racial Thought and Practice*

1. Winthrop D. Jordan, *White over Black: American Attitudes toward the Negro, 1550–1812* (Chapel Hill, N.C., 1968).
2. *An Essay on the Causes of the Variety and Complexion and Figure in Human Species.* ed. Winthrop D. Jordan (Cambridge, Mass., 1965).
3. Introduction to Smith, *Essay*, p. xiv; for useful summary of the red sons of Israel theory, see Brodie, *No Man Knows My History*, pp. 34–37.
4. 1 Nephi 12:23.
5. *Journal of Discourses* 11 (1866): 272; *Juvenile Instructor* 26 (1891): 635–36.
6. Book of Mormon, 3 Nephi 2:15–16.
7. Tanner, *Mormonism Like Watergate?* p. 9.
8. George M. Fredrickson, *The Black Image in the White Mind; The Debate on Afro-American Character and Destiny, 1817–1914* (New York, 1971), pp. 61–70, 90–96; Klaus J. Hansen, "The Millennium, the West, and Race in the Antebellum American Mind, *Western Historical Quarterly* 3 (October 1972): 384–85.
9. Fredrickson, *Black Image in the White Mind*, pp. 71–96; William R. Stanton, *The Leopard's Spots: Scientific Attitudes Toward Race in America, 1815–*1859 (Chicago, 1960), 100–112.
10. On the first position see especially Lester E. Bush, Jr., "Mormonism's Negro Doctrine: An Historical Overview," *Dialogue* 8 (Spring 1973): 11–68; on the second see Ronald K. Esplin, "Brigham Young and Priesthood Denial to the Blacks: An Alternative View," *Brigham Young University Studies* 19 (Spring 1979): 394–402.
11. Begun in 1966, *Dialogue* has raised a number of other important and controversial issues, such as the authenticity of the Book of Abraham, sexuality, and feminism. Another influential essay on the Negro doctrine is Stephen G. Taggart, *Mormonism's Negro Policy: Social and Historical Origins* (Salt Lake City, 1970); the most complete overview and synthesis of cur-

rent scholarship is Newell G. Bringhurst, "A Servant of Servants . . . Cursed as Pertaining to the Priesthood: Mormon Attitudes toward Slavery and the Black Man, 1830–80" (Ph.D. diss., University of California, Davis, 1975). Bringhurst argues that priesthood denial was not implemented until 1849 (p. 53).

12. Abraham 1:26.

13. Quoted in Marty, *A Nation of Behavers,* p. xi.

14. Roberts, *Comprehensive History,* 1:326–28; Smith, *History of the Church,* 1:378.

15. William H. Chafe has pointed out that social control of blacks and women had identical motivations (*Women and Equality* [New York, 1977]).

16. *Journal of Discourses* 5 (1857): 157.

17. Appleby, p. 88.

18. *Millennial Star* 10 (1848): 247; William Mulder, "Mormonism's 'Gathering': An American Doctrine with a Difference," *Church History* 23 (September 1954): 248–64.

19. By the end of 1845, 4,733 British Mormons had sailed to America. By 1900, 51,000 European Mormon converts had immigrated to America, including 38,000 from Britain. Allen and Leonard, *The Story of the Latter-Day Saints,* pp. 145–51.

20. Significantly, Elijah Abel was not assigned to a tribe of Israel in his patriarchal blessing. Bush, "Mormonism's Negro Doctrine," p. 52, n. 30; Gordon I. Irving, "The Law of Adoption: One Phase of the Development of the Mormon Concept of Salvation, 1830–1890," *Brigham Young University Studies* 14 (Spring 1974): 291–314.

21. Max Weber's observations on the relationship between tribalism and ethnicity may help to illuminate the Mormon quest for tribalism: "Almost any kind of similarity or contrast of physical type and habits can induce the belief that a tribal affinity or disaffinity exists between groups that attract or repel each other. . . . The belief in tribal kinship, *regardless of whether it has any objective foundation,* can have important consequences especially for the formation of a political community" (my italics; "Ethnic Groups," in Talcott Parsons et al., *Theories of Society* [Glencoe, Ill., 1961] 1:305 ff., quoted in Marty, *A Nation of Behaviors,* pp. 167–68). The Mormon kingdom served as kind of melting pot designed to eliminate national and ethnic distinctions. See Hansen, *Quest for Empire,* pp. 119–20.

22. *Journal of Discourses* 10:110; Journal of Wilford Woodruff, January 16, 1852 (Historical Department of the Church of Jesus Christ of Latter-day Saints).

23. Ibid. According to Lester Bush, this is the first public announcement of the Negro doctrine ("Mormonism's Negro Doctrine," p. 25). "The earliest record of a Church decision to deny the priesthood to Negroes" is in the Journal History, February 13, 1849 (Bush, p. 25).

24. Ibid.

25. Joseph Smith Hyde, *Orson Hyde* (Salt Lake City, 1933), p. 56; *Seer* 1 (April 1853): 54–56; *Contributor* 6 (1885): 296–97; Bush, "Mormonism's Negro Doctrine," pp. 27, 35–36.

26. Taggart, *Mormonism's Negro Policy,* p. 79; Bush, "Mormonism's Negro Doctrine," pp. 45–58.

27. Bush, "Mormonism's Negro Doctrine," p. 47.

28. *Ensign* 8 (July 1978): 75.

29. Bush, "Mormonism's Negro Doctrine," p. 49.

30. Doctrine and Covenants, "Official Declaration," pp. 256–57. An excellent objective account is Henry J. Wolfinger, "A Reexamination of the Woodruff Manifesto in the Light of Utah Constitutional History," *Utah Historical Quarterly* 39 (Fall 1971): 238–49; Kenneth W. Godfrey, "The Coming of the Manifesto," *Dialogue* 5 (Autumn 1970): 11–25, represents the Mormon point of view in light of modern scholarship; Gordon C. Thomasson, "The Manifesto Was a Victory," *Dialogue* 6 (Spring 1971): 37–45, is an excercise in apologetics.

31. Richard P. Howard, "A Tentative Approach to the Book of Abraham," *Dialogue* 3 (Summer 1968): 88–92.

32. Most notably to the presidential aspirations of George Romney (Republican, 1968) and Morris Udall (Democrat, 1976).

33. I am referring to the article by Eugene England, "The Mormon Cross," *Dialogue* 8 (Spring 1973): 78–86. See also Hugh Nibley, "The Best Possible Test," *ibid.,* pp. 73–77.

34. "Sources of Strain in Mormon History Reconsidered," in Marvin S. Hill and James B. Allen, *Mormonism and American Culture* (New York 1972), p. 163.

7   *Epilogue: Mormonism and the*
                                     Shifting Sands of Culture

1. See especially Jan Shipps, "From Satyr to Saint: American Attitudes Toward the Mormons, 1860–1960" (paper presented at Annual Meeting of the Organization of American Historians, 1973).

2. *The Protestant Ethic and the Spirit of Capitalism,* trans. Talcott Parsons (New York, 1930), pp. 13–14, 16–27.

3. *The Structure of Scientific Revolutions,* 2d ed. (Chicago, 1969).

4. Larson, *The "Americanization" of Utah for Statehood,* illustrations between pp. 184–85.

5. In *Errand into the Wilderness* (Cambridge, Mass., 1956), pp. 3–4; particularly illuminating in this context is David Brion Davis, "The New England Origins of Mormonism," *New England Quarterly* 26 (June 1953): 147–68.

6. Journal of Wilford Woodruff, quoted in Roberts, *Comprehensive History,* 3:276.

7. To the Mormons, the Civil War seemed to be the fulfilment of a remarkable prophecy by Joseph Smith in 1832, that had predicted the outbreak of a civil war between North and South; Doctrine and Covenants, sec. 87. See also Hansen, *Quest for Empire,* pp. 165–69.

8. Journal History, January 19, 1863 (Archives, Church of Jesus Christ of Latter-day Saints).

9. Hansen, *Quest for Empire,* pp. 180–81.

10. To George H. Brimhall, April 18, 1906, Brimhall Papers, Brigham Young University Archives.

11. Leonard J. Arrington, "Scholarly Studies of Mormonism in the Twentieth Century," Dialogue 1 (Spring 1966): 15–32. Most notable among these histories are Neff, *History of Utah, 1847 to 1869* (Salt Lake City, 1940); and Leland H. Creer, *Utah and the Nation* (Seattle, 1929). Two carefully reasoned studies refuting the concept of Mormonism as a frontier religion are Whitney R. Cross, *The Burned-over District* (Ithaca, N.Y., 1950), pp. 138–50; and S. George Ellsworth, "A History of Mormon Missions in the United States and Canada, 1830–1860" (Ph.D. diss., University of California, Berkeley, 1951), pp. 327–42.

12. *The Social Teachings of the Christian Churches,* trans. Olive Wyon (2 vols.; London, 1931), 2:461–65; see also Thomas F.

O'Dea, "Mormonism and the Avoidance of Sectarian Stagnation: A Study of Church, Sect, and Incipient Nationality," *American Journal of Sociology* 60 (1954): 285–93.

13. *A Nation of Behavers,* p. 71.

14. See, for example, the periodical *Truth,* founded in 1935 by Joseph W. Musser and edited by him for twenty-one years. A number of fundamentalist communities who practice polygamy are found in Arizona and Mexico. Yet perhaps the largest number of practicing polygamists (who are, of course, excommunicated from the Mormon church if found out) reside in metropolitan Salt Lake City, where plural wives can find jobs as school teachers, nurses, store clerks, and the like.

15. *From Boundlessness to Consolidation* (Ann Arbor, 1969); Robert H. Wiebe, *The Search for Order, 1877–1920* (New York, 1967); Alfred D. Chandler, *The Visible Hand* (Cambridge, Mass., 1977).

16. Mark W. Cannon, "Mormons in the Executive Suite," *Dialogue* 3 (Autumn 1968): 97–108.

17. D. Michael Quinn, "The Mormon Hierarchy, 1832–1932: An American Elite" (Ph.D. diss., Yale University, 1976).

18. "D. Michael Quinn on the Mormon Hierarchy as a Western Elite: The Achievements and Limitations of Recent Mormon Historical Writing" (unpublished comments at Western History Association meetings, Portland, Oregon, October 3, 1977), p. 7.

19. *Time* 114 (December 17, 1979): 45.

Note on Sources

The majority of primary sources of Mormon history are located in the archival collections mentioned in my acknowledgments in the Preface. Of these, the sources housed in the east wing of the Church Office Building of the Church of Jesus Christ of Latter-day Saints in Salt Lake City are by far the most numerous and most important. They include about one million volumes of minute books and other records; some three thousand diaries; a day-by-day scrapbook, the so-called Journal History, comprising more than a thousand volumes; more than six thousand manuscript collections of church leaders and organizations, such as the Papers of Brigham Young, which includes about 30,000 pages of correspondence, as well as the Manuscript History of Brigham Young, containing about 48,000 pages; ledgers and account books; records of the State of Deseret and of Utah Territory, 1851–58; immigration records; marriage and divorce records; office journals of the Church Historian's Office; and nearly all publications of the church from 1830 to the present. For a more detailed description of these records, see Leonard J. Arrington and Davis Bitton, *The Mormon Experience: A History of the Latter-day Saints* (New York, 1979), pp. 341–42. An excellent collection of primary materials, drawing upon a wide range of sources, is William Mulder and A. Russell Mortensen, eds., *Among the Mormons: Historic Accounts by Contemporary Observers* (New York, 1958).

Perhaps the most useful working bibliography, especially on books and articles about Mormonism, is in James B. Allen and Glen M. Leonard, *The Story of the Latter-day Saints* (Salt Lake City, 1976), pp. 639–700. Indispensable for the serious researcher is Chad Flake, ed., *A Mormon Bibliography, 1830–1930:*

Books, Pamphlets, Periodicals, and Broadsides Relating to the First Century of Mormonism (Salt Lake City, 1978), which indicates the depository in which the imprints are housed. Davis Bitton, *Guide to Mormon Diaries and Autobiographies* (Provo, Utah, 1977), introduces the researcher to 2,894 firsthand accounts.

It is unfortunate that because of its turbulent history the church's primary records are far less complete prior to 1846 than after the exodus to Utah, although Smith did appoint a number of scribes and "historians" to produce a kind of official record of his history. The first of these, the "History of Joseph Smith," was published in *The Times and Seasons* in Nauvoo between 1842 and 1846, and then reprinted in the *Deseret News* in Salt Lake City, 1851–57, as well as in the *Latter-day Saints' Millenial Star* (Liverpool, 1852–62). B. H. Roberts, a self-taught historian and a member of the hierarchy, brought out a new edition in six volumes under the title *History of the Church . . . Period I, by Joseph Smith* (Salt Lake City, 1902–12). Although a partisan record, it is indispensable for the serious historian. It is to be regretted that high Mormon officials have been less than encouraging in the production of a modern, scholarly edition of the papers of Joseph Smith. If that monumental event should ever come to pass, a great deal of credit will have to go to Dean C. Jessee, who has made a significant beginning in the restoration of an authentic record of Joseph Smith in pioneering studies such as "The Early Accounts of Joseph Smith's First Vision," *Brigham Young University Studies* 9 (Spring 1969): 275–94; "The Original Book of Mormon Manuscript," ibid. 10 (Spring 1970): 259–78; and "The Writing of Joseph Smith's History," ibid. 11 (Summer 1971): 439–73.

Also useful is Joseph Smith III, Heman C. Smith, and F. Henry Edwards, eds. and comps., *The History of the Reorganized Church of Jesus Christ of Latter Day Saints* (6 vols. to date; Independence, Mo., 1967–), which presents the history of the "Latter Day Saints" from the perspective of the second largest of the several Mormon churches.

One of the earliest and most detailed histories by a committed Mormon is B. H. Roberts, *A Comprehensive History of the Church of Jesus Christ of Latter-day Saints* (6 vols., Salt Lake City, 1930). This has now been superseded by Allen and Leonard, *The Story of the Latter-Day Saints,* which, though it skirts a number of controversial issues, treats the history of Mormonism with an objectivity remarkable for a work issued by the official publishing house of the church. Regrettably, high Mormon officials who took umbrage at such candor forced withdrawal of the work from the market, but not before about 30,000 copies were sold. The most recent history by committed Mormons with professional credentials is Arrington and Bitton, *The Mormon Experience.* Less comprehensive but more interpretive than *The Story of the Latter-day Saints,* Arrington and Bitton's work sees Mormonism adapting to the modern world in five stages of "creative adjustment." Written for a primarily non-Mormon audience, and published by Knopf, the book is less vulnerable to potential displeasure by the hierarchy, in spite of a candid discussion of controversial issues. I especially recommend chapter 2, "The Appeals of Mormonism," as an amplification of my necessarily telescoped treatment of that topic. For a perceptive and stimulating study of early Mormonism, see Gordon Douglas Pollock, "In Search of Security: The Mormons and the Kingdom of God on Earth, 1830–1844" (Ph.D. thesis, Queen's University, 1977).

For a handy collection of articles that have stood the test of time, by influential non-Mormon scholars such as David Brion Davis, Mario De Pillis, and Thomas F. O'Dea, see Marvin S. Hill and James B. Allen, eds., *Mormonism and American Culture* (New York, 1972). Sociologist of religion Thomas F. O'Dea's *The Mormons* (Chicago, 1957), is still indispensable. Observant readers will notice that my interpretation of the transformation of Mormon culture was influenced by anthropologist Mark Leone, whose work has now appeared in book form, *The Roots of Mormonism* (Cambridge, Mass., 1979). Though highly suggestive, and in parts even brilliant, Leone's work overstates the case for the fluidity of the Mormon belief system. I hasten to add that one of the most creative and imaginative of historians of Mormonism, Jan Shipps, will argue in a forthcoming study that I myself have overstated the case for the "bourgeoisification" of Mormon culture.

These works fit into what a number of commentators have called "the new Mormon history," a tradition exemplified by Leonard J. Arrington's *Great Basin Kingdom: An Economic History of the Latter-day Saints, 1830–1900* (Cambridge, Mass., 1958) and continued by young scholars such as Lawrence Foster, whose *Religion and Sexuality: Three American Communal Experiments of the Nineteenth Century* (New York, 1981) includes the most exhaustively researched, broadly conceived, and sophisticated study of Mormon polygamy extant. Much of this work has been promoted by the the Mormon History Association, founded in 1966, and published in its *Journal of Mormon History*. Other journals publishing extensively in Mormon studies are *Brigham Young University Studies*; *Dialogue: A Journal of Mormon Thought*; *Sunstone: A Journal of Mormon Scholarship, Issues, and Art*; and the *Utah Historical Quarterly*. National and regional publications such as the *Journal of American History, Church History, Western Historical Quarterly, Pacific Historical Review,* and *Arizona and the West* have also been hospitable to Mormon scholarship.

Sooner or later, one should hope, such work should filter down into the textbooks. With one notable exception, this has not been the case. David Brion Davis's "The Mormons as a Test Case," in *The Great Republic* (Boston, 1977), pp. 532–41, is a remarkable achievement, deftly placing Mormonism into the context of American culture.

Another area that has been little touched by the new Mormon history is biography. Fawn M. Brodie's *No Man Knows My History: The Life of Joseph Smith the Mormon Prophet* (New York, 1945; 2d ed., 1971), still stands as the most literate of all Mormon biographies. A number of scholars have raised serious questions about the limitations of her research, her fundamental assumptions, and her use of evidence, most notably Marvin S. Hill, "Secular or Sectarian History? A Critique of 'No Man Knows My History,'" *Church History* 43 (March 1974): 78–96; and Jan Shipps, "The Prophet Puzzle: Suggestions Leading Toward a More Comprehensive Interpretation of Joseph Smith," *Journal of Mormon History* 1 (1974): 3–20. Donna Hill has attempted a sympathetic Mormon interpretation based on current scholarship in *Joseph Smith: The First Mormon* (New York, 1977). As I have argued at a recent Mormon history conference, however (Canandaigua, New York, May 2, 1980), Fawn Brodie has lobbed the ball into the Mormon court, and Mormon scholars have not yet succeeded in returning it. Brodie has raised serious questions abou the *historical* authenticity of the book of Mormon. Believers, of course, need no such proof. But if Mormons want to play by the rules of historical scholarship, Brodie presents an obstacle that has not yet been removed.

Other leading Mormons, of course, do not present these difficulties. It is, therefore, all the more surprising that few good biographies exist. The greatest need is for a serious and sophisticated study of Brigham Young. M. R. Werner's *Brigham Young* (New York, 1925) is rather superficial and now out of date. Stanley Hirshson's *The Lion of the Lord: A Biography of Brigham Young* (New York, 1969) is mistitled because it is based primarily on biased newspaper reports. For a well-written biography of Young's successor, see Samuel W. Taylor, *The Kingdom of God or Nothing: The Life of John Taylor, Militant Mormon* (New York, 1976). For a perceptive look at polygamy, see Taylor's biography of his much-married father John W. Taylor, *Family Kingdom* (rev. ed., Salt Lake City, 1974). A prolific author on Mormon topics, Taylor has also written *Nightfall at Nauvoo* (New York, 1971) and *Rocky Mountain Empire: The Latter-day Saints Today* (New York, 1978). Because he embellishes his history with the techniques of the novelist, and because of his personal perspective on the Mormon past Taylor has not been popular among Mormon historians. His frank opinions have also made him less than popular among devout Latter-day Saints. Nevertheless, his emphasis on what he regards as the larger truths of the Mormon past rather than on the collection of facts makes his contribution invaluable to the serious student of Mormon history.

Useful guides to selected aspects of Mormon history are Marvin S. Hill, "The Historiography of Mormonism," *Church History* 27 (December 1959): 481–26; Leonard T. Arrington, "Scholarly Studies of Mormonism in the Twentieth Century," *Dialogue: A Journal of Mormon Thought* 1 (Spring 1966): 15–32; Robert B. Flanders, "Writing on the Mormon Past," ibid. 1 (Autum 1966): 47–61; and "Some Reflections on the New Mormon History," ibid. 9 (Spring 1974): 34–41; Rodman W. Paul, "The Mormons as a Theme in Western Historical Writing," *Journal of American History* 54 (December 1967): 511–23; Thomas G. Alexander and James B. Allen, "The Mormons in the Mountain West: A Selected Bibliography," *Arizona and the West* 9 (Winter 1967): 365–84; Davis Bitton, "Mormon Polygamy: A Review Article," *Journal of Mormon History* 4 (1977): 101–18; Thomas G. Alexander, "The Place of Joseph Smith in the Development of American Religion: A Historiographical Inquiry," *Journal of Mormon History* 5 (1978): 3–17; and Richard D. Poll, "Nauvoo and the New Mormon History: A Bibliographical Survey," ibid., pp. 105–23.

Index